THE STORY OF ENGLAND

by the same author

★

THE MURDER OF SIR THOMAS OVERBURY

THE STORY OF
ENGLAND

FROM THE TIME OF KING ALFRED
TO THE CORONATION OF
QUEEN ELIZABETH II

by

WILLIAM McELWEE

FABER AND FABER LIMITED

24 Russell Square

London

First published in mcmliv
by Faber and Faber Limited
24 Russell Square London W.C.1
Printed in Great Britain by
Latimer Trend & Co Ltd Plymouth

CONTENTS

★

	PREFACE	*page* 11
I.	KING ALFRED'S ENGLAND	13
II.	FROM KING OF WESSEX TO 'EMPEROR OF BRITAIN'	28
III.	THE CATASTROPHE OF ANGLO-SAXON ENGLAND	44
IV.	THE NORMAN CONQUEST	58
V.	MAKING A NATION	72
VI.	THE COLLAPSE OF MEDIAEVAL ENGLAND	92
VII.	RESTORATION OF GOVERNMENT AND REORGANIZATION IN A NEW WORLD	111
VIII.	FROM REFORMATION TO THE VERGE OF CIVIL WAR	130
IX.	CIVIL WAR, RESTORATION, AND REVOLUTION	147
X.	POLITICAL STABILITY ACHIEVED	165
XI.	REFORM AND REACTION	186
XII.	THE ERA OF REFORM	203
XIII.	VICTORIAN ENGLAND	217
XIV.	THE WORLD WAR AND ITS AFTERMATH	235
XV.	ENGLAND'S FINEST HOUR	250
	SOME SUGGESTIONS FOR FURTHER READING	261
	INDEX	264

GENEALOGICAL TABLES

THE WESSEX KINGS OF ENGLAND | *page* 27
THE END OF THE HOUSE OF ALFRED | 43
THE NORMANS AND ANGEVINS | 71
YORK AND LANCASTER—THE END OF THE | 90–1
PLANTAGENETS
THE TUDORS | 129
THE STUARTS AND THE HANOVERIAN SUCCESSION | 163
THE HANOVERIANS | 185
THE FAMILY OF THE PRESENT QUEEN | 234

ILLUSTRATIONS

✦

PLATES

1. Canute and Emma dedicating a shrine   *facing page* 50
2. Three scenes from the Bayeux Tapestry   63
3. Two fourteenth-century manor houses   96
4. 'The Thames from above Greenwich' in James I's   113
   reign
5. Georgian prosperity, an artists' club   176
6. Eighteenth-century philanthropy, Mr. Howard   193
   offering relief to prisoners
7. The English scene at the end of the Napoleonic   208
   Wars
8. Victorian prosperity, 'The Derby Day'   225

MAPS

1. Alfred's England   *page* 21
2. Reconquest of England by the House of Alfred   34
3. The Civil War   153
4. Growth and shift of the population during the   168-9
   Industrial Revolution
5. French and English in North America   180

PREFACE

★

In this short volume I have tried to make a continuous story in a readable form of England's development from the time of King Alfred to the present day. This has obviously involved much compression and some distortion, since much that is both interesting and important has had to be left out. But I hope it may serve to give those who have picked up a piecemeal knowledge of English history from the haphazard study of scattered periods at school some sense of that continuity of our national life which is one of the most important things about it.

In the interests of readability I have avoided footnotes altogether and I have attached to the narrative only such genealogical tables and maps as I think absolutely necessary for the understanding of the story. There are also at the end of the book some quite arbitrary and personal suggestions for further reading. A list of sources for a work of this kind would be too long to print and I must content myself with a single acknowledgement, to Keith Feiling, lately Chichele Professor in the University of Oxford, not only for what he taught me at Christ Church, but for his recently published *History of England* on which I have drawn very heavily indeed in writing this book.

Stowe,   WILLIAM MCELWEE
   April 1954

Chapter One

KING ALFRED'S ENGLAND

The Beginnings of the Story

✯

On about March 23rd of the year 878 a small band of West Saxons, perhaps a few hundred strong, found its way to the island of Athelney through the great marshes which then stretched behind Glastonbury to the Bristol Channel, and there set about fortifying a temporary base against the Danes. They were the faithful remnant, bodyguard and household, who had been on the run with King Alfred since the second week in January, when Guthrum the Dane, treacherously breaking both his own very recent promises and the normal rules of war, had surprised them in the midst of their Christmas festivities at Chippenham. The Danish attack had been skilfully co-ordinated. Simultaneously with the advance of Guthrum's main army from Gloucester the Danish pirates based in Dublin and Wexford and on the Welsh coast had concentrated under King Hubba, the terror of the Irish seas, and had descended on the north coast of Devonshire. It is often difficult to penetrate the severe recitals of fact of the early chronicles on the one hand, and the legend-encrusted, over-enthusiastic contemporary lives of heroes on the other, to the real men who made early history. But there are occasional vivid glimpses; and something of Alfred's personal quality in this crisis comes through even the official narrative of the Anglo-Saxon Chronicle. There was panic everywhere, and many of the West Saxon leaders had fled overseas on the first impact of the sudden, overwhelming Danish success. 'Most of the people', says the Chronicle, 'they reduced, except Alfred, the King.'

Alfred was thirty when the Danes 'stole away' from Gloucester for this Twelfth Night raid on Chippenham, and he had already reigned for seven years in Wessex—that is, over all England south of the Thames. Even before he succeeded to the throne he had begun to be a legend. Good-looking and bookish and not physically strong, the youngest and very much his mother's favourite son, he had shown at the Battle of Ashdown seven years before that he was never-theless one of the greatest leaders in action the West Saxons had ever had. Then, at a moment when his brother, King Ethelred, was hearing mass behind the lines and would not be disturbed, he had spotted the Danes on the Downs above them forming up for what must be a devastating downhill attack. On his own initiative he led the main force of the Saxons up the hill and, 'charging like a wild boar', caught the Danes off balance and held them until Ethelred, who was no coward but only a little over-punctilious about his devotions, came up with the reserves to complete a spec-tacular victory.

That was in 871, the year in which the men of Wessex fought nine pitched battles and innumerable minor engage-ments before the Danes at last drew off to harry less formid-able enemies elsewhere; and it was in the middle of this campaign that Ethelred died, of exhaustion, and perhaps of wounds got in the great defeat of Marden just before Easter. Alfred's reign, thus begun in the midst of military crisis, had been one of intermittent crisis ever since. He had bought a few years of peace and had used them well. He had reorganized the 'Fyrd', the county militia, or Home Guard, in which every Saxon freeman had to serve, dividing it into two halves which could be called out alternately, so that half could stay and till the fields and the army no longer melted away at harvest time, as it had tended to do in earlier campaigns. He had also, by enlarging the number of King's

Thanes—men who held land and rank on condition of un-restricted military service when needed—created a small regular force that was always available. It is probable that he began the naval reconstruction programme for which he was later famous, since in 875 he personally defeated a small Viking squadron at sea. Above all, he had begun to gather round him the band of devoted counsellors and subordin-ates who were later to help him so enormously in his work of reconstruction. In consequence he had some dependable men in charge in Hampshire, Wiltshire, and Dorsetshire, who did not fly oversea when the storm broke in 876. In Devon he had Ealdorman Odda, who at once set about collecting his county levies to deal with the seaborne in-vasion of King Hubba, and throughout his retreat to Athel-ney he was in close touch with Ethelnoth, the Ealdorman of Somerset. Something of the spirit which animated this band of Alfred's helpers can be caught in a phrase used years later about Ethelnoth by Werferth, who had gallantly accepted the Bishopric of Worcester six years earlier, when the post looked like a sure road to martyrdom, and who may well have been with Alfred in Athelney. Having need to refer to the Ealdorman of Somerset in a dry, legal charter, he calls him 'Ethelnoth, the friend of us all'. With men of this quality still at large and in touch with him, Alfred's situa-tion in Athelney was not so desperate as it seemed. Hateful as it is to abandon a legend, it is highly improbable that he ever burnt the cakes there. He was never anything like so hard driven as to have to take solitary refuge with a cow-herd who did not even recognize him. But he did drop a brooch there, with his name on it, which was picked up on the farm still called Athelney in 1693, and is now in Oxford. He and his band were certainly hard pressed, but the counter-attack was well under way and in the mean-time, once they had built their stockade, in the phrase, again, of the Anglo-Saxon Chronicle, they 'kept fighting against the foe'.

One preliminary success had been won even before the

Athelney fort was complete. With a number of Thanes and as much of the Fyrd of Devonshire as he could raise, Odda had moved to meet Hubba as he came marauding down the Bristol Channel. Unfortunately the Danes came ashore in superior force and Odda had to entrench himself, probably at Kenny Castle, near Appledore. There he was besieged by the Danes and, rather than wait to be starved out, he decided 'to take the chance of death or victory' in a surprise sally at dawn. He was completely victorious. Hubba was killed and with him nearly 1,000 of his men, and only a remnant got away to their ships. This cleared one front, and Alfred could now concentrate against Guthrum's main force, entrenched at Chippenham. He moved out in the second week of May, and the excellence of his planning is shown by the fact that at Egbert's Stone, near Warminster, at the end of his first day's march, he joined up with all the levies from Somerset, Dorset, Wiltshire, and Hampshire and was able to move forward the next morning at the head of an army large enough to offer battle to Guthrum's main force.

Turning points in history are rare, but the decisive nature of this particular crisis in English history can scarcely be disputed. Had Alfred gone under, the rudimentary civilization which it had taken the Anglo-Saxons 400 years to build on the ruins they had themselves made of Roman Britain would have been blotted out. The Christianity painfully established by Augustine and his followers would have disappeared, and the whole land would have passed to heathen barbarians even more savage and primitive than the Angles and Saxons had been when they first landed. The whole story of England would have been different: almost certainly tragically so. That is why English history and legend have so fastened on the picture of the young king driven into hiding in the Somersetshire marshes, and that is why, too, the story of England may well begin in Easter week of 878. For when Alfred emerged with such dramatic suddenness to recover his kingdom, he began a process of conquest which was not halted until his grandson could fairly claim that he ruled over the whole of England, for the first time effectively united.

It is not easy either to imagine or describe the England which, from his island stockade, Alfred was setting out to subdue. Only occasional disastrous floods, when the railway line seems to run through great inland seas, can give the modern Englishman a glimpse of the extent to which the rivers dominated English geography in the days before embankment and scientific drainage. The great tidal estuaries of Thames and Severn, Dee, Mersey, and Solway were enlarged and prolonged by miles of almost impassable marsh. From the Wash 1,300 square miles of fen stretched inland to Stamford and Huntingdon, and another great fen prolonged the Humber inland to cut Lincolnshire off to the north-west. The great swamp which sheltered Alfred at Athelney remained an undrained, trackless haunt of outlaws and lost men for centuries, and the lower reaches of even the smaller rivers such as Lea, Medway and Colne, could be a formidable military obstacle.

Above all this, roughly west and north of a line drawn from Durham to Exeter, the high rocky barrier which stretched from the Pennines along the Welsh mountains to Dartmoor made another great area difficult for a conqueror or administrator to penetrate and control. And where the passages between the high hills were not blocked by marshes they were filled with forests almost as impenetrable. What we know to-day as 'the wooded, dim, blue goodness of the Weald' was then dense jungle which defied movement and agriculture for hundreds of years and penned in the South Saxons along a strip of coast and downland so effectively that they had to leave the conquest and colonization of Surrey to the Middle Saxons from north of the Thames. Only a narrow gap separated the Andredsweald from the New Forest; and beyond that a belt of thick forest ran up the centre of Somersetshire. The Forest of Dean stopped all progress beyond the lower Severn. Forest made much of modern Warwickshire and Oxfordshire and the whole of eastern Hertfordshire and southern Essex uninhabitable, and further north, in Cheshire, Nottinghamshire, and Yorkshire, blocked every gap between swamp and hills.

These were the basic factors which conditioned the lives of every Englishman from king to cattle-thief for long after Alfred's time, and it is essential to keep the nature of the country always in mind in order to understand what they did and tried to do, and perhaps even more, what they failed to do. The surviving fragments of woodland which for us are the pleasant background for a picnic were then vast thickets of bramble and thorn into which a man must cut his way with an axe: the dark haunt of every known and unknown terror. Death from exposure or starvation was a normal occupational risk of those who lived among the bleak hills where hikers now walk for pleasure. The woods round London were full of wild boar. The brown bear was still a terror in north and west and in our richly cultivated midland shires shepherds were ceaselessly on guard against wolves. In such a background there was little room for the gentler virtues and none for modern sensibilities and humanitarianisms. Life was inevitably a hard, dogged struggle, even in times of peace and prosperity, and it bred men, whether they were Saxons or Danes or Celts, who were tough and self-reliant, not easily disciplined, necessarily callous and often brutal. Its Saxon invaders did not find this a friendly country. Their poetry is shot through with a sense of the hostility of nature: glimpses of forest trees crashing in the cruel winter gales, of eagles' and ravens' nests on exposed crags, and of the loneliness of the great marshes where pelicans and bitterns still bred. To all except the robber and the outlaw the forest was the greatest of all enemies.

This mere difficulty of moving from one part of the island to another explains a great deal of early English history. It accounts largely for the fact that when the raiding bands began to settle down after the chaos of the Saxon

18

invasion, they coalesced into seven kingdoms instead of one, and that, after 300 years of fighting each other, no one of these kingdoms had been able to establish a permanent supremacy over all the others. But there were, of course, important factors which worked the other way. The rivers and fens which so often impeded the movements of landsmen had already been used by barges for commerce in Roman times and had carried the shallow draught ships of both Saxon and Dane into the very heart of the country: once in Alfred's reign a Danish fleet anchored twenty miles up the Lea, north of London. Moreover, however fierce the hostility between the various kingdoms and sub-kingdoms, Saxons, Angles and Jutes all retained the most remarkable sense of kinship. Their ruling families were all bewilderingly inter-related and all claimed descent from a common stock. The indiscipline of the rank and file was tempered from the start by the necessary loyalties of a band of adventurers, and in the settlement and exploitation of their conquered lands they had further developed an already strong sense of obligation to the community and of the rights of individuals within it. They might be at times very difficult to govern. But they were easy to lead, given the right leader.

Finally, and potentially most important of all to anybody who wished to govern a united England, there were the old Roman military highways, as yet largely unexploited by the Saxons, but destined to provide her with a system of communications which as much as anything saved her from the disastrous anarchy which overtook, for example, Germany in the Middle Ages. But that was almost all that Rome did leave behind her in Britain. There was not in this country the massive legacy of a great civilization which in Italy and France, even in its decay and collapse, did so much to temper the barbarism of invading Goths and Franks. The first Saxon invaders found only the skin-deep culture of a military occupation, most of which vanished with the departure of the last Roman troops in the year 407.

The tribes of the north and west had never really been disturbed, once they had accepted Roman garrisons and the necessity of Roman tribute. For three centuries they had continued to live their own ancestral pattern of life, and when the legions withdrew from the richly cultivated south and east their immediate reaction was to move in and destroy what had always remained to them an alien and hostile influence, in some cases joining hands with Saxon invaders to do so. The provincial capitals, after a period of slow decay, were sacked and abandoned; for a time even London seems to have been uninhabited and some of the big towns, like Silchester, were never reoccupied. By A.D. 500 it is fair to say that nothing of Rome survived save the roads and occasionally some still useful fortifications, as at Lincoln and York.

The elements which Alfred and his successors were to try to weld into a nation were, therefore, Celtic and Saxon; though how much Celtic blood survived in the mixture remains largely a matter of argument and guesswork. It seems that often the first stage was one of almost peaceful penetration, the Saxons mingling with the local population, and Saxon language and ways of life only gradually predominating. Elsewhere the small bands of newcomers often preferred to carve out pioneering settlements for themselves from the forest and waste, though remaining apparently on good terms with local British communities. At Cirencester they shared a cemetery; in Canterbury they lived in separate quarters of the same town. But in the two centuries of fighting which followed, as the numbers of invaders grew and British resistance solidified, the war seems to have become one of extermination. Under leaders like the entirely shadowy and legendary Arthur the Britons fought to a finish, and over most of England they were driven out or killed. But even so there must have been many who survived as slaves, and their women must have added a large element of Celtic blood to the stock which finally settled down in the Saxon villages, since not all the Saxons arrived with families and cattle loaded complete into their boats.

It was very unlikely that the population of half a million or so, which is estimated to have lived in central and south-

Alfred's England

Forests, Rivers and Marshes, with principal Roman Roads

Forests → Marshes →
Roman Roads →

eastern Britain in later Roman times, was entirely blotted
out.

The question, in any case, is largely academic. For practical purposes in Alfred's time the British had become the
Welsh, irreconcilable and apparently unconquerable behind
their mountains, though in West Saxon Devon and Cornwall British stock and language still predominated. The
England which he had to deal with was Anglo-Saxon, and
most of the Celtic influence and culture traceable in it was
due to later counter-penetration by Welsh missionaries or
craftsmen. Here and there, on the fringes, there might be
fragmentary survivals of communities still largely neolithic
in their way of life. In Devonshire there were villages which
retained the organization of the old Roman villa and only
very late adapted themselves to the necessary minimum of
the Saxon manorial system. The general picture, nevertheless, was a uniform one, of village communities dotted all
over the country where dry soil and good water were to be
had, pushing their way up every river valley and cutting
into every forest, thrusting such Britons as survived back
into the lower slopes of moors and downs.

It is in their villages that the Anglo-Saxons must first be
studied; for all their larger institutions, their courts, and
their conception of law and kingship, grew out of the ideas
underlying their village life. And the villages in turn grew
out of the war bands—family and clan groups—who had
set out to conquer an inheritance less barren than the sandy
wastes of Frisia and Schleswig into which the wanderings of
European peoples had crowded them. The family unit was
at the bottom of everything. The Venerable Bede will give
the area of the Isle of Wight as '1,200 familes', measuring
the land by the number of families it can support, and the
hide, the basic land measurement of the Saxons, was variable
according to the quality of the soil, because it represented
the amount of land which would keep one family.

Two main principles thus dominated the land-holding
system at the time of the settlement. Firstly, a family's hold-

ing was a sort of perpetual trust; it could not be given away or sold. Secondly, though freehold, each family share was only a part of the land of the tribe or clan—'Folkland' they called it. It took the form of a number of scattered strips in the common fields of the village, sometimes changed each year by lot, more often permanently held. Each village had its three great open arable fields, two of which were tilled each year, while the third lay fallow and was available for common grazing. The enclosed pasture was treated in the same way, fenced off in strips for hay in the summer and thrown open to common grazing in the winter. Finally there was the waste: woodland or scrub, where there was sometimes additional grazing, pasturage for swine, and firewood for all. In the village each family had its homestead and farmyard.

Though every larger household had its slaves, descendants of the Britons, or prisoners-of-war, or sometime free families which had lost or forfeited their birthright, it remained essentially a free society; in some ways freer, perhaps, than any which has lived since in this island. Property was a trust—a share of the common wealth, hedged about with rights, it is true, but also inalienably attached to certain obligations. A piratical venture depends absolutely on each doing his share and getting his share, and this was the habit of mind carried over into the first village settlements. But piracy and war, though they depend on the principle of free association, do not tend to create equality, and Saxon society was already essentially unequal and aristocratic in its organization before it left Germany. Equal shares for all of the same status would be the rule; but by no means equal status for all. The Saxons brought with them a hereditary nobility intensely conscious of its position, and a great sense of kingship and of the blood royal. But here again the war band's necessities stamped their pattern on the national institutions. Kings, as far as we can discover, were drawn without exception from the royal line, but not necessarily by primogeniture. An infant cannot lead a war band and a primitive kingdom in troublous times needs a competent man of action on the throne. So the Witan—an undefined assembly of nobles and wise men—the tribe's natural leaders, would choose the most suitable member of the royal family available. Thus, though the tendency was for the eldest son to succeed, the other principle long remained, and Alfred himself owed his throne to it. His brother, Ethelred, dying in mid-campaign, left two young sons; but the Witan unhesitatingly chose Alfred, and within three weeks he was in the field at the head of his own army.

This twin system of families equally free but permanently differentiated in status underlay all Anglo-Saxon law, and gave men, oddly enough, a scale of value calculated on a financial basis. In a brutal age the law aimed not so much at punishing a murderer as at compensating the victim's family, and so avoiding the blood feud which became such an unmitigated curse in many parts of the world. Among all Germanic peoples different classes thus came to be assessed at their compensation value: the wergeld which had to be paid to a man's relations if he were murdered. Infinitely variable in the early days, the categories of wergeld had, by the year 700, settled in England into three main divisions. The more important nobles, the King's Thanes, were assessed at 1,200s., or 200 head of cattle; lesser nobles and larger landowners at 600s.; and the ordinary yeoman farmer at only 200s. It cost only half as much at the different levels to kill a Welshman, and a descending scale of values existed for all personal injuries down to the thirty copper pieces payable for the loss of a big toe-nail. In due course a similar scale of values came to be applied to the oaths taken in the law courts. A man's family or clan must ride in to the law court of shire or hundred to swear on his behalf, and the more men of substance he could muster among his 'oath-helpers' the better his chances of survival.

Such, in very rough outline, was the basic Saxon system of law and land tenure. But in an age when common sense invariably prevailed over constitutional procedure it was ceaselessly modified from the moment it was established. A man without powerful family backing would seek the protection of a magnate, who thus became his 'Lord', and in troubled times more and more men tended to do this, until to be a 'lordless' man was to be altogether unfortunate. Soon the 'Lord' who swore to a man's title to his lands began to be regarded as the ultimate owner of that land and so, insensibly, there emerged a feudal relationship of over-lord and vassal tenant. Village after village passed into the protection of, and so into dependence on, a manor, with the lord's home farm or domain among the common strips and maintained by his neighbours' labour in return for the protection he afforded them. The system never hardened into one of rigid castes and seems always to have had the flexibility characteristic of English society in all later periods. If a man prospered and acquired more land, his status rose accordingly. If he fell, it fell with him.

There were many other elements at work to modify the primitive pattern. The King's need to endow a class of Thanes as semi-professional soldiers led him to invent a method of alienating the theoretically inalienable 'Folkland' by charter, so creating what soon became the general rule— 'Bookland', held on defined terms of service. Other large landowners soon saw the convenience of this, and the need to endow the Church speeded the process up, so that, before long, except in Kent, which clung to the old ways, almost all land had become Bookland, tangled in feudal obligation. There were other and more important ways in which the advent of Latin Christianity, practically triumphant all over England by the end of the seventh century, helped to break up the primitive Saxon code of behaviour and law. The Church could not reckon men's value by wergelds, but only in terms of souls equal before God. She could invoke sanc-tions more sacred than any other, so that, in the transitional phase, the value of a Christian communicant's oath became superior in the law courts to all others. She claimed endow-ment in land, but necessarily rejected many of the obligations traditionally attached to ownership. Above all, she was universal, looking beyond Canterbury to Rome, with machinery for governing her hierarchy more complex and dependable than the rudimentary institutions of a Saxon king. As such she did much to destroy the chronic localism of Saxon habits of thought, and very early became the greatest of all potential allies for a monarchy which aimed at uniting the whole of England.

This, then, was the general pattern of the society which Alfred set out from Athelney to save. It was only in his own Wessex that it at that moment survived. Under Danish attack the old kingdoms of Northumbria and East Anglia had disintegrated and of Mercia, whose kings had once ruled the Midlands from Trent to Thames and across to the Welsh border and had claimed overlordship over all England, only the south-western corner remained. Already many Danes were parcelling out the land and settling down among the Saxons they had conquered. But the reconquest and reorganization of all that was a task for the remoter future. For the moment all that Alfred could hope for was to save Wessex, and that he brilliantly achieved when, three days after leaving Athelney, he met the main Danish host at Edington. There was hard fighting lasting for several hours before the Danes broke. But then Alfred followed them swiftly, drove the remnant into their Chippenham camp and, after a fortnight's blockade, forced them to surrender. Guthrum agreed to leave Wessex and, before doing so, to be baptised a Christian with twenty-nine of his leading men.

The Treaty of Wedmore, as this agreement is generally called, looked on the surface a precarious agreement. Guthrum had broken similar promises made only a year before, and Danes were apt to treat enforced baptism with levity. But this time Guthrum had had enough. He withdrew to East Anglia, leaving all that was south and west of the Watling Street to Alfred. So England, and probably a great deal more than England, was saved. The inept descendants of Charlemagne seemed powerless to protect Germany and

France against the Danes, and with that other great scourge of Christendom, the Saracens, pressing hard on southern Italy and Spain, western civilization was in real danger of final extinction. The immediate effect of the victory was, of course, to send more Danes to pillage easier victims in northern Europe. But Alfred had shown at last that they could be defeated and stopped, and that deliverance was possible from the fury of the Northmen. More important still, he was now to show how such a victory should be used.

THE WESSEX KINGS OF ENGLAND

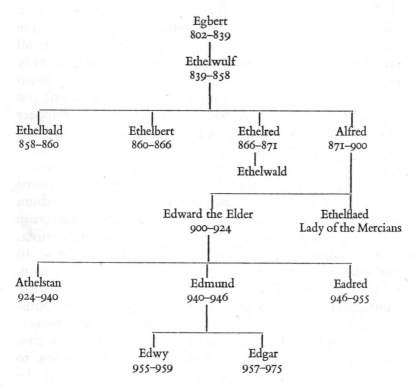

27

Chapter Two

FROM KING OF WESSEX
TO 'EMPEROR OF BRITAIN'

★

rom 878 until 892, apart from one seaborne raid in
885, which tempted Guthrum momentarily to break
his promises of Wedmore, Alfred had peace. It was in
the exploitation of those years, rather than in his brilliant
victories, that he showed what a remarkable man he was.
Instead of the efficient military despotism which his popularity and prestige would have made easy to establish and
which circumstances would have seemed to justify, he flung
himself into building a civilized nation with all the accumulated energy of seven frustrated years. 'Throughout all
England,' he wrote himself, 'everything was harried and
burnt.' A century before his time England had poured
scholars and missionaries into Europe and the Canterbury
school had been teaching Greek as well as Latin, Music, and
Astronomy. Now there was scarcely a priest south of the
Thames who could construe Latin, and the governing class
was quite illiterate. The story of how he himself had learnt
to read Anglo-Saxon poetry in order to win a coveted
illuminated book as a prize from his mother may well be
true; but he had to summon scholars from outside Wessex
to translate Latin for him after he had come to the throne
and it was not until he was nearly forty that he was able to
read it on his own. A formidable education programme, a
tidying and tightening up of the legal system, and a military
reorganization were the objects which Alfred set himself to
achieve in the few years at his disposal.

'My task', he wrote towards the end of his life, in one of the explanatory comments which he liked to insert in works he was translating, 'was that I should virtuously and fittingly administer the authority committed to me. Now no man can administer government unless he have fit tools and the raw material to work upon. And a king's raw material and instruments of rule are a well-peopled land and he must have men of prayer, men of war, and men of work.' Of the men of prayer who helped him to launch his programme, Werferth and Plegmund, later Archbishop of Canterbury, came from Mercia, and Asser, his muddle-headed, well-meaning biographer, whom he made Bishop of Sherborne, from South Wales. But to restart the monastic movement in Wessex he had to have foreigners: John the Old Saxon to be abbot of his new foundation at Athelney, and Grimbald the Frank for his projected minster at Winchester. Even so, he was not very successful. West Saxons had lost the impulse towards cloister life and in the end he had to fetch monks, too, from France, with disastrous international consequences at Athelney, where the Frankish monks tried to murder their German abbot. Nevertheless, by the end of his reign, with these two monasteries and a Nunnery at Shaftesbury, he had established a few centres of piety and learning which were to have a powerful influence in the next three generations.

His educational efforts were much more effective. He set up a court school for the sons of his Thanes, at which all should learn to read and write Anglo-Saxon before they were schooled in arms and taught to hunt, and where those might 'be taught Latin whom it is proposed to educate further and promote to higher office'. Asser paints a delightful picture of some of the older officials, Ealdormen and King's Reeves, who had to preside over law courts, going painfully through 'the unaccustomed and laborious discipline' of learning to read in order to keep their offices, and there must have been some hardship. But the result was to give England an educated lay aristocracy, to whom European culture and science were accessible; and 100 years later there were still English magnates who could write Latin freely.

What was most remarkable about this transformation was Alfred's personal share in it. In effect he pushed it through single-handed, collecting the nucleus of teachers, and with their assistance himself producing the translations which made available for the first time in Anglo-Saxon Bede's great *History*, Orosius's *History of the World*, Gregory the Great's *Pastoral Care*, Boethius's *Consolations of Philosophy*, and some selections from St. Augustine. His inserted explanatory notes and his prefaces give us glimpses of a delightful mind, humble, but determined that others should be enabled to enjoy the advantages which he had wrung from books in the midst of wars. He translated freely, 'sense for sense', as he put it himself, rather than 'word for word', drawing freely on Saxon analogies to make the meaning really clear. Thus the doctors who argued with the child Jesus in the Temple were 'the wisest Witan that there were in Jerusalem', and we get a new idea of the early conception of the feudal relation between lord and vassal when we read of the Apostles as 'Christ's Thanes'. Alfred's whole philosophy he summed up in what was probably one of the last sentences he ever wrote: 'Therefore he seems to me a very foolish man and very wretched who will not increase his understanding while he is in this world and ever wish and long to reach that endless life where all shall be made clear.'

Alfred's educational and literary achievement is easy to assess, and very impressive it was for a man who was actively engaged in war for sixteen years out of a reign of twenty-eight. Though every chronicle speaks of the high quality of his justice and the skill with which he 'righted wrongs', it is not easy to discover what he actually did to reform his civil administration. His re-issue of the Laws of Wessex, though it incorporated the local codes of Kent and of such of Mercia as he controlled, and so produced a first foundation for what might be called the Law of England, was a muddled and very conservative piece of work which changed little in the primitive codes of his ancestors. The few alterations were what might be expected in an age of perpetual emergency, tending to exalt the power of the King and his servants. Treason became a crime for which no money payment could atone. The King's messengers and court were specially protected and fugitives from his justice might not be sheltered. There were doubled penalties for army deserters and for major offences committed when the Fyrd was out.

In fact Alfred's real contribution was to make the existing system work, and he did so by taking charge of it himself. The tendency of the age was authoritarian, as always in wartime, and, though Alfred was no tyrant, he was certainly a benevolent despot. In the lower courts the Reeves and Ealdormen who presided ceased merely to register the decisions of the assembled freemen and became more and more exponents of the law. Alfred himself settled cases whenever they were brought to him, using his personal prestige always to good ends, but in so doing exalting the power of the Crown to something quite new in the Anglo-Saxon world and producing a much clearer conception of governmental power. We rarely hear of his consulting the Witan, and he called no Church synods to settle difficult points. He settled them himself. 'We admonish you', Pope John VII wrote to the Archbishop of Canterbury, 'to set yourself as a wall for the house of God not only against the King, but also against all who are minded to act perversely'. A petition addressed years later to Edward the Elder gives a vivid picture of how Alfred 'stood and washed his hands at Wardour within the bower' while they stated their case, and then came out to give his decision. 'And, sire,' the document ends, 'if every judgement which King Alfred gave us is to be upset, when shall we come to any conclusion?' It was an age of good justice, but not of constitutional reform.

But all this work would have gone for nothing without some improvement in the Wessex defences. Even the victorious campaigns of 871 and 878 had been totally ruinous because of the difficulty of bringing the highly mobile, hard-hitting Danish army to battle before it had done irretrievable harm. It was not a large army—probably never more than 10,000 men, even when all the bands were concentrated for a big killing—and once pinned down it could be defeated. But it used astonishingly modern combined operations tactics, sending the fleet round the coast to take the enemy in the rear, while the landing parties, always mounted, though they fought on foot, moved inland with bewildering speed to surprise what resistance was gathering before it was properly concentrated.

Alfred's counter-measures were quite simple and obvious, but he was the first European ruler to think the problem out clearly. He enlarged and strengthened the fleet so that, although he could not hope to intercept a main attack before it landed, he could prevent the coastal, outflanking movements which had been so distracting. He increased the number of his Thanes and mounted them, so that he had a small mobile striking force to pin down an invasion which got ashore. Finally he set about fortifying his towns, which seem up to that point to have been quite defenceless; and where there was no town he created new, fortified camps. To provide these new 'burhs' with garrisons he allotted to each a given hidage of land, granted to men on condition that they maintained a house in the burh and were available for the defence of its walls.

We can see the beginnings of the success of these measures in the short Danish raid of 885, which was held up besieging Rochester until the King came up with the fyrd to drive it off, while the fleet held off the East Anglian Danes in some hard fighting in the Thames estuary. But the real test came in 892, when the whole of the 'Great Army', driven off from Germany by the Emperor Arnulf, descended on Kent and Sussex, bringing their wives and families with them for what was clearly intended to be the final conquest and settlement of England. With two fast-moving armies in the field and four Danish fleets operating round the coast, the war became one of bewilderingly rapid manœuvre and fascinating complexity, and at every crisis we find one or other of Alfred's reforms working effectively. When the Sussex division of the Danes set out round the Andredsweald to join their other force in Hertfordshire, Edward, Alfred's eldest son, outmarched them and caught and defeated them at Farnham. A distracting raid by two fleets on Devonshire was foiled by the burh of Exeter, which held out successfully until Alfred came up with the main army. The main attempt by the whole Danish army to break south across the Thames in 893 was headed off by the largest levy of the fyrd ever seen—it is pleasant to find our old friend, Ethelnoth, once again turning out at the head of the men of Somerset—and ended up spending a miserable winter in the deserted ruins of Roman Chester. In the meantime the Atheling Edward had captured their base at Benfleet, ships, wives, plunder and all.

Each year of the war only served to emphasize yet more the impotence of the Danes to make any effective penetration of Wessex. Chichester further proved the value of the new burh policy by standing a siege, and the fyrd seems to have been largely employed protecting the harvesters from raids. Perhaps the most impressive evidence of Alfred's new military strength was provided by the Danes who marched from Chester to regain their base in Essex in the spring of 894 by way of North Wales, Northumbria and East Anglia, 'so as the fyrd might not reach them'. The summer of 895 ended with their whole force blockaded in Thorney Island; and in 896 the host broke up and departed, having, 'by God's mercy,' says the chronicler, 'not utterly broken down the English nation'. So for the last four years of his reign Alfred was left in comparative peace to finish his translations, to potter with the goldsmiths and craftsmen whose work he loved, and to design and try out his new ships 'nigh twice as long as those of others'. One last glimpse of him we get, when he invested his immensely promising six-year-old grandson, Athelstan, with a scarlet cloak, a

jewelled belt, and a Saxon sword with a great scabbard, and
on October 26th, in the year 900, at the early age of fifty-
two, he died.

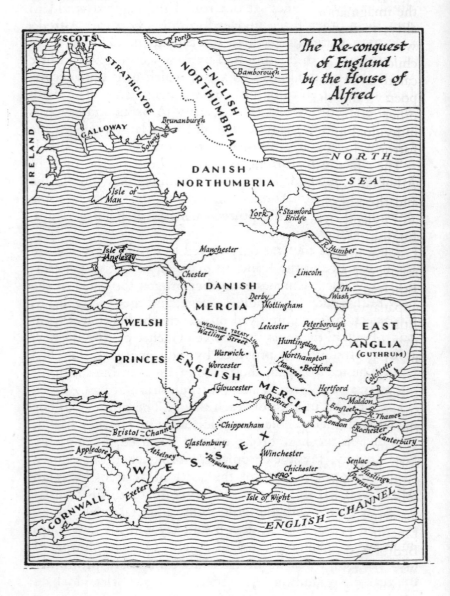

The Re-conquest
of England
by the House of
Alfred

Edward the Elder, who succeeded him, was a remorselessly efficient soldier and administrator, but not the colourful figure that his father had been. His achievements caught the imagination of his contemporaries, but not his personality; so that we know what he did, but little of what he was. We know that he had three wives and fourteen children; that, like all Alfred's children, he was well educated and 'used books frequently', especially old Saxon poetry; and the coins he struck, quite different from any other Saxon coins known, superior in quality and highly individual in design, suggest artistic interests of which, unfortunately, we have no other record.

The thirty-nine years of the reigns of Edward and Athelstan were the period when defence changed to attack, and the kingdom of Wessex expanded into a kingdom of all England. Apart from the firm base south of the Thames, English Mercia was by now securely held, and with it London and the lands north-east of it, which Alfred had recovered from Guthrum in 886 and had handed over to Ethelred, the surviving Ealdorman of Mercia, as a life appanage. He also gave him his very capable daughter, Ethelflaed, for his wife; and her force of character was such that, in that unfeminist age, she came generally to be recognized as co-regent with her husband of English Mercia, an area which stretched from the Watling Street to the Welsh mountains and north as far as Manchester, and which had suffered most severely in the last great Danish war because the burh system had not yet been extended there.

Danish England, which Edward now set himself to absorb piecemeal, was a loose and disorderly confederacy. Guthrum and his sons ruled a kingdom in East Anglia, which included Essex. There were Danish 'Earls', each with his army settled in the surrounding territory, at Stamford, Lincoln, Derby, Nottingham, Leicester, Northampton, Bedford, Cambridge and Huntingdon. In the north there was a total anarchy, to which settled Danes, indigenous Saxons, the Kings of Scotland and Strathclyde, and Danish raiders from Ireland, Norway and Orkney all contributed. Behind that again there was still the Great Army, strengthened by fresh outlaws from a newly united Norway, and not yet drawn in to what was to be its permanent settlement in northern Europe in Normandy. The Welsh princes could on the whole be ruled out. Though still quite untrustworthy, they had rightly decided that the Danes were the worst menace and gave at least a temporary allegiance to the English kings. On the other hand, their perpetual civil wars made them useless as allies.

In two things Edward showed a touch of his father's original genius. In the first place he spotted at once that an incursion of the Danes from East Anglia and Northumbria presented quite a different problem from the homeless Great Army, and, instead of chasing after the invaders' field army, he marched straight into Danish territory, ravaging as far north as the fens, and so forcing the enemy to come back to defend their homes. That won him his first war, in the first two years of his reign. Secondly, he perceived that the burh system, devised by Alfred for defence, could now be turned into a most effective method of attack. He would use his field army as a covering force while he built and garrisoned burh after burh in enemy territory, so achieving a sort of creeping annexation to which the Danes could find no effective counter.

The great war of his reign opened in 910 and lasted for ten years. Ealdorman Ethelred of Mercia died in that year and Edward took back under his direct control London and the territory which he reorganized as the new shires of Buckinghamshire, Oxfordshire, Hertfordshire and Middlesex. The rest of Mercia he left to his sister, Ethelflaed, in the somewhat undefined position of 'Lady of the Mercians'. She became at once the most enthusiastic and efficient collaborator in his burh-building policy, and their joint advance, brilliantly planned and co-ordinated, proved irresistible. She had already, jointly with Ethelred in the year before he died, reoccupied and fortified Chester so as to make communication more difficult between Dublin and York. She now first secured the Welsh frontier and the Severn valley by burhs at Shrewsbury, Bromesberrow, and Bridgnorth, and then pushed forward into Danish territory with three more at Warwick, Derby and Leicester, while Edward at the same time thrust his new burhs into East Anglia and the eastern Midlands at Witham, Maldon, Bedford, Colchester, Northampton, Huntingdon and Towcester. The Danes failed to produce any concerted resistance to this insidious form of aggression, except for one intervention by the Great Army in 913 which entirely failed to breach the defences on both sides of the Bristol Channel. After that the 'Army' disappeared from English history for sixty years, and the only remaining foreign complications were the Danes at Dublin and the Picts and Scots.

As a result of this forward policy southern Essex gave in and accepted Edward's rule in 911, Bedfordshire was secured by 914, and in 916, after some very hard fighting by Ethelflaed in Derby and by Edward himself round Towcester and Colchester, the rest of Essex, East Anglia, and the lands which were subsequently organized into the shires of Northampton, Huntingdon, Cambridge and Derby, all surrendered. In 917 brother and sister took the field together for the last time. Ethelflaed overran Leicester, while Edward took Stamford, Nottingham and Lincoln. Though these were the areas most thickly colonized by Danes, there was no resistance. The remorseless, unspectacular, efficient advance of the last seven years had broken the enemy's spirit. The Northumbrians accepted Edward's overlordship without fighting, and by 920, when the war finally ended, even the Reeve of Bamborough, whose shadowy authority stretched from the Tyne to Edinburgh, the Strathclyde Welsh, who owned the rest of Lowland Scotland, and Constantine, King of Scots, himself had taken 'King Edward for father and lord'.

In 917, in the midst of their joint triumphs, Ethelflaed had died, and Edward, passing over the rights of her daughter, whom he sent into a nunnery, annexed all western Mercia to the Crown. So for the last four years of his life he was practically in control of all England south of the Humber and Mersey, theoretically ruler of the whole of Great Britain. There was of course much consolidation to be done in the East Midlands and East Anglia, where the Danes remained for some years liable to rise in aid of any invasion by their fellow countrymen. As for the submission of Northumbria, that was scarcely more valuable than the homage of Wales, Strathclyde and Scotland—a recognition, merely, of the fact that Edward was for the moment too formidable a foe to be challenged in the open.

So it was left for Athelstan, the most spectacular of all the House of Wessex, to finish the conquest of the north. He quickly lost patience with the feuds and civil wars of the Viking sub-kingdom of York, marched in and annexed the whole of Northumbria. This closed at least one happy hunting ground of Danish exiles and younger sons from Dublin or Norway, but it made Athelstan too powerful for the comfort of his neighbours. The Scots and the Welsh, who had looked to his father to protect them from the Vikings, now began to look to the Vikings to protect them from him. A great preventive raid into the far north of Scotland failed in its object, and in 937, at Brunanburh, just north of the Solway, he had to face a combine of all his enemies: Scots and Strathclyde Welsh, and Danes from Ireland, Orkney, and Norway. This epic fight which provoked the Anglo-Saxon Chronicle, otherwise a dreary, sparse record at this period, to break into epic verse, was still remembered a century later as 'the great battle'. After a whole long day of 'hard hand play', of 'clashing of bills' and 'conflict of banners', the enemy broke and fled in all directions. 'The grey-haired warrior, the old deceiver,' Constantine of Scotland, 'crept home again', and a remnant only of the Irish Vikings regained their ships, so hot was the pursuit.

So Athelstan was at last genuinely King of all England and, for the moment at any rate, 'Emperor of Britain' and

'Lord of all Albion'. His sisters were married to the Emperor and the King of France, the King of Provence, and Hugh Capet, the great Count of Paris. His court was a much sought refuge for foreign exiles, and foreign rulers asked to borrow his fleet to keep the Northmen out of their river mouths. It was a far cry from the stockade at Athelney, and a remarkable achievement by three great men in less than sixty years.

But it was a precarious achievement, depending too much on the ability of the House of Wessex to continue to produce great leaders generation after generation. This for an exceptionally long time it did. But they were all short-lived, and the beginning of each reign produced a crisis which showed how much more time was needed to solidify the united elements of England into a nation. When Athelstan died, only two years after Brunanburh, his nineteen-year-old brother, Edmund, had to face a rising of all the newly conquered districts, and for two humiliating years was forced back behind Alfred's old frontier of the Watling Street. He recovered the line of the Humber in 942 and finally expelled Eric Bloodaxe and Anlaf of Dublin and all the other wrangling Vikings from Northumbria in 944. But at this promising moment he foolishly intervened in a brawl at his own dinner-table and was stabbed to death. This placed the Witan in a dilemma, since they had to choose between his six-year-old elder son and his brother Eadred, who, though brilliantly intelligent, suffered from chronic indigestion and could eat no meat. They chose Eadred and he rose nobly to the occasion. In spite of his indigestion he fought the formidable Eric Bloodaxe to a standstill and after eight years achieved what neither of his brothers nor his father had ever managed, a final pacification of Northumbria. But then, within two years, he too died, leaving the throne to the nephew, still only fifteen years old, who had been passed over in 946.

There followed four disastrous years. The young King Edwy fell into the clutches of an intriguing widow remotely connected with the royal house, called Ethelgifu, who seems to have had behind her a clique of courtiers and magnates, and who planned to secure herself in power by marrying the infatuated boy to her own fifteen-year-old daughter. Matters came to a head at the Coronation banquet when Edwy left his guests almost immediately and withdrew to Ethelgifu's bower. The insulted magnates sent the Abbot of Glastonbury and the Bishop of Lichfield to beg him to return, and there were scandalous stories of the scene they discovered and the row which followed before they at last picked the Crown of England from the corner where it had been kicked, put it on the King's head, and brought him back to the feast.

But Edwy married the girl, nevertheless, and the government controlled by his mother-in-law lasted for two years, by the end of which it had aroused a storm of opposition. The Mercians and Northumbrians broke away and made Edwy's fourteen-year-old brother, Edgar, their king, while the other party hung on to Wessex, and for two years we have the foreboding picture of England divided between rival gangs of powerful magnates, each with a puppet king. But fortunately Edwy then died, and three years later Edgar freed himself from his backers and took firm control of his own kingdom.

Edgar's reign, seventeen years of unbroken peace and prosperity, was the golden age of Saxon England. Its tragedy was that it was so short. For, dying at the age of thirty-two, he left two vital processes still incomplete: the establishment of a really firm control over the magnates who had shown during the minority that they were developing a dangerously independent hereditary power; and the long overdue ecclesiastical reform launched by St. Dunstan from Canterbury and St. Oswald from York.

Dishearteningly little progress had been made since Alfred's first attempts to rehabilitate monastic life in England. In the houses which had survived the ravages of the Danes, canons, mostly married, lived secular lives untroubled by rules or discipline. The parish priests nearly all had wives and often passed their benefices on to their sons. The machinery for collecting tithes and Peter's pence—the annual contribution due to Rome—was haphazard or non-existent. Sundays and feast days were not regularly kept. But at last the great European religious revival, largely the achievement of the reformed Benedictines of Cluny, touched England too, and a spontaneous movement towards reform gave the leaders their chance. Reformed communities at Glastonbury and Abingdon led the way for the monks; and among the laity religious and charitable fraternities in towns and villages showed that there was real strength behind Dunstan's work. Unfortunately, however, not all the Church's leaders were as patient as Dunstan and Oswald, and the grim ferocity with which a man like Ethelwold of Winchester hounded out all canons who would not abandon their old ways and take the full monastic habit provoked a reaction which was later to have serious consequences. Many of the ejected canons had powerful connections outside the Church and so represented a vested interest which it would have been wiser not to challenge so brusquely.

One event which showed clearly the new importance of the ecclesiastical world was Edgar's coronation at Bath, postponed, nobody knows why, until fourteen years after his accession. We see there the first beginnings of the rite which has since so powerfully affected the English conception of kingship, with the King being led to the altar by the two archbishops while the choir sang 'righteousness and judgement are the habitation of thy seat', and all the ceremonial of the oaths and the anointing, and the investiture with crown, ring, sceptre and sword. When it was all over, the King set sail from Bristol with a great fleet, rounded Wales and anchored at Chester to receive the homage of the Scots and Welsh and the Vikings of Man and the Western Isles, and to be rowed to church by eight kings. It was only just over 100 years since Alfred's hasty election and crowning between two pitched battles, and the achievement looked solid enough. But what had been gained by these four generations of able and devoted men was to be thrown away again by the weakness and stupidity of one within thirty years of Edgar's death.

THE END OF THE HOUSE OF ALFRED

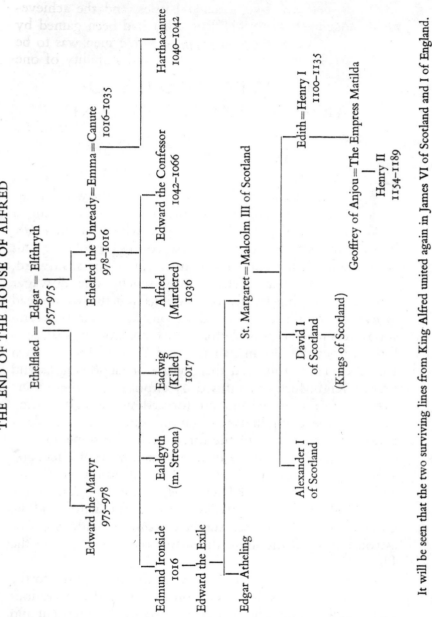

It will be seen that the two surviving lines from King Alfred united again in James VI of Scotland and I of England.

Chapter Three

THE CATASTROPHE OF ANGLO-SAXON ENGLAND

★

The beginning of Edgar's reign had shown that already some of the magnates were establishing a hereditary power and wealth which might easily become uncontrollable. Still worse confusion followed his early death. He left two sons by different mothers: Edward, aged thirteen, and Ethelred, only seven. The dowager Queen's ramifying family connections and the widespread grievances of the dispossessed canons and their powerful supporters made it possible for her to try, though unsuccessfully, to get the Witan to pass over Edward for her own Ethelred. There followed three years of faction fights and private feuds, further confused by expulsions and counter-expulsions of reformed and unreformed monks, culminating on a March evening in 978, when the sixteen-year-old King rode in after hunting to the forecourt of his step-mother's castle at Corfe. Her butler brought out a horn of wine, and as her thanes pressed round him for a toast one seized his hand as though to kiss it. There was a sudden shout from the King: 'What do you, breaking my right arm?' and he crashed from his horse, stabbed from behind. So, disastrously, began the long, disastrous reign of Ethelred the Unready.

There was startlingly little reaction in the country to the murder. There was no opposition to Ethelred's succession; surprisingly enough he was even crowned by Dunstan and Oswald. The murderers went unpunished, one of them,

44

Aelfric, being even promoted Ealdorman five years later. Dunstan very soon withdrew from politics. The greater Ealdormen, men mostly of royal blood ruling over dangerously large blocks of territory which they were rapidly turning into hereditary appanages, seem to have withdrawn each into his own sphere of influence and to have left the central government to the Queen-mother and her camarilla, so long as they in turn were left in peace. There seems to have been no official government policy: Aelfhere of Mercia, for example, restored all the dispossessed canons in his jurisdiction, while Ethelwine of East Anglia backed the reformers. It is not surprising that before long they began to quarrel among themselves.

In this atmosphere Ethelred grew up, a vain, selfish, vicious young man, without strength of mind or character, pleasure-loving and treacherous, easily frightened and cruel in his revenges. He did, indeed, attack, and largely eliminate the greater magnates, but only to replace them with worthless favourites of his own, treacherous and cowardly like himself: Aelfric, his brother's murderer, and Eadric, nicknamed 'Streona', 'the Grasper', who married his daughter, and who betrayed everyone he served, in battle or out of it. There was nothing fundamentally wrong with England; it was no worse than when his father had shaken himself free of leading strings twenty years before. But Ethelred's first recorded action showed what his subjects were in for. Instead of taking legal action in a dispute with the Bishop of Rochester, he harried his lands and besieged his cathedral city and Dunstan had to bribe him with a hundred pounds of silver to withdraw. That was in 986; and already, six years before, there had been the first warning Danish raids in Kent and Devonshire.

Two causes combined to produce a second great plague of Northmen at the turn of the century: a new united kingdom of Denmark and Norway had filled the seas with a fresh crop of outlaws; and the Irish under Brian Boru were forcing the Danes of Dublin and Wexford to seek easier game in the Bristol Channel. It was precisely the same sort of attack that Alfred had beaten off with improvised and infinitely feebler resources. With a hundred years of experience and victory behind them, a fleet more powerful than ever before, and a well-tried military organization, the English could have defeated the Danes with ease. But, as the Chronicle, echoing the Old Testament, lamented: 'When the leader groweth feeble, then is the army sore hindered.' It was a heartbreaking, bitter period to live through; heartbreaking even to describe, with chance after chance missed through cowardice, treachery, or criminal incompetence.

Even the first ten years of only tentative, sporadic raids showed that Ethelred and the men he trusted were totally incapable. Every harbour and river mouth became a happy hunting ground for pirates and the local inhabitants were left to fend for themselves. 'Anything that may be counselled,' wrote the indignant chronicler, 'never stands for a month,' and 'when the enemy is eastward, then are our forces kept westward.' The first really big attack, under the celebrated Olaf Tryggveson, fell on Ipswich in 991 and showed the general pattern of events which was to be repeated almost annually for more than twenty years. Byrhtnoth, the ageing Ealdorman of Essex, lived splendidly up to the old traditions, refused to buy them off, and with his own fyrd met the crews of ninety-three ships in a battle which was to make another great epic poem, Maldon, where he and almost all his thanes were left dead on the field. But now nothing was gained by their heroism. King and Witan decided to buy Olaf off with £10,000, and so added the gruelling taxation of Danegeld to all the other miseries England was asked to bear.

The London burh garrison fought off a big attack in 994, inflicting on the Danes 'more harm and evil than they had ever supposed any citizens could do to them', but the only result was that they moved to Southampton and sat there ravaging until Ethelred paid up another Danegeld. Year after year we hear of local officials, Ealdormen and High

Reeves, gallantly doing their duty—in Hampshire, Dorset, and Wiltshire in 1001, and in East Anglia in 1004—and generally paying for it with their lives, while the King, when he was not skulking out of the way, was operating in the wrong part of the country. Three times at least a great fleet was fitted out for decisive action. Aelfric brought about the defeat of one by betraying the plans to the enemy. The second frittered away the summer without doing anything. Half of the third took to piracy and by the time they had finished fighting among themselves they were out of provisions. On land Ethelred never took the field himself, and his treacherous or incompetent generals—Aelfric or Streona—either could not bring the Danes to battle, or fought half-heartedly. 'The leaders first of all began the flight,' says the chronicler, bitterly and repeatedly. Meanwhile the Danegelds that brought no respite rose steadily: to £24,000 in 1002; £36,000 in 1007; and to £48,000 in 1012. At Court it was an endless story of intrigue and murder for private ends, of heirs blinded or mutilated. By the end there were at least three known murderers who had been rewarded with earldoms.

They planned a nation-wide fast on water and herbs and they had a special mass said against the heathen. But the most futile expedient of all was the general massacre of all the Danes they could lay hands on on St. Brice's Day, 1002, which, since the sister of Sweyn, King of Denmark and Norway, was among the victims, brought the official forces of two nations into the scale the next year; and that in turn led to the landing of Sweyn in 1013 with the settled intention of permanent conquest. Only London offered resistance. Men would fight for Ethelred no longer and even Wessex recognized Sweyn, drunken, heathen pirate though he was, almost with relief. Ethelred still had a fleet of thirty ships, but he used it only to convey himself and his family to Normandy with such plunder as he had been able hastily to collect by ravaging Kent. Yet, incredible though it must seem, he was restored by the Witan when Sweyn suddenly died, and there were two more years of misery and civil war, and some exceptionally scandalous murders by Streona with the King's connivance. When Ethelred at last died in 1016 he left to his gallant son, Edmund Ironside, London only and a handful of still faithful thanes. The rest was held by Sweyn's son, Canute, who would have completed the conquest earlier but for troubles in Denmark and Norway.

The best commentary on the ineptitude of Ethelred and his government is provided by the staggering events of the year 1016. Almost friendless, with every man's loyalty corrupted by thirty years of betrayal, with no fleet and no army, Edmund all but snatched victory in a single campaign reminiscent of the great early days of Alfred. In a lightning dash into Wessex he raised enough men to cut to pieces a Danish detachment at Penselwood. Then, in a hard-fought battle, he cleared his way back to London, which was still holding out, defeated Canute at Brentford, followed him into Kent and defeated him again at Otford. Driven back into its ships, the all-conquering Danish army had become a mere marauding fleet plundering the Essex coast and one more great victory might have settled the matter. But at this crisis Edmund made the fatal mistake of trusting Streona, who had just changed sides for the second time; and at Ashington Streona deserted with all the Mercian levies as the battle started, leaving the rest to be butchered. Even so, enough had been done to save half a kingdom. Canute made peace, leaving Edmund all Alfred's old kingdom with the addition of Essex and East Anglia. So the whole future of England seemed once again in the balance when, a few weeks later, Edmund died. Possibly Canute had him poisoned: it would have been quite in keeping with what we know of his ways. But more probably he was simply worn out by that gruelling summer.

Edmund left an eighteen-year-old brother under whom there might have been yet another of those miraculous recoveries which had happened so often in the history of the

House of Wessex, but the Witan was too exhausted and dispirited to face the certainty of renewed war, and let Canute talk them into electing him king of all England. Edmund's infant sons, twins not a year old, Canute sent off to Olaf of Sweden with a private word that it would be convenient if they were never heard of again. The surviving brother attempted insurrection, was betrayed by his friends, hunted down and killed. There remained, however, Ethelred's second wife, Emma, who had carried her two sons, Alfred and Edward, out of his reach to her own family in Normandy. Cynically he offered to marry her, on condition that she abandoned her children and any claim they might have to the throne. The offer was accepted in the spirit in which it was made, Emma cheerfully abandoning her sons provided Canute in return declared illegitimate his two sons by the daughter of a Mercian Ealdorman. So it was agreed that any son the two might have should succeed in England, and the last possible dynastic threat from the old Saxon royal house seemed to have been provided for.

Up to the moment of his accession Canute had shown himself as barbarous as any of his Danish ancestors, exceptional only for his cunning. Before leaving for Denmark on Ethelred's brief restoration in 1014 he had put ashore at Sandwich his Saxon hostages with their noses, ears and hands cut off, and those of his enemies whom he could not easily or openly murder had a way of dying suddenly and mysteriously. But he was an intelligent, methodical man on the make. He wished to be respected as a Christian and civilized sovereign and he had the wit to acquire the necessary veneer. Moreover, Denmark had gone for the moment to his brother, so that he had no official force behind him, and England could not be held down permanently by an army of freebooters. From all points of view Canute had to make himself acceptable to his English subjects; and since he was an adept at compromise and a master of sententious propaganda, and, moreover, an extremely competent administrator, he succeeded admirably and managed to come down in legend and history as the wise, good king, who kept the peace, served the Church, and rebuked vanity.

The tidying-up process with which he began his reign shows at once the long-headed, calculating skill which were to characterize the next nineteen years. The execution of a large number of Saxon magnates and the levy of a Danegeld twice as large as Ethelred's largest might have heralded merely a brutal military tyranny. But gradually the policy became apparent. His victims were mostly Ethelred's treacherous friends. 'I will repay your service,' he said to Streona, 'with the reward you have deserved,' and thereupon called in Earl Eric of Northumbria to cut off his head. 'But those who had been faithful to Edmund he much loved.' He used the great Danegeld to pay off his army and send it home, keeping only a bodyguard of Housecarles to man his small standing fleet, and Saxons soon began to infiltrate even into that. The great earldoms were divided evenly between Danes and Saxons, most of Northumbria and eastern Mercia going to Danes. All that he did was impartial and sensible. When in due course he inherited Denmark and conquered Norway, he opened up markets which enormously expanded English trade, especially that of London. When he went on pilgrimage to Rome he used his great international prestige to extract lower tariffs for English continental trade and better terms for English pilgrims. He became a great patron of the Church and an ostentatious devotee of the English saints.

In fact he gave England peace and prosperity and a return of self-respect. That it was all done entirely cynically made no difference to his subjects. His proclamation, sent from Rome in 1027 to report progress, was a characteristic masterpiece of sanctimonious propaganda, mixing news of commercial advantages with pious aspirations which came oddly from a man who had just had his brother-in-law murdered after a quarrel over a game of chess. But these proclamations achieved their object, and he died in 1035 not only respected, but loved.

1. Canute and Emma dedicating a shrine, from a contemporary MS.

(*By kind permission of the Trustees of the British Museum*)

He left an even more tangled dynastic situation than his Saxon predecessors. His only legitimate son, Harthacanute, though only sixteen, was already ruling Denmark and had been promised England. His elder illegitimate son, Sweyn, was struggling to hold down Norway. Over in Normandy there were Emma's other children, Alfred and Edward; and far away in Hungary, where the kindly Olaf of Sweden had sent them to be out of reach, were still the sons of Edmund Ironside. But on the spot there was the younger illegitimate son, Harold Harefoot, just eighteen, ambitious and locally popular in the north. By choosing Harold the Witan made war with Denmark almost certain and civil war in England highly probable.

There followed another of those interludes of chaos which in Saxon history seemed almost the rule after any long and successful reign. Emma stood out for the rights of her Harthacanute and secured for him the kingdom of Wessex, whose powerful earl, Godwin, son of the man whose mutiny and piracy had wrecked the great naval effort of 1009, came temporarily to her side. But Harthacanute was delayed by war in Norway and Godwin found it increasingly hard to hold his kingdom for him. The landing of Alfred from Normandy, nominally to see his mother, but accompanied by the rather large bodyguard of 600 knights, gave the Earl a chance to change sides. He feasted Alfred at Guildford and billeted his men in small parties about the town to be massacred later in the night. Alfred, handed over to Harold, was blinded and sent to die as a monk at Ely. This gave Harold the whole kingdom for three years until he died, in 1040, just as Harthacanute, accompanied by his mother and his half-brother, Edward, was about to land and claim his crown. On a basis of amnesty all round he was now duly chosen king. But he, too, very shortly died, leaving Edward as the only immediately available heir. So there succeeded in 1042 the last of the male line of Alfred to sit on the throne of England, Edward, nicknamed the Confessor.

On the whole Edward, feeble though he was, was an improvement on Canute's sons, all of whom had reverted to type. Harold Harefoot had been stupid and cruel. Harthacanute's first act on landing had been to have his brother's body dug up and cast naked on to the Thames mud; and he had died drinking at a marriage feast. Edward was not virile enough to be vicious. Rosy-cheeked and prematurely white-haired, almost a churchman, since he had taken vows of chastity which he kept even after his marriage, he could take infinite trouble over things which did not matter, but was quite incapable of grasping or using power. He dealt firmly with the mother who had neglected him for twenty-six years, forcing her to disgorge the wealth accumulated from two complaisant husbands and to retire on a modest competence to Winchester. But this was an isolated occasion. He was dignified and far more civilized than any of his immediate predecessors, with the effeminate manners acquired from the Norman-French clerics. He loved ritual and ceremonial and he made in all ways an admirable figurehead. When his will was crossed he could be petulant, but he was never in a rage, and provided he was left undisturbed to his fasts and prayers, to give lavish gifts to the Church and prefer a reasonable number of his Norman friends to high office, he was content to leave government to others. The Witan was consulted about everything and executive power fell mostly to Earl Godwin who, in spite of having 'martyred' the King's brother, had managed another adroit change of sides and was now the King's father-in-law and very much the over-mighty subject.

The Saxon England which enjoyed, under Godwin and his sons, a last twenty years of somewhat uneasy peace, was a very different place from the kingdom which Athelstan had triumphantly united a century before. In the first place, in spite of Danish depredations, it was a great deal richer. Indeed the Danes were much greater traders than the Saxons, who, according to Tacitus, had always hated town life, and under their influence York grew steadily on the

proceeds of Scandinavian trade, and a brisk trade with the
Dublin Danes began to turn Chester into something more
than a military outpost. But it was above all in London,
refounded by Alfred as a garrison town and still governed
by a military guild, that the Danes made themselves most
felt. The beginnings of the great English woollen export
trade brought in exchange wine from France and Germany
and cloth from Flanders. There were busy wharves all down
the river front and the empty spaces inside the city walls
were fast filling up with small houses and shops. It was the
great growth of wealth and population and of a sturdy independence which made London the last stronghold against
the Danes in 1016; but it was also London which chiefly
benefited from Canute's continental empire and the new,
profitable markets which his European prestige was able to
open up.

The growth of trade and industry in the towns and the
beginnings of international commerce inevitably altered
life in the villages too. The purely self-supporting agricultural community began here and there to give way to a
rudimentary specialization. Fishing and mining villages, the
salt workers of Droitwich and the iron workers who were
slowly hacking their way into the Weald, could find
flourishing market towns for the exchange of their produce.
Everywhere men were becoming less isolated and more
prosperous, but they were also becoming less free. The
formation of a military aristocracy on whom all men were
to a greater or lesser extent dependent had been inevitably
accelerated by 150 years of war. When the heathen had
burnt and harried their way through the countryside it was
only too easy for the rich and powerful to grab the lands of
poorer neighbours, for titles were hard to prove and even
harder to enforce. The lordless man was obliged to 'commend' himself to his most powerful neighbour as much to
protect himself from his own countrymen as from the Danes,
or to secure a loan to rebuild his homestead and re-stock his
farm after a raid. Thereby his absolute freehold was lost. He

had to attend his lord's court and perform the services which would alone enable the lord in his turn to carry out the military and administrative duties which he owed for his land to the King.

This attachment of duties and services to the holding of all land, which was the essence of feudalism, was the only way in which it was possible to expand the rudimentary machinery of local government to the needs of a national kingdom. There was no other system which could provide 'burh' garrisons and if the Church was to be endowed bishops and abbots had to be allowed to apply the same system in the lands they held of the King. At the same time the needs of war speeded up the process whereby cash sales superseded barter, and rents and services began to be paid in money rather than kind. The primitive method by which the King must travel round literally eating and drinking his fines and taxes and the produce of his manors, reckoning them in terms of lambs and eggs and vats of honey, clearly would not sustain the governmental and military machine needed by an Edward the Elder. A national fleet meant a national system of taxation, which put a further strain on the small independent man. If he surrendered and took his land instead on loan or 'lease' from the local abbey or the nearest King's thane, then he secured the backing of a capitalist whose interest it would be to tide him over a crisis—war damage, or a bad harvest. When Ethelred's really crushing taxation for Danegeld was superimposed on all this, the lordless man went to the wall altogether.

Thanks to the piecemeal and fluctuating nature of the unification of the country, this pattern was infinitely varied. The amount of independence each man had forfeited and the type of service he might now have to perform depended on local conditions or the whim of the king or rich landowner at the moment when he was endowing a new monastery. There was a great difference between the south and west and the Danish districts where the surviving earls had a more compact power than their Saxon counterparts and the soldier conqueror settled on the land achieved a superior position which still further depressed that of his Saxon neighbour. Even more confused were the various jurisdictions which sprang up all over the country. Below the Shire Courts, at which twice a year the Thanes and the Reeves with their village deputations met the Earl and the Bishop, there was a confusion of old free courts and private jurisdictions, established haphazard as the kings progressively faced the difficulty of governing anything as large as England from Winchester or London. There was an absence of system—a ramshackle quality about the whole structure —which the Normans were to find extremely confusing and irritating in a few years' time.

The Confessor's weakness, which allowed England to become the battleground of wrangling earls, prolonged for another twenty years the conditions which were producing this confusion. Godwin, son of the pirate, exploited power ruthlessly for his own profit, suppressing monasteries and grabbing the land of his weaker dependents. His sons, Sweyn in the Welsh Marches and Harold in East Anglia, were no better. Sweyn in the end was forced to leave England as a result of his abduction of the lovely Abbess of Leominster; and a few years later, in 1051, the whole family followed him into exile, having quarrelled with the group of Norman clerics and advisers round the King, taken to arms, and found that they had insufficient backing. But Godwin and Harold fought their way back in 1052, burning most of the towns on the south coast on the way, and from then until the end of the reign dominated King and country. They engineered the outlawry of Robert of Jumièges, the Norman-bred Archbishop of Canterbury, and in defiance of the Pope installed their friend Stigand, Bishop of Winchester, in his place. From Godwin's death in 1053 it was Harold who governed England, and there is every reason to suppose that he was scheming from the start to get the crown for himself.

It has sometimes been the fashion to present Harold as a

last incarnation of all the Saxon virtues who would, but for the mischance of a single arrow, have revived the glories of Alfred and Athelstan and saved a freer England from being involved in Norman and Angevin continental quarrels. The known facts do not support such a view. The England which he governed held no great promise of progress and civilization; and Harold himself, during his eighteen years or so of public life, showed that he had none of the wisdom and magnanimity of Alfred and few of the strong man qualities of Athelstan. From the very start he was playing a losing hand. Both his personal power and that of the government steadily declined between 1053 and 1066. Welsh and Scottish interference forced him in the end to accept Edwin and Morcar, the grandsons of Leofric, Canute's Earl of Mercia, as Earls of Mercia and Northumbria, so that half England was in the hands of the one family which could rival his and which he could never wholly conciliate. Abroad there were other dangers which he could do nothing to conjure. The King of Norway nursed claims on the English throne based on promises made by Harthacanute. King Swyen of Denmark had similar claims. Duke William of Normandy had extracted some sort of promise of the succession from the King when he visited England in 1051, and this claim Harold had to some extent promised to support in order to get away from William when an unlucky chance blew his ship ashore on the French coast in 1064, though whether he swore to help on a casket of relics, as the Norman story went, will never be known. Finally, he had somehow to get round the undoubted rights of Edgar the Atheling, grandson of Edmund Ironside, whom Edward had fetched back from Hungary. The election of Canute was the only doubtful precedent he could offer the Witan for choosing a King outside the royal house.

The death of Edward the Confessor, the crisis for which he had been preparing, came on 5th January, 1066. In one way he was lucky it was no later, since Edgar was still just young enough to be represented as unfit to take over the kingdom. But it was a bad moment from other points of view. Harold Hardrada of Norway was at last free of war and was planning to use the claims of Harold's own brother, Tostig, who had been expelled for misgovernment from the earldom of Northumbria, as an excuse for invasion. Worse still, Edward's long illness had given William of Normandy plenty of warning, and he too was beginning to get ready. Nevertheless Harold committed himself to the gamble, and the opening stages went with smooth efficiency. King Edward was buried early on the morning after he died. At high mass that same morning Harold was chosen by the Witan and crowned King of England.

Chapter Four

THE NORMAN CONQUEST

How it happened and what it meant

✯

Anatural love of lost causes and admiration for a game fighter against odds must not obscure the fact that, had Harold been a truly great patriot, he would have backed the cause of the sixteen-year-old Edgar and so rallied a loyalty far more whole-hearted than any member of his own predatory family could command. Had he been more able, he would not, after thirteen years in charge of the kingdom, have found himself facing the possibility of three separate sea-borne invasions without a fleet. By personal energy and courage he did indeed produce, in his short nine months' reign, a last flicker of what had been the glories of Alfred and Athelstan. But the hard facts of 1066 were that he was trying desperately to heal political rifts in the state for which he and his family had been as much as anybody responsible, and to meet attack from the most efficient and up-to-date power in Europe with a military machine whose organization and tactics were obsolete.

Personal energy, however hectic, could not remake England in four months. When, in May, Tostig with thirty shiploads of pirates and adventurers, fell upon the Kent coast and the Isle of Wight, the fleet was not ready and Harold himself was in the north trying to shore up Northumbrian loyalty and, by marrying the sister of Edwin and Morcar, to animate to enthusiasm their somewhat tentative patriotism. He beat Tostig off easily enough, though only to send him round to wait off the Scottish coast for the great fleet Harold Hardrada had promised to fit out. Even when the fleet was at sea off the Solent and an army massed on the south coast, from June until September, his diplomatic isolation and the dual threat from Scandinavia and Normandy threw him on a defensive which lacked all initiative. There was nothing he could do but wait—the worst possible game for territorial levies with half their minds on the harvest, and for the primitive administrative machine which found it hard to keep the fleet victualled.

No errors of staffwork, miscalculations of time and distance or of necessary supplies, marred William's smooth preparations. For him the opportunity had come at the most favourable moment possible. He was on excellent terms with France. His more dangerous neighbours were all either tangled in troubles of their own or prepared to come in with him on a profit-sharing basis. Thanks to Harold's maintenance of the schismatic Stigand as Archbishop of Canterbury, the Pope was easily persuaded to send a consecrated banner to bless the enterprise and so lend colour to the propaganda which represented the predatory raid as a righteous crusade against 'the oath-breaker'. Every adventurer in Europe flocked to him, and the Norman barons, though they refused in Council to commit the Duchy officially to so risky an enterprise, almost all volunteered privately for English land and wealth in proportion to the size of the contingents they brought. Meanwhile the Normandy ports were feverishly at work collecting and building the 800 transports and store ships needed to carry a force of 12,000 men, their horses and supplies, across the Channel. By the beginning of September William had completed the concentration of his troops on the Dives and on the 12th began to move forward to St. Valéry-en-Caux where his fleet was assembling. Four days earlier Harold, finding his crews mutinous for want of provisions, had to send his ships round to London to refit and revictual; and three days later the united fleets of Tostig and Harold Hardrada sailed into the Humber.

It was Harold's misfortune to come up against two of the most formidable and picturesque heroic figures in Europe simultaneously. William, bastard son of the tanner's daughter Arlette, had had to fight every inch of the way to get control of his own duchy and keep it. He was now forty; a tall, stark, unfriendly man, a great fighter whose bow no one else in Europe could bend, a born leader and organizer, cold in his rages and deadly in revenge. Harold Hardrada was another mighty warrior; a soldier of fortune who had commanded a brigade of guards at Byzantium and fought his way as far as Novgorod, winning the King of Russia's sister as his wife. He was seven feet tall, cunning, fearless and immensely strong: the sort of leader under whom Norsemen were most dangerous. Harold was no match for these men in reputation or stature: 'A little man,' the Norse poet said, 'and he sat proudly in his stirrups.' Yet within a month he all but defeated both of them.

Once the crisis was on him the fretful energy of four months of baffled inactivity and the knowledge that only quick, spectacular success would maintain his precarious hold on English loyalty drove Harold forward with bewildering speed. The moment he heard that Hardrada was ashore he marched north with his 3,000 or so Housecarles, leaving the south coast to be watched by such of the fyrd as had not deserted, but depending, as he knew, on the north wind which had blown the Norsemen down from Scotland to keep William penned in St. Valéry until he got back. Nine days later, at dawn on the 25th, he marched into York, having picked up enough Midland levies on the way to muster a sizeable army. Edwin and Morcar had been heavily defeated outside the city on the 20th and Hardrada and Tostig had withdrawn, with 150 citizens as hostages, to Stamford Bridge, seven miles away on the Derwent, to await hostages from the rest of Northumbria and draw in Tostig's northern friends. A detachment of the army lay ten miles away from the main body; some of them had left their horses and armour with the ships; and the first they knew of Harold's presence was the flash of the English armour, 'like glistening ice', as the sun broke through the early morning haze. Even so it was a hard fought day. This was the largest army the Norsemen had ever thrown into England and it was not until late in the evening that the gallant last stand of the rearguard round the bridge was overcome. But by then Harold Hardrada and Tostig and most of their troops lay dead. Three hundred ships had sailed into the Humber; the survivors could only man twenty-four for the return.

For a moment it seemed like Alfred and Ironside rolled into one. But circumstances had forced Alfred and Ironside to improvise; faulty organization was at the root of most of Harold's difficulties. His other antagonist was a man whose provisions did not run out when contrary winds delayed his sailing and whose movements were planned and executed with unhurried precision. Three days after Stamford Bridge William's army landed unopposed at Pevensey. 'Had I been there', Harold cried when the news reached him at York on October 2nd, 'they never had made good their landing.' But it was not the fault of an unlucky change of wind that his fleet was immobilized in the Thames; and it was almost certainly a mistake now to use against William's methodical invasion the same headlong tactics as had been so spectacularly successful against Hardrada. For within five days Harold was back in London—a march of 200 miles. Four days later, on October 11th, he moved out again, and on the 13th emerged from the forest on to the spur of high ground north of Hastings where Battle Abbey now stands— another sixty miles in less than three days.

With the best will in the world Edwin and Morcar could not have brought their dismounted levies south at that pace, and only fragments of the available forces from East Anglia and the southern Midlands were there. Deliberately Harold challenged William to battle with less than half the troops he might have had by waiting a day or two. His brother, Gyrth, would have had him delay, devastating the surrounding country and forcing William to leave his base at Hastings and come through the forest to seek them out. Meanwhile, he thought, English resistance would harden behind them. But Harold's haste and William's cautious hugging of the coast for the past fortnight, when London and the south had lain at his mercy, only make sense if both of them calculated that English loyalty and resistance, if given time, were more likely to disintegrate than to stiffen. Clearly each of them thought that his best chance of success lay in one great victory; for, when Harold began to dig himself in on the immensely strong position which he had chosen at Senlac, William joyfully marched forward to attack it. At nine in the morning on October 14th the Norman archers opened the battle.

Only a lucky chance would have given the English victory. Against a heavily armed, well-disciplined force of professional soldiers—the cream of fighting Europe—they had few archers and no cavalry; and more than half their men were raw country levies, armed mostly with shield and spear, some having only scythes or clubs. But the position Harold had taken up, about 1,000 yards wide, with both flanks protected by steep slopes and the dense forest at his rear, reduced the Norman tactical advantages to a minimum and made it one of the hardest fought battles in history. It was clear by the middle of the afternoon that frontal attacks could not break the shield wall which still stood firm along the entire length of the ridge. The great two-handed axes of the household troops and thanes massed round Harold's standards in the centre had done fearful execution. William had had two horses killed under him, and once he had to ride the length of his line unhelmeted to stop a panic rumour that he had been killed. As a last expedient he tried a feigned flight of his whole right wing, remembering how he had been able, earlier in the day, to ride down some of the Saxon levies who had dashed down the hill against

2. Three scenes from the Bayeux Tapestry of the Battle of Hastings. *Top:* The rival tactics. Shield wall and horsemen. *Centre:* William raises his helmet to show he is still alive. *Bottom:* Harold mortally wounded as the shield wall breaks

(Victoria and Albert Museum. Crown copyright)

orders to pursue a broken charge. The stratagem was the turning point of the day. Huge masses of the Saxons, thinking the battle won, poured down the slope to be cut to pieces by the Norman cavalry in the valley and there were not enough left to hold the ridge. But the better disciplined regular troops on the high ground in the centre still stood firm. Unless he could overcome them and kill Harold himself, his victory would be worth little. He broke them in the end by pulling back his troops and, between cavalry charges, directing into the mass a dropping fire of arrows against which their shields were no protection. Whatever may be said of the decadence of Saxon England, it died magnificently. 'The only movement', says the Norman chronicler, 'was the dropping of the dead; the living stood motionless.' Pierced through the eye, Harold leant in agony on his shield as the horsemen at last broke through the thinning defence to cut him down. True to the ancient tradition of the race, the Housecarles stood and died to a man round his body.

Both Harold and William had been right in thinking that a single battle would decide the fate of England. The forces behind Harold disintegrated at his death as completely as those behind William would have done had it been a Saxon axe rather than a Norman arrow that had struck home. Prudently avoiding any direct trial of strength, William marched ravaging round London through Wallingford to Berkhampstead; and there a deputation from the Witan, ironically headed by Stigand, offered him the crown. A wavering attempt to put Edgar on the throne had broken down, and Edwin and Morcar withdrew north to await events. On Christmas Day William was crowned in the Confessor's new abbey at Westminster, and within a few weeks the northern earls accepted the accomplished fact and sent in their submissions. Hastings had not been a battle between two nations; it had been two men fighting for a crown.

But it had been a battle between two civilizations. There

was little in Anglo-Saxon England which did not offend the tidy, rather clerkly Norman mind, accustomed to institutions which were clear-cut, logical, centralized and uniform. A Norman's status could be determined with almost mathematical precision. The baronies of roughly equal size, whether they were held by nobles or the Church, had to bring their sub-tenants in groups of five knights to the Duke's army; and the knights were maintained in their manors by the labour dues uniformly owed by the serfs. The law followed the same pattern. Every tenant had his court, which the sub-tenant must attend, and himself attended the court of his over-lord. At the top of the scale the Duke exercised rights of wardship over the heirs of his tenants-in-chief and of giving their heiresses in marriage, and claimed fixed money grants on certain occasions: an aid on the marriage of his eldest son; a relief from each heir who succeeded. At the bottom the peasant had to have permission from the lord of the manor to marry, and his son paid as a 'heriot' his best animal in order to succeed to his father's holding. There was a clearly defined criminal code and the Duke's court controlled the whole legal system, reserving from the local courts such types of case as might involve the public peace, granting or witholding the right to build castles, and enforcing the Duke's right to garrison them when necessary. A similar chain of courts and officials controlled the affairs of the Church, radiating also from the Duke, who called Church Councils and, subject to a remote Papal approval, appointed the bishops. It was, in fact, a planner's dream: the organization of life into an efficient military and judicial machine controlled by a single man.

This was the pattern which the Normans sought to impose on the haphazard, hand-to-mouth feudalism of the Saxons. They were not wholly successful, but what they achieved amounted to a social revolution. In the villages, where nine-tenths of the population lived, they would recognize only three categories of men: freemen, villeins, or cottars. The innumerable gradations of the Saxon village,

the partial sacrifices of free tenure, and the odd, single obligations, some personal, some attached to a holding, which
resulted in one man owing suit to the courts of two different
lords, were all swept away. A man was either free or not free.
If free, he could sell, transfer, lease and bequeath his land as
he pleased. Though he must commend himself to a lord and
pay rent or service for the protection he received, he could
transfer his allegiance if he wished. If not free he must either
be a villein or a cottar. The villein normally farmed thirty
strips in the common field and worked three days a week,
and extra days at busy times, on the domain of the lord of
the manor. The cottar had only three to five strips, worked
only one day a week for his lord, and was free to hire out
his labour for the rest as he chose. Both were tied to the
manor, but were protected in life and limb. Each had a
cottage and a garden; and the status of each descended to his
children.

Since the system was imposed by aliens on a conquered
people, inevitably the partially free were scaled down
rather than up. Four centuries of Anglo-Saxon civilization
had meant for the average peasant farmer a slow but steady
loss of freedom. For the vast majority the Norman conquest
completed the process. The Saxon village and agriculture
were left, but on each a manor and a manor court were imposed. The tangle of obligations and the variations from
village to village of sizes of holding, rules of service, and
type of legal jurisdiction were all ruthlessly sorted into a
single pattern. Within twenty years, when the Domesday
Book was compiled by the Conqueror's order, so that the
Treasury officials at Winchester could know the value,
population, acreage and stock of every manor south of the
Tyne, only one per cent of the old Saxon holders still owned
their land. About one-eighth of the whole population were
freemen, most of them concentrated in the old Danish
areas of Lincolnshire and East Anglia. Of the remainder,
more than half were villeins; about a third cottars. But on
the other side it must be remembered that the reformed

Church which the Normans also brought with them refused to tolerate the Saxon slaves who had been merely the property of their lords. If the conquest levelled the Saxon thane and Danish freeman down to the status of a yeoman farmer and the Saxon yeoman down to villeinage, it at least raised the slave to a cottar with homestead and land and limited, but defined, rights; and by the end of the century slavery was no longer known in England.

Though the idea of a semi-slave status which tied a man to a piece of land and which descended unavoidably to his children shocks the modern mind, it would be a mistake to think of the villeins as necessarily an unhappy and discontented class. A close-knit community with clear obligations for everybody was an advantage to the small farmer in troublous times which far outweighed independence if it meant combined action to meet bad harvests and the ravages of war. Few men wanted to wander from their native villages and the personal ambition of most was limited to the hope that they might live to a reasonable age and rear a family without major disaster. The theoretically rigorous scale of week and boon work was in practice lightened by the many holidays imposed by Church festivals, local fairs and the like. And, though it was in their manorial system that the Normans most nearly realized their ideal pattern of society, they soon found that 'the custom of the manor' was a two-edged weapon which Saxon villeins were well able to use to get what they believed to be their rights. In the long run the lord was as dependent on his villeins as they on him, and their contentment and prosperity were vital to his. In England there was an additional force at work. The Normans, however invulnerable in bulk, were only 100,000 men and women engulfed in two million Anglo-Saxons. Individually they were always in a tiny minority; and the Saxon peasant, with his sturdy sense of the tolerable limits of power and of his own immemorial rights and customs in a village which had existed long before the manor and would outlast it, was in a stronger bargaining position than any other in Europe. Moreover, he had, deeply ingrained, the habit of corporate action and this, rather than the tyranny of an aristocracy, was the dominant fact in manorial courts.

Personal factors were also at work from the very first to modify the Norman system in its higher reaches. On the one hand the fact of the conquest gave the new king an almost clean slate. As he granted power and lands he could and did take precautions against their misuse against himself. The eldest son, and he only, might succeed to the privileges which gradually accumulated round the tenure of land direct from the king. The homage by which sub-tenants promised to serve their lord must never be allowed to override the loyalty and duty owed by both to the over-lord. The Conqueror rewarded his more powerful and faith-ful supporters generously, but so scattered their manors that it would not be easy to raise a private army against him, only allowing large compact fiefs on the borders of Wales and Scotland where strong marcher lords were needed to hold the frontier. So that there we have one of the threads which can be traced through English history for more than five centuries after the conquest: the tendency of the king to mistrust and to seek to curtail the power of his barons; to enforce his own writs and intrude his law and authority into areas where the barons in turn hung grimly on to what power they had and sought, where possible, to extend it.

But on the other hand, always working to prevent any conflict between king and barons being pushed to extremes, there was the basic fact that the conquest had been a joint-stock enterprise in which the king and barons depended absolutely upon each other. The king could not govern the country without the co-operation of the great feudal land-owners. Equally the feudal lords could not destroy the power of the king without destroying the basis of their own. But, while in other countries both sides were constantly prepared, under the stress of temporary grievance or blind hatred, to commit this form of indirect self-destruction, the fact of the conquest in England, for two or three vital generations at least, forced king and barons, however they might bicker, to a fundamental collaboration, because always both were conscious that the vast bulk of the people were subject, alien and potentially hostile. In the last analysis they had to stand together.

Politically speaking the history of England, though not always happy, has generally been happier than that of other nations. She avoided in the seventeenth and eighteenth centuries both the excesses of French over-centralized, over-powerful monarchy and the chaos left behind by feudal disorder in Germany; and in modern times she has so far managed by ceaseless adaptation of her system to harmonize the need for government with increasingly exacting demands for self-government. Some historians have seen the remote origin of this good fortune in the almost magical chemical blend of Norman-French blood with Anglo-Saxon to produce in the Englishman, nicely balanced, a sense of order and a love of liberty. To others the impact of Norman efficiency and logic on the Saxon love of liberty and of traditional rights has seemed the decisive factor. Both were undoubtedly important consequences of the conquest. But most important of all, perhaps, were the two hard facts that for the century that followed king and barons were dependent on each other for survival in a conquered land, and that both were obliged, since they were so small a minority, to adapt themselves to some extent to the wishes of the folk they governed. At least as important as the social revolution effected by the Normans in England were the gradual modifications imposed on their system by the English outlook and habit of thought. The two combined to give the nation a start politically over others which it has never wholly lost.

But while it is possible now to reach this comforting conclusion on the ultimate benefit to England of the conquest, to argue that the lot of the villein in practice was less hard than in crude feudal theory, and that in the cultural sphere

the Norman link with European civilization was of incalculable benefit, none of these considerations alter the fact that
the conquest itself was harsh and created widespread misery.
The complete break-up of the old governing class, the ob-
trusion of new foreign lords and officials, and the ruthless
enforcement of a new and much more regimented way of
life could scarcely do otherwise. When, in 1069, Edwin and
Morcar, Edgar Atheling, and all the surviving northern earls
rose in rebellion with Danish backing, butchered 500
Norman knights in Durham, and burnt York city and
minster, the Conqueror took a fearful revenge. Every
village and town, farmhouse and standing crop between
York and Durham was burnt; the cattle were driven off and
the surviving population was left to starve. For a century or
more the north remained in large part an uninhabited,
ruined, weed-grown waste; and that, too, was one consequence of the conquest. 'Cold heart and bloody hand Now
rule the English land,' a northern poet sang. Against the
fifteen great cathedrals which the Normans built within
forty years and the wholly beneficial reforms which brought
the English Church into line with the rest of western Christendom, must be set centuries of war in France which wasted
English blood and treasure to no English purpose. The historian may say, rightly, that the conquest was ultimately of incalculable benefit to England. To the Englishman of the time
it did not appear as a kindly and civilizing influence.

An exception to this generalization must, however, be
made in favour of the reform of the English Church carried
through in a much more kindly, sensible spirit by Lanfranc,
with whom William replaced Stigand at Canterbury. It can
be argued that life for the ordinary man in town and village
was often more cheerful and pleasant under the anarchic,
happy-go-lucky Saxon way of life and that too big a price
had to be paid for Norman orderliness. There was nothing
to be said for the slackness and the scandals which constantly
pervaded the English Church in spite of the efforts of men
like Dunstan, Oswald, and Wulfstan, the saintly bishop of

Worcester at the time of the conquest. By persuasion rather than by coercion England was now brought into line with the standards of a reformed Christendom. The married clergy—an overwhelming majority— were allowed to keep their wives, but no more clerical marriages were tolerated. Prelates could no longer live lives of pleasant, secular luxury, as Stigand had; and where he could not find native leaders who could establish in Abbeys and Bishoprics a proper standard of discipline, piety, and learning, Lanfranc could draw on the vast resources of the Continent. There was grumbling, and perhaps some real hardship. But henceforth Alfred's 'men of prayer' could at last fulfil their proper function in the community.

It must be remembered, of course, that the conquest, abrupt and devastating though its effects were, was not a single event carried through in a year. The processes which it set in motion were far from complete when the Conqueror died in 1087, and already it was working out far less symmetrically than the Norman mind would have preferred. The fact, for example, that the lands of the northern Saxon earls did not fall in until after the great rising of 1069 meant that the distribution of lands among William's supporters was a piecemeal process which resulted in a confusion of feudal holdings very unlike the uniform baronies of the Normandy pattern. In all sorts of ways local circumstances and the obstinacy of Saxon custom modified the planners' intentions even while they were being carried out. But by 1087 the decisive changes which made the conquest, for good or ill, such a landmark in English history, were all but complete. The citizens of London could see the Tower rising by the river bank. All over England not only castles, but cathedrals and great abbey churches gave Englishmen an outward and visible sign of the new order; and at Winchester the clerks were collecting and rearranging under orderly, Norman, feudal headings the information furnished by the sworn witnesses, half Saxon and half Norman, to the Domesday commissioners.

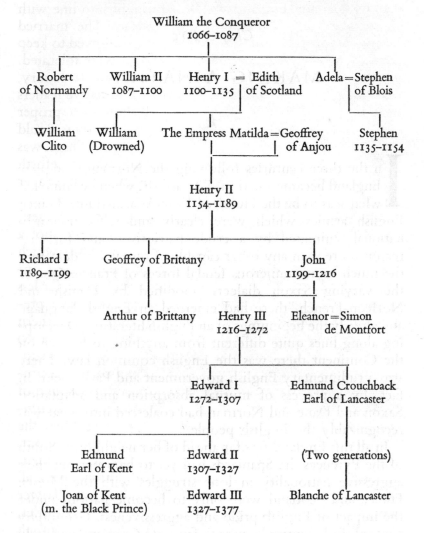

William the Conqueror
1066–1087

Robert of Normandy — William II 1087–1100 — Henry I 1100–1135 = Edith of Scotland — Adela = Stephen of Blois

William Clito — William (Drowned) — The Empress Matilda = Geoffrey of Anjou — Stephen 1135–1154

Henry II
1154–1189

Richard I 1189–1199 — Geoffrey of Brittany — John 1199–1216

Arthur of Brittany — Henry III 1216–1272 — Eleanor = Simon de Montfort

Edward I 1272–1307 — Edmund Crouchback Earl of Lancaster

Edmund Earl of Kent — Edward II 1307–1327 — (Two generations)

Joan of Kent (m. the Black Prince) — Edward III 1327–1377 — Blanche of Lancaster

71

Chapter Five

MAKING A NATION

★

In the three centuries following the Norman Conquest
England became a nation. Edward III, when he launched
what was to be the Hundred Years War, led into France
English armies which were clearly and self-consciously
national, animated by a crude patriotism, and for that
reason more than any other capable of repeatedly defeating
the much more numerous feudal forces of France. Out of
the varying Saxon dialects, modified by Danish and
Norman-French, there had emerged an English language
and already the beginnings of an English literature. Developing along lines quite different from anything to be seen on
the Continent there was the English common law. There
was a rudimentary English government and Parliament. In
fact, by a process of mutual absorption and adaptation
Saxon and Dane and Norman had coalesced into what was
recognizably the English people.

In all this England was far ahead of her neighbours. South
of the Pyrenees the Spaniards had yet to hammer out their
aggressive nationality in lone struggles with the Moors.
France and Scotland were only to become nations under
the impact of English pride and aggressiveness. Geography
and political ineptitude were to frustrate Germany and Italy
for centuries. Yet the processes which led up to this startling
English advance were so obscure that they scarcely show at
all in the political history of the period following the conquest. They have to be sought in an economic expansion
which played havoc with the careful categories of the

72

Domesday commissioners; in certain Saxon habits of thought and behaviour which made a proper feudal system unworkable from the start; in a unique development of the king's system of government to meet circumstances which were unique in Europe. For what might be called the history-book events of the period were almost entirely concerned with outside distractions which might have been expected to frustrate all economic and constitutional progress: baronial rebellions and civil wars; a struggle with the growing power of the Roman Church, postponed by the good understanding of William I and Lanfranc, but in the long run unavoidable; troubles on the Welsh and Scottish borders, inherited from Anglo-Saxon England and unsolved for centuries; frontier wars with France, resulting first from the possession of Normandy and later of the vast Angevin empire which stretched from the Somme to the Pyrenees. Yet in the story of English development these apparent distractions played a vital part by forcing the king to rely increasingly on a measure of English popular support and to make a series of administrative experiments which largely determined the pattern which English life has followed ever since.

Superficially, then, the history of Norman England presents a picture very little different from that of Saxon England. Norman barons were as disorderly and self-interested as Godwin and his sons. The careers of Robert of Bellême, who delighted in starving his captives to death or watching them roast over a slow fire, or of Geoffrey de Mandeville who terrorized the Fens in Stephen's time, matched the worst tales that could be told of the reigns of Ethelred or Canute. A strong king, however personally unjust or immoral, who could keep such men in order was a good king; with a weak man on the throne large parts of the kingdom collapsed instantly into anarchy. So even the Anglo-Saxon chronicler, still working away at his manuscript up at Peterborough, after listing all the oppressions and cruelties, and particularly the injustices resulting from the

73

new forest enclosures, of that 'stark' man, William I, concludes: 'The good peace that he made in this land is not to be forgotten.' His son, William II, the Red King, squat, ungainly, and wholly without personal dignity, almost illiterate, vicious, blasphemous and tyrannical, because he allowed nobody to torment his subjects but himself, earned the same commendation: 'He kept good peace.' His brother, Henry, who ruled from 1100 to 1135, was better educated and really intelligent, but no less callous and brutal. It was in his reign that the practice of disembowelling and quartering the half hung traitor originated, and he sentenced a poet who had lampooned him to be blinded and imprisoned for life. Nevertheless, such English opinion as was articulate hailed him as 'the Lion of Justice'. 'Good man he was, and there was great awe of him. In his day no man dared to harm another.'

The problem of government, in fact, was reduced to terms of brutal simplicity easily grasped by the ordinary villager. All three of these kings called with confidence on Saxon levies to help them against the barons, and Henry I even took the fyrd to Normandy to defeat his brother Robert at Tenchebrai in 1106 and, by conquering Normandy, in some sort to revenge Hastings. When, in 1080, the leaders of Bishop Odo of Bayeux's baronial rebellion marched defeated out through the ranks of the Saxon farmers and townsmen who made up Rufus's army, there were shouts of 'Halters, bring halters', and 'Lord, King, do not trust the traitors'. The issue was perfectly clear to them; and the king, though he used the barons to govern England, could always count on the English at a pinch to save him from the barons. With this in mind Henry I had started his reign by republishing the laws of the Confessor; and he had married the niece of Edgar Atheling, so bringing the blood of Alfred back on to the throne. The son who was thus to have been the embodiment of the fusion of Norman and Saxon, William Atheling, was unfortunately drowned by the incompetence of a drunken pilot in the White Ship, leaving only his sister, the widowed Empress Matilda, to represent both Saxon and Norman royal lines. But the barons would not be governed by a woman; and the chronicler's famous comment on Stephen, Henry's nephew whom they put up against her, summed up the whole attitude of the age towards the problem of government: 'A mild man and soft and good, and did no justice.' 'The eighteen long winters' men called his reign, when he and Matilda fought a long drawn-out war which neither was competent to win, and local tyranny and private wars made life intolerable for almost everybody, amidst barbarities worse, because more cold-blooded and deliberate, than those of the Danish invasions two centuries before.

But in 1154 England's luck turned again and Henry II, Matilda's son, gave the country thirty-five years of peaceful and ordered progress of which enough records survive to show what colossal progress had already been made, as it were out of sight, during the preceding century. In the first place it is clear that, in spite of the wars and rebellions and the barbarities, it had been a century of rapidly increasing prosperity. Towns were growing fast and rapidly emancipating themselves by means of royal charters from dependence on the local manor, such tiresome obligations as the use of the lord's mill and baking oven, and the intrusion of a tax-gathering sheriff. London, already a self-governing community with its hundred churches and its overflowing population, even got the right to appoint the sheriff; and many lesser towns got, especially during the reign of Henry I, the most cherished right—that of paying an annual lump sum, which they could raise as they pleased, to the exchequer instead of all the tolls, taxes and dues which caused endless dispute with local feudal authority. A steady expansion of the export of cloth and raw wool, the first beginnings of exports from the Tyneside coalfields to France, and a rapid growth of internal trade were among the important consequences of the 'good peace' kept by the Norman kings, and were not seriously interrupted in many places even during Stephen's eighteen long winters. For if, round Peterborough in that disastrous period, 'men said openly that Christ slept and His saints,' at Norwich they were finishing the nave of the great cathedral; there were barons who established local peace and used it to endow great abbey churches; good coins were being minted at York; the King's justices still toured the home counties to supervise the local courts.

The best proof of increasing prosperity outside the towns was the steady expansion of the population. Labour was beginning to be plentiful and cheap, so that many lords were trying to change the services of the villeins into money rents which could be used to hire whole-time labourers, which would be both cheaper and more efficient; and many villeins were shrewd enough to resist the attempt, preferring to hire the cheap labour themselves while they did their week's work on the domain. In many villages there began to be too many men for the available strips, and new holdings were being carved out of the waste: compact farms, paying money rents to the manor, tenanted not only by smaller freeholders on the make, but by villeins who had made a little capital in silver money by grazing sheep on the common. This new class of landless labourers created by the rise in population not only enabled the villein to farm a new holding while continuing to work his thirty strips in the village field, but often made it profitable for the lord to let off a portion of his domain for rent rather than farm it himself on the unprofitable labour service basis. The knight's fee, the large, compact holding designed to produce a fully armed, mounted man for the feudal army, was tending to split up and to pass to five or six different farmers, thereby creating a host of new financial and legal problems when men were required to produce the fraction of a knight for military service. There was a ramifying process of sub-infeudation as sub-tenants in their turn acquired sub-tenants for parts of their holdings, and the consequent disputes over land titles, often involving the tenants of different lords, threw an increasing burden on the royal courts. The royal household—a few officers of state and a handful of officials and treasury clerks—was forced to expand and adapt itself to meet these new needs, and in doing so produced the embryo beginnings of the law courts and the civil service.

In the first place the government was having to handle much larger sums of money. The only way to deal with the much sub-divided knight's fee was to raise a sum in cash instead of the actual armed horseman and hire a professional to do the job; and even in peace time more efficient collection of taxes and better administration of royal estates produced an increased revenue, to which Henry added large sums extracted from the Jews in return for toleration and protection, and a considerable income in 'tallages' from the towns, which were illegal, but which they found it politic to pay. At the same time it was necessary to provide quick legal remedies for those who could get no justice from their lord's court or even, often, from the Shire court.

It is astonishing to find how much of the work of the first two Henries survives to this day in fact as well as in name. To get a picture of this earliest form of English government one has to think back to a time when the King's Bench really was just that: the seat from which, like King Alfred before him, the king dispensed an over-riding justice. The modern court grew out of the gradual specialization of the five councillors appointed to sit in the King's absence. But such a court still moved with the royal household from hunting lodge to hunting lodge, or across the Channel to campaign in Poitou, and to meet this obvious inconvenience Henry tried the experiment of leaving a duplicate court permanently at Westminster which in due course was to become the Court of Common Pleas. A similar practical simplicity characterizes the origins of the Exchequer in the days when the Chancellor really sat behind a chequered cloth at the great annual accounting and the sheriffs of each county stacked on its squares the piles of silver coin representing the feudal dues and the king's share of fines and tolls; when wooden tallies notched and split were the only record of the fixed sums due from each, and addition and subtraction were the only arithmetical processes available to the accountant. It was only in Henry I's time that the abacus —a contraption of wires and beads which we know as an educative nursery toy—was imported from the Moors to make multiplication possible.

Working with such primitive tools as these, Henry II evolved a machinery of government of astonishing complexity and efficiency. To force the feudal courts to do justice and to substitute his own when they failed he used a system of standardized writs, for which a man threatened with eviction or unable to get his just rights by ordinary process could apply to the Chancellor. These were in effect a sharp order to the local authority to see justice done or the King's court would step in to do it. It was primarily to supervise the working of this system, to keep sheriffs up to the mark and to keep men contented and loyal by giving them quick justice, that the Assize judges toured the shires every year; and in their gradually established right to deal exclusively with cases of murder, robbery, arson and forgery was sealed the ultimate doom of feudal jurisdiction in England. Moreover, out of this reaching down of the royal justice to make direct touch with the village freemen who came as delegates to the shire courts to swear to the customs of their manor or hundred there grew the two most important and most peculiarly English of all our institutions: the common law and the jury.

The germ of both can really be seen in the manor courts where the villagers' sworn evidence of what was the custom of the manor was the judgement of the court. English law thus became something that already existed, independently of the will of feudal lord or sovereign, of Church law or the theoretical principles to be deduced from Roman law. It was this law, already embodied as immemorial custom and constantly elaborated by decisions in the courts and interpretations by judges, that the king used to curb baronial or local misgovernment, and so forged a weapon which could be—and soon was—used against himself in protection of local rights and liberties. In practice Henry II was extremely autocratic; but he could not effectively enforce such a law as the instrument of his power without binding himself under it as effectively as anybody else. At the same time the use of the sworn evidence of all sorts of different groups of people as a method of finding out facts was enormously extended. It had been used to make the Domesday survey and Henry used it constantly; for example in the Inquest of Sheriffs in 1170, when all the knights and freeholders of every shire were put on oath to reveal any misdeeds of the sheriffs, most of whom in consequence lost their jobs. It soon became the standard method of settling disputed titles to land, invaluable to the king, since it ensured that decisions, even if unjust, were at least popular, and it removed the obvious injustices of the Norman method of ordeal by battle. It was a short step to use a jury to decide whether accused criminals should be committed for trial; and in an age in which evidence and judgement were thought of as a single process, to perceive that it was even a more satisfactory way of determining guilt or innocence than ordeal by fire or water. For the time, of course, all this concerned the freeman only. Three-quarters of the population were still bound to the lord's court and without redress outside it. But it was not to be very long before the villeins began to get free and so automatically ensure for themselves the same protection of the law as other men enjoyed.

This immense stride forward—the biggest single step in the growth of the English constitution—was largely Henry's personal achievement. To the red hair and tempestuous energy of his Angevin ancestors he added a first-class academic brain; and when darkness put an end to his furious hunting he transferred his fidgety energy indoors, pacing round, fiddling with dagger or hunting knife, while he helped to draft a charter or to alter the wording of a writ. He ruled more than half France under different titles, but as time went on he found England not only his greatest source of wealth but also his most fascinating problem and the country he liked best to live in. His family life, on the other hand, was a nightmare. His infidelities and his occasional spectacular rages, when he would weep and curse and roll on the ground, drove his wife, the strong-willed Eleanor of Aquitaine, to whom he owed half his great French ap- panages, almost crazy with irritation, until she joined with his sons in open war against him. He was at war with one or more of them all the last years of his life; and it was the treachery of his favourite, spoilt, sneering John, which finally drove him to turn his face to the wall and die, re- viling Christ for having dishonoured him. Few men live more vividly in the pages of contemporary gossip writers than Henry, and there was something intensely human even in his blasphemous furies. 'God,' he cried, as he watched his beloved birthplace, Le Mans, go up in flames before the advancing troops of his son, Richard, in 1189, 'Thou hast taken from me what I prized most, and I will take from Thee what Thou prizest most in me, my soul'; and a month later, as he exchanged the kiss of peace with Richard, he hissed in his ear, 'May God not let me die till I am worthily revenged on you.' This was the temperament, and it was the most famous of these characteristic rages, that led him rashly to cry shame on the knights and courtiers who fed at his expense and had allowed him to become 'the laughing- stock of a low-born clerk'.

It is difficult not to feel that there was justification for Henry's fury with Becket. The fundamental dispute be- tween them was one which had already got Rufus and Henry I into trouble with Archbishop Anselm and which cropped up at one time or another in every country in Christendom. Broadly it turned on the boundary between royal and papal power: on the difficulty of reconciling the King's laws with the Law of God. It was a problem for which, between theoretical extremists, there could be no solution. In practical politics it boiled down to two main arguments, on both of which a reasonable compromise could be reached. On the first, the question of the appointment of bishops and their right to deal direct with Rome over the king's head, Henry I and Anselm had reached working agreement. It was over the second, the Church's claim to try all clerical persons in spiritual courts, even for offences against the criminal law, that Henry and Becket fell out. Becket, from the moment that he stopped being the King's chancellor and intimate friend and became Archbishop, took an extreme position. Clerics included beadles and vergers and choirmen, and in no circumstances could any of them be brought before lay judges.

It was not an academic dispute. Henry's judges worked out that over 100 murders had been committed in the first ten years of his reign by clerics, all of whom had gone almost unpunished under the mild penalties which were the maximum a bishop's court could inflict. In the end, after years of bitter strife, in which each side used every petty weapon of persecution at its disposal, Becket reluctantly accepted Henry's solution that 'criminous clerks' should be unfrocked by the ecclesiastical courts and then handed over for justice, so dodging the issue. But he went back on the agreement. Contemporary Englishmen saw the Archbishop's conduct as a brave stand for the Faith. Modern historians would mostly agree that his opposition was honest, but tactlessly and stupidly carried out. To Henry it was simply the base treachery of an old friend which goaded him to his fatal outburst just after Christmas of 1170. The sequel is well-known, and whatever may be thought of Becket's earlier behaviour, it is impossible not to admire him as he stood before the high altar with his trembling chaplains and contemptuously defied FitzUrse and his three fellow-gangsters. The murder of Becket was the one great set-back of Henry's reign. He lost the battle over criminous clerks and he himself had to do penance before the shrine of St. Thomas of Canterbury, who soon became England's most popular saint.

In the eighty years which covered the reigns of Henry II's two sons, Richard I and John, and of his grandson, Henry III, England reaped the harvest he had sown. Richard was an absentee, John villainous and unpopular, Henry III a weakling. Any of these at any earlier period would have left the more loyal and law-abiding magnates helpless, because leaderless, while the the rest seized the opportunity to pillage and harry their neighbours. But Henry had created an administrative machine which did not break down when there was no strong king to drive it. The local self-government which he had forced on the shires and towns by his assizes and juries and charters, making them tax themselves, police themselves, and sit in judgment on their own delinquents, did not break down even when baronial civil war was actually raging. At the centre officials, trained to a more or less specialized routine and largely unconcerned with policy, quietly went on with their jobs. Furthermore, there was now a large moderate party among the barons themselves whose conservatism looked no further back than the reign of Henry II, who had no wish to revert to anarchy, had a real sense of the national interest, and would range themselves behind the more senior responsible officials to preserve the law as Henry had made them understand it either against their own irresponsible brethren or against the king himself. Finally, behind all this again, there was a new force: town merchants and the lesser gentry and more prosperous freemen in the shires, the bulk of the tax-paying classes, who already represented a formed public opinion which it was increasingly difficult to ignore. The habit of consulting them in all sorts of local assembly was already growing up, and it would not be long before their representatives would be summoned to take part in the Great Council—that expansion of the ordinary king's council to include all the tenants-in-chief, which Norman kings had always called together for consultations on important occasions, and which was beginning to be called Parliament. The doctrine, first enunciated by Edward I, that 'what touches all shall be decided by all' was the inevitable consequence of Henry II's principle that all freemen were equal before the law.

No two brothers ever contrasted more sharply than Richard and John. Richard lived life in terms of southern French chivalry: of songs and tournaments and romanticized war. He was the finest fighter and one of the better generals of his day, often brutal, but impulsively generous; always, whatever he did, a popular hero. In his reign of ten years he spent only ten months in England. He taxed the country to the bone to raise his army for the Third Crusade, and it cheerfully subscribed again five years later the enormous sum required for his ransom when his own high-handed quarrelsomeness had landed him in an Austrian prison. He returned to a tremendous welcome and plunged back into French wars until, five years later, a crossbow bolt put an end to his spectacular career. John was much cleverer, a competent general and a cunning politician, and he played quite skilfully for popularity, especially in resisting the Pope's exaggerated claims to interfere in English affairs. But all men shrank away from him. Behind his pale, sneering face and his high, cackling laugh there was only venomous cruelty. He was shifty, indolent, and greedy, and behind him he left a trail of ruined homes and broken marriages; of families mourning the hostages he had starved to death. He grovelled when he was beaten, betrayed everyone who trusted him, and brutally murdered his own nephew, Arthur of Brittany.

While Richard was away the government continued to function peacefully and efficiently under Archbishop Hubert Walter, in spite of John's treacherous attempts at usurpation. But John's personal government from 1199 to 1212 was calculated to destroy all that Henry II had achieved. He raised unprecedented taxes and squandered them on foreign favourites and futile campaigns in France which lost him almost the whole of his inheritance. He made every powerful marcher lord in Ireland and Wales into a bitter personal enemy. He defied the Pope and brought down on England five years of Interdict, of silent bells and closed churches, and the dead buried without blessing in unconsecrated ground, only in the end to surrender far more to Papal pretensions than had ever before been granted. So he faced baronial revolt in the end without friends, money, or prestige. For the first time since the Conquest the people were on the side of the barons against the king.

Thus Magna Carta, which John was forced to sign at Runnymede in 1215, and which was to be used for centuries by reformers as a basis for claims which its authors would scarcely have understood, was essentially a conservative document. It was an attempt by the moderates to stop John's capricious tyranny without going to the opposite extreme of feudal decentralization and disorder. There was nothing new in all its sixty-two clauses, which sought only to define clearly the liberties and rights enjoyed by all free men under Henry II's law. But this, of course, in itself was a tremendous step forward, for it meant that moderate conservatives for the next century took their stand not on what that enlightened king had destroyed, but on what he had achieved, and the Great Charter became the permanent foundation of the English constitution.

In their immediate object of achieving a peaceful compromise the authors of the Charter failed. John decided to fight it out and the baronial extremists invited the Dauphin of France to come over and take the throne. But in September 1216, just when he might have won, John's gluttony brought on an attack of dysentery which fortunately killed him. The moderates got control of the regency set up for the nine-year-old Henry III, the French were evicted, and the Charter was confirmed. But Henry grew up into a disastrous ruler, childish, extravagant and irresponsible. He rebuilt Westminster Abbey, but most of his money went in personal luxury or in futile foreign adventures, as when he financed an attempt to put his son on the throne of Sicily.

He alienated the barons by heaping riches and honours on worthless foreigners, and by trying to govern through these same men in Household appointments he exasperated the regular official class. At a time when Rome was demanding more money and more power than ever before, he pursued a policy entirely subservient to the Pope and so threw into opposition the tax-paying classes and the whole of the clergy. Even Henry II's system could not survive such wanton stupidity; and there was crying need for administrative reform.

This was in fact what Simon de Montfort and his friends were trying to achieve when they seized power in 1258 and expelled the foreigners. But it was not possible to run royal government without a king, and Simon, though popular enough in the towns and with the lower clergy, was too overbearing to have much support in his own class. His attempt to force reform simultaneously on barons and king only provoked a civil war. The first battle, at Lewes in 1264, he won. The king became virtually a prisoner and the movement which had started out to free England from misrule by foreigners and to re-establish the Charter degenerated into a military dictatorship which grew steadily more unpopular. It was doomed from the moment, in May, 1265, that the heir to the throne, Prince Edward, tricked his guards, escaped from captivity, and took the field on a programme of the old laws, the Charter, and a properly constituted Council staffed by Englishmen. By skilful manœuvre he cut Montfort off behind the Severn from his midland supporters and with vastly superior forces caught and killed him at Evesham. From then on, though Henry III lived until 1272, Edward governed the country.

Edward I was pre-eminently a soldier. He was over six foot tall, physically and morally as straight as a ramrod, and made harsh by too strong a sense of his own righteousness. He was always in training and had little sympathy for the weaknesses of others. Yet, though by temperament an autocrat, he had learnt from Montfort's failure the necessity of compromise and the value of good will to a government. So his reign caught up all the threads of the past century: the steady extension of the council's legal and administrative machinery inherited from Henry II; the habit of consulting all who were interested in any particular piece of legislation, which Montfort had fostered largely for partisan purposes; the problem, much worse in the last two reigns, of the over-mighty baron; the permanent difficulty of undefined frontiers with Wales, Scotland, and France; the endless squabble with the still growing pretensions of the Papacy.

But for his obstinate determination completely to conquer Scotland, Edward might have been wholly successful in all these activities. He did indeed carry through the overdue administrative reform, dismissing corrupt and tyrannical sheriffs, coroners who took unauthorized fees for viewing corpses, and judges who connived at the maintenance of suits in court by bodies of armed retainers. The police system was tightened up and military service was extended. Some 280 new kinds of writ were devised by his lawyers to meet the new needs of a more civilized society. Great statutes sharply defined the terms on which land might go to the Church and stopped the intrusion of Church courts into civil suits, regularized the sale and transfer of land, entailed all the estates of the Crown's tenants-in-chief, and established Assizes three times a year; and at each stage the representatives of the classes concerned were called to consult with the Council, not as a matter of right, but as a convenience, so that, though there was as yet no Parliament in the modern sense, the habit of consultation was being formed and the principle would soon follow. By 1284 Wales was finally conquered, the last Principality of the north being turned into a kind of marcher earldom vested in the king's eldest son. The Gascon frontier was secured, and the threat of the over-mighty marcher earl was bought off, for the time being at least, by marrying most of them into the royal family.

Had Edward's reign ended in 1295 it would have been a

record of almost unbroken success. The last twelve years of Scottish war were not only a failure in themselves, but endangered all the rest. Unable to induce the Scots to accept his interpretation of English overlordship, he annexed the kingdom. But, though it was easy enough to defeat the Scottish spearmen in battle, provided archers and heavy cavalry were correctly handled, to garrison and hold down the whole country was beyond England militarily and financially. The result of the resistance led first by Wallace and then by Robert Bruce was to make Scotland a nation and England bankrupt. When, in 1307, Edward forced himself from his bed for a last attempt he had taxed every source in England to the bone, mortgaged his future to Italian bankers, and so strained his relations with his subjects that he had had to clap into the Tower a knight of the shire for Lancashire for moving in a petition in Parliament the startlingly modern view that redress of grievance ought to precede supply. Moreover, thanks to his prolonged absences, many of the abuses he had remedied had crept back into the administration, which in some ways was more corrupt than ever. Two days after crossing the border he died, leaving nothing to show for it all but the Scottish coronation stone embodied in St. Edward's chair—a legacy, even to-day, of doubtful value. Castle after castle fell back into Scottish hands, until only Stirling remained, and that had promised to surrender if not relieved by June 24th of 1314. By desperately hard marching Edward II brought an army of 20,000 men to the crossing of the Bannock Burn below Stirling with one day to spare. Foiled at the road crossing, the exhausted army moved downstream and got over, to spend the night in a bog, and to find themselves in the morning chilly and demoralized, with no room to deploy and no ground suitable for heavy cavalry. Rather than give them a chance to improve their position, Bruce moved at once to attack with about half their numbers, and in fact the English had already lost faith in their leadership. 'Yon folk kneel to ask mercy,' Edward said to one of his cronies, as each clump of Scots spearmen fell on its knees to say the Lord's Prayer before going into action. 'They ask mercy,' came the answer, 'but not of you.' The English did everything wrong. A series of disorderly cavalry charges suffered heavy loss among the Scottish spears; the archers, sent forward without cover, were scattered by the enemy light horse, and when Bruce counter-attacked, the whole mass of Edward's army broke and fled. It was the most spectacular defeat of English history.

It was the only spectacular event of Edward II's dreary reign. That large, good-looking, lethargic man had no grasp of the problems of government and was only really happy in the company of craftsmen, learning to thatch or shoe a horse, or rowing with the Thames watermen. He formed a disastrous attachment to a Gascon knight, Piers Gaveston, who was detested by his father and by all the barons, whom he married to his niece and loaded with inappropriate honours, letting him, for example, carry St. Edward's crown at his coronation. Already exasperated by the capricious ruling of the country through Household servants, the barons found Gaveston's mockery and his talent for apt nicknames the last straw. 'Joseph the Jew' was his name for the Earl of Pembroke; Lancaster, the King's cousin, was 'the play actor'; Warwick, the fiercest of them all, 'the black dog of Arden'. Gaveston paid for his wit with his life when Lancaster and Warwick caught him in 1312 and beheaded him in defiance of a safe-conduct; and seven years later Edward, with a rare spurt of energy inspired by hatred, revenged him by executing Lancaster without a trial in his own castle of Pontefract. In between these occasional bouts of civil war government was carried on alternately by a managing committee of barons who called themselves the Lords Ordainers and by the King and his favourites in the intervals when they escaped control. Neither provided very good government.

Towards the end things got a little better, since the king's last favourites, the Despensers, father and son, though greedy, were extremely competent and understood the necessity of collaborating with Parliament. But the legacy of squalid intrigue and civil war was too great. In 1325 Edward was fool enough to let his wife, who loathed him, take his eldest son to negotiate with the King of France. At the same time, Roger Mortimer, Earl of March, escaped from the Tower, also to France. Within a year the Queen and Mortimer were openly living together in sin and raising money and troops in the Netherlands to invade England. By November, 1326, the friendless Edward was a prisoner in Berkeley Castle and a few months later he was murdered. There followed four years of misgovernment by the Queen-mother and her paramour until one dramatic night in Nottingham Castle, when Edward III, now eighteen, seized Mortimer in the bedroom next to his mother's and, deaf to her cry of 'Fair son, have pity on the gentle Mortimer', sent him up to be hanged on the thieves' gallows at Tyburn. So began the last brief flowering of mediaeval England, before she sank into the confusion of transition to a modern age.

YORK AND LANCASTER
THE END OF THE PLANTAGENETS

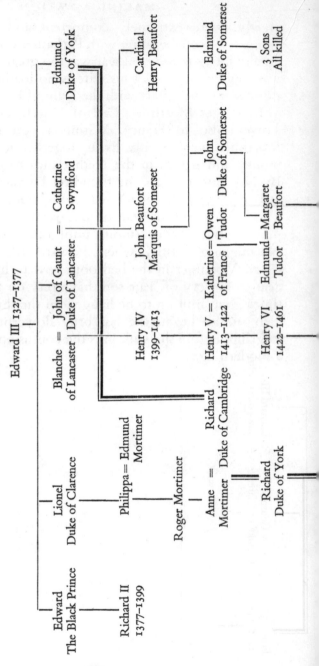

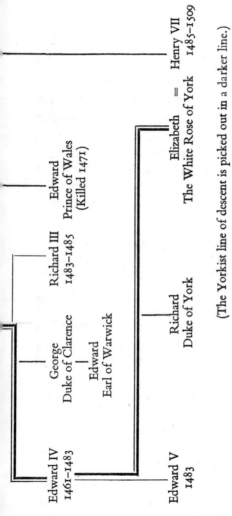

Edward IV
1461–1483

George
Duke of Clarence
|
Edward
Earl of Warwick

Richard III
1483–1485

Edward
Prince of Wales
(Killed 1471)

Edward V
1483

Richard
Duke of York

Elizabeth = Henry VII 1485–1509
The White Rose of York

(The Yorkist line of descent is picked out in a darker line.)

Chapter Six

THE COLLAPSE OF
MEDIAEVAL ENGLAND

★

In the century and a half which separated the outbreak of
the Hundred Years' War in 1338 from the end of the
Wars of the Roses in 1485 mediaeval England collapsed.
Clearly such a complicated process cannot be anchored to
one single event, nor tied to a single cause. For various
reasons the institutions which made up the fabric of society
broke down one by one. The Black Death made the village
agricultural system unworkable and so brought down the
complex feudal superstructure which had been raised on it.
The craft and merchant guilds lost their control of town life,
as wealth increased and international commerce expanded.
The Church could not adapt her teaching and organization
fast enough to the changed conditions created by the emergence of a single English language and literature and a large
body of educated English laymen. The system of government so painfully built up found the greater barons at last
uncontrollable and ceased to be able to guarantee to ordinary
men the rule of law on which all other peaceful progress
depended.

Edward III himself stood exactly at the turning point.
Personally he was the embodiment of the society of the
later middle ages, both in its triumphs and its absurdities.
The ideal of chivalry, which sought to divert to the protection of the weak and the defence of Christendom the
strength and passions of a ruling class for whom fighting
was a sport, can be seen with all its charm and all its limita-

tions in the stories which have come down to us of this reign. Edward III founded the Order of the Garter. He preferred to risk his victory at Crécy by holding back his reserves at a critical moment to give his son a chance to win his spurs; and that same son, the Black Prince, gave the world the perfect example of knightly courtesy and humility when he waited personally on his prisoner, King John of France, at dinner on the night after the battle of Poitiers. But chivalry had its class limitations. Only the intervention of his wife prevented Edward from behaving brutally to the burghers of Calais, and the Black Prince personally ordered the massacre of every inhabitant of Limoges in 1369 as a piece of pure terrorism. At the same time Crécy, in 1346, and Poitiers ten years later—the victories which became the patriotic legends round which early English nationalism was built—were not triumphs of the knightly class at all, but of archers; and at Crécy the first cannon sounded even more decisively the knell of the feudal baron.

The French war, which was the background of English history from 1338 until 1453, started as usual in the attempt to gain a defensible frontier in Gascony, which was a valuable market for our corn and cloth as well as a source of wine and salt. After a shaky start, when the king, hard-driven for money and troops, tried high-handed methods of finance and government, and so provoked a sullen resistance from the governing and tax-paying classes, the nation settled down to fifteen years of almost unbroken success. A genuine national enthusiasm marked this phase. Parliament, now that Edward had learnt to leave it to do things its own way, voted the necessary supplies for three years at a time. The objectives, moreover, were solid national gains—Gascon trade and Calais, an invaluable depot for the growing wool and cloth trade with the Flemish cities. The victories, won by English archers against the massed chivalry of France, were not the achievement of a remote, courtly, Norman-French aristocracy, but were such as might be sung in popular ballads in taverns. By the end of this phase, in 1360, the Treaty of Brétigny gave Edward all south-western France and Calais in absolute sovereignty. The kings both of Scotland and France had been English prisoners, and it looked as though the frontiers were secure for a generation to come. But the financial effort had been too great and a series of outbreaks of bubonic plague—the Black Death—suddenly killed off more than half the population. The Black Prince sickened and died; the king became slowly senile. Castle by castle, the French recovered all that they had lost, and by Edward's death in 1377 they were raiding and burning Sussex villages.

It seemed that nothing was left but Calais and a legend of victory. But in fact the peaceful development of English institutions under cover of the war had been startling. Because he had to have money—at one point he was so hard pressed that he pawned his crown to German bankers—Edward acquiesced in a large expansion of parliamentary power and activity. The right of the shire and borough representatives to be summoned had by now become an accepted fact, and their custom of withdrawing to discuss matters submitted to them apart had created the beginnings of a House of Commons. Indeed, during the stormy opening years of the reign, Parliament was putting forward claims with an entirely modern ring about them, demanding to audit the king's war taxes and to choose and dismiss his ministers for him. Thereafter Edward, by nature easy-going, found it simpler to work with them, and allowed them to establish an absolute control of taxation. His big measures were all put through as Acts of Parliament: Provisors, which stopped the appointment of English ecclesiastics by the Pope; Praemunire, which forbade all appeals to courts outside the kingdom; most important of all, the Treasons' Act which, by defining treason more narrowly, prevented the arbitrary arrest of opponents of the government for 'reasons of state', and ensured for the accused a trial by his peers. Finally the administrative machine of Henry II and

Edward I received one of its finishing touches by the creation of J.P.s—local magistrates with summary powers to
deal with felonies and trespass and to regulate prices and
wages. Thus local government passed largely into the hands of
the same class which was already asserting a claim to financial
control of national affairs in the House of Commons.

The most decisive single factor in English history in the
later middle ages was the Black Death. It imposed on all
activity in Edward III's reign the same pattern that it imposed on the war: a rising tide of prosperity, success, and
progress, followed by sudden collapse. How many people
died will never accurately be known. Italian merchant ships
trading with the east brought it with the rats to Genoa, and
from there it spread northwards to reach Weymouth in
August, 1348, and to rage through England for the next
two years. Probably more than a third of the population
died in those two years alone. The monks, crowded in their
dormitories, were perhaps the hardest hit; Westminster
Abbey lost half its brethren; out of sixty at St. Albans only
thirteen survived. But all classes suffered. King Edward lost
a daughter, and three Archbishops of Canterbury died.
Altogether, in this and subsequent outbreaks during the
next ten years, something over half the people died. Inevitably perhaps, those who were left in a position to do so
ate, drank, and were merry. The sufferings of the poor
seemed worse against a background of fantastic new
fashions in clothes and unheard-of luxuries among the rich.
In a disintegrated society spiritual values wavered and the
hold of a Church whose prelates were too rich and worldly
and whose Popes had moved to 'the sinful city of Avignon',
to become pensioners of the French King, weakened alarm-
ingly.

Though the more congested populations of the towns
may have been harder hit at first, it was in the villages that
the long-term effects of the plague were most decisive. For
three centuries life in the country had been characterized by
a steady growth of the population, producing, as the waste

land was eaten into by pioneers, a growing shortage of land and surplus labour. Manorial lords had been able to tighten up villein services, and an over-numerous, land-hungry peasantry had been largely defenceless economically and socially. Within two years the situation was abruptly reversed. In some places there were not enough men left to get the harvest in. The wages of the surviving landless labourers rose sharply from ½d. a day to 2d. or 3d. and the value of the villein's labour rose correspondingly. Naturally he sought by every means to escape it, while the lord was obstinately determined to retain and enforce it. The village field could only be kept in cultivation by the amalgamation of villein holdings, which created a new class of comparatively substantial tenant farmers who still more resented the obligation of weekly work. Refusing to face the economic facts, Parliament backed the conservative stand of the manorial lords with Statutes of Labourers, which forbade commutation of labour services for money, ordered that wages should be pegged at the 1347 figure everywhere, and fixed more and more hideous penalties—branding, slavery, and death—for run-away villeins. But there was no adequate police force or system of communications to make it easy to catch the run-away, especially when any other landlord or town employer was only too glad to take him on without any awkward questions. So the young, the unmarried, and the enterprising emancipated themselves; and one by one the lords were forced, in order to keep any labour at all, to exchange the weekly services for money rents which they could use to hire labour. Furthermore, as wages continued to rise, many found that they were getting in much less than they paid out, and so began to break up the domain altogether and let it out in tenant farms. So, in less than a century, villeinage disappeared, compact holdings displaced the scattered strips, and the peasant became, not indeed a freeholder, but a freeman, with all the advantages and disadvantages of existence in a freely competitive market.

3. Two manor houses which indicate the peaceful rise of the gentry in the fourteenth century. *Above:* Markenfield Hall, Yorks, 1310. *Below:* Woodland Manor, Mere, Wilts, 1380

(*Photographs by 'Country Life'*)

But the resistance of manorial lords, Parliament, and J.P.s, though in the long run ineffectual, was strong enough to force a temporary crisis. Unions of landless labourers organized strikes and riots against the parliamentary wage-scale. Villeins free from labour services fought on for complete freedom: from heriots and fines on marriage and from compulsory use of the lord's mill and bake-oven. Unlike the French peasantry whom starvation and despair drove to massacre their lords, these were men whose wages were rising faster than prices and who were freer than ever their fathers had been, and whose very freedom made the last vestiges of personal serfdom intolerable. When at last other causes converged on this discontent to produce the Peasants' Revolt of 1381, the objective was at least as much legal as economic. The peasants wanted above all things equality before the law.

Indeed, the social protest represented by the Peasants' Revolt went deeper even than that. The protests of the intellectuals against the vices of a decaying social system percolated in rhyming slogans down even to the illiterate masses and there met with a growing and widespread discontent with the institutions of the Church of Rome. Chaucer, whose decision to forsake the official French of literature and diplomacy and write his greatest work, the *Canterbury Tales*, in English was one of the significant events of the century, was a courtier and civil servant none the less; not a critic, but a member of the established order, though he poked fun at it. But even he had little good to say of the various types of clergy whom he included among his Canterbury pilgrims. His monk, fat and jolly, and a passionate huntsman, and the elegant, socially conscious Abbess, preoccupied with table manners and lapdogs, typified a worldly monasticism which no longer did its job. The Summoner who carried out the moral supervision exercised by spiritual courts, and so lived largely by blackmail, and the Pardoner with his bag of 'pigges bones' which he sold as relics of the saints, were scandals only too well known. The only praiseworthy figure was the poor parish priest who stayed and did his job while others rushed to London for rich preferments and pluralities. The Avignon Popes lacked the prestige, and the bishops, almost all absorbed on the King's Council in the business of secular government, lacked the time to reform abuses which made the Church so easy a target for criticism. Langland, Chaucer's great contemporary, and unlike him a man of the people, in his *Vision of Piers Plowman* directly attacked abuses at which Chaucer only raised a satirical eyebrow. All virtue is gradually seen to reside in the humble labourer on whose toil the whole superstructure of wealth and dignity in Church and state is raised, and the question is squarely put: what scriptural authority justifies this exploitation of the man who grows the bread on which all else depends? This was direct propaganda, and the rioting peasants later in the century used the name of Piers the plowman as a rallying cry.

Moreover, within the Church itself, there were forces at work to reinforce the criticisms of the poets. The begging friars, who drew their inspiration from the blessedness of Christian poverty as taught by St. Francis, were licensed to preach where they pleased, expounding a religion which also found no justification for social inequality, and their every sermon on the sinfulness of riches was inflammatory propaganda. But many of the friars were rich and worldly themselves, and it was the poor preachers who followed John Wycliffe, the first English religious reformer, who did most to focus popular discontent. Wycliffe was not a heretic until he attacked the doctrine of the real presence in the mass in 1380. His followers, the Lollards, were ultimately persecuted out of existence, but the thing which he had created when he started giving the people readings from his translation of the New Testament and expounding from it the simple truths of the sermon on the Mount of Olives lived on to become English puritanism, which was thus tied up from the start with revolutionary views of Church and state.

Political collapse brought all these seething economic and social discontents to a head in 1381. The temporary eclipse of English fortunes in France had filled the country with unemployed ex-soldiers, who with the robbers and the outlaws and the run-away villeins, formed yet more bands haunting the edges of the forests ready to join in any trouble that was going. The reckless policy, started by Edward I, of joining the most dangerous baronial families to the royal house by marriage, had surrounded the throne with too powerful semi-royal feudatories whose cousinship to the king seemed to make private war somehow less treasonable. Moreover, they had formed the habit of raising their own troops of indentured soldiers as contingents for Edward III's armies in France, and their military strength, no longer bound up in a network of feudal loyalties, was bound to become a danger the moment there was any weakness at the centre of government; the dotage of Edward III and the minority of his grandson, Richard II, automatically created a dangerous situation.

A severe and inequitable poll tax brought matters to a head in 1381. Fired by the celebrated priest, John Ball, who preached a primitive Christian communism in which tithe and tax should have no part and 'the King's Son of Heaven shall pay for all', the men of Kent harried tax collectors and magistrates for their lives and finally marched on London under the leadership of an old soldier named Wat Tyler, to be joined there by the men of Essex and admitted into the City by artisans who had their own grievances against the gradual monopoly of civic power by the richer merchants. Starting as an orderly, idealistic movement, directed only against the king's evil counsellors, and often even backed by the local small gentry, the rising soon degenerated into looting, rioting, and murder. They opened the prisons; the Tower was betrayed to them; they assassinated the Archbishop of Canterbury and the Treasurer; and there was a wholesale massacre of Flemish weavers for taking bread out of the mouths of honest Englishmen. The government, paralysed by indecision, conceded the commutation of all labour services for fixed rents of 4d. an acre and promised a general amnesty, whereupon, at a further conference in Smithfield, Wat Tyler demanded the confiscation of all Church lands and the abolition of all manorial rights, including the game laws. Insolently arguing this, he leant forward to put a hand on the king's bridle, and Walworth, the Mayor, misinterpreting the gesture, cut him down. Only the nerve and quickness of the fourteen-year-old king saved the royal party from instant massacre; for he rode at once across to the rebels crying that he himself would now be their leader, and was able to lead them out of the city. From this moment the forces of law and order recovered courage and the rebel bands were quickly dispersed.

The story in the rest of the country followed the same general pattern: a triumph of revolt lasting only until somebody had the courage to use the available forces against it. Thus the Bishop of Norwich with a handful of men-at-arms subdued the Norfolk peasants and restored order in Cambridge, where the mob had set fire to Corpus. By the late autumn order had been restored almost everywhere, but the government's revenge was not so brutal as might have been expected, thanks to the general feeling that the peasant grievances had been at least partly justified by misgovernment. Even John Ball had his trial by jury, and in all only about 200 of the leaders were hanged. On the other hand none of the promises made to the rebels were kept and the revolt achieved nothing. There was no large-scale release of villeins. Servile tenures simply continued to disappear at the same rate as before under the hard pressure of economic fact which no statutes of labourers could alter. Those landlords who could not work their estates on a money basis by the old system began to turn over to sheep farming, so saving labour and also making fortunes, since the European market, first for English raw wool, and then for English cloth, seemed unlimited. The peasants in the end gained the personal freedom which has ever since lain at the root of all English law and politics, though mostly at a colossal material sacrifice. The bulk of the released villeins became, not small farmers, but landless labourers or half-skilled artisans on the margin of unemployment in the towns. The final broad effect of the Black Death and the events it provoked was to make the rich much richer and the poor poorer.

As the agrarian system on which mediaeval England had rested broke down, the political collapse which had seemed imminent every time the throne passed to a minor or weakling at last took place. The reign of Richard II, begun so promisingly in a gallant gesture at Smithfield, was the beginning of the end. For Richard never grew up. His spoilt petulance which only the Queen, Anne of Bohemia, was able to control, turned as he grew older to an ungovernable temper in which he was capable of drawing his sword on a councillor who disagreed with him. In a dilettante, extravagant way he was civilized, loving fine clothes and jewels, and patronizing poets, but he never learnt to control himself or others, or mastered the fundamentals of government. His conception of sovereignty was that of a renaissance tyrant, who expected events to conform to his whim and did not recognize law, either as a thing to be enforced or obeyed. From his personal circle, his half brothers, his tutor, and his one great friend, Robert de Vere, Earl of Oxford, he built a government of the Household, arbitrary, extravagant, and capricious, which roused a baronial opposition similar to that which had sought to control Henry III and Edward II. But the 'Appellants' who played to Richard the role of Edward II's Ordainers had behind them a much more truculent Parliament, with a House of Commons beginning to be conscious of its strength and intensely resentful of local misgovernment and high taxation. It is significant that Richard tried to persuade the Pope to canonize Edward II, and not surprising that he, too, was deposed and murdered.

But the forces which Richard's incompetence released

were infinitely more dangerous than the partly public-spirited baronial opposition committees of earlier periods. Of the five Appellants who marched arm in arm into the Merciless Parliament of 1387 to denounce the treasons of Richard's ministers, one was his uncle, Thomas of Gloucester, and another his cousin Henry, son of John of Gaunt and heir to two dukedoms and three earldoms. The Plantagenets, entangled by marriage with the already much too powerful baronial families, were turning on each other; and the skirmish of Radcot Bridge in that same year, 1387, in which the Appellants scattered the royal troops under de Vere, started a century of intermittent civil war in which both dynasty and baronage were to destroy themselves.

Two years later Richard recovered control of his own kingdom, but he had learnt no lesson. Extravagance, arbitrary government, and heavy taxes unaccounted for put ordinary men, London citizens and country knights and yeomen, on the side of the disruptive barons. 'The axe was sharp and the stokke was hard', men sang in the taverns in 1390, 'In the XIII yere of King Richarde'. He had his uncle murdered; he terrorized Parliament with a guard of Cheshire archers mounted in Palace Yard into condemning two more of the Appellants, and exiled the remaining two. When finally, on John of Gaunt's death, he sequestrated all the lands of the Duchy of Lancaster which should have gone to his exiled cousin, Henry, he roused an almost universal opposition. In 1399 Parliament compelled him to abdicate, and Henry of Lancaster took the throne as Henry IV. The story, put about by Lancastrian supporters the following year, that Richard had starved himself to death in Pontefract castle was not widely believed.

The Lancastrian kings, Henry IV, V, and VI, never recovered from this usurpation and murder; and their ruin was also the final catastrophe of mediaeval England. Their more than doubtful title to the throne and the violence with which it had been asserted put them under the perpetual handicap of having to truckle to forces which it was their business to dominate. It had been England's fortune in the past that the misgovernment of occasional weaklings on the throne had been more than remedied by strong-willed successors: Henry II's reforms had followed Stephen's eighteen long winters; Edward I and III had each more than recovered the ground lost by their fathers. Henry IV had the will and the ability to re-establish the rule of law, but could not do so because his own seizure of power had been in defiance of it. He dared not raise sufficient taxes for fear of antagonizing Parliament on whose authority his best title to the throne rested. He dared not assert control too vigorously over barons whose military support had made his *coup d'état* possible. So for fourteen bankrupt years, increasingly crippled by ill health, he wrestled with treason and rebellion, to die, bitter and disappointed, still planning the Crusade which he felt might have expiated his seizure of the crown.

The same evil inheritance dogged his son, the last truly great man of the remarkable Plantagenet line. Henry V's virtues were not endearing: an iron self-discipline, a rigid piety, and a puritanical conviction of the rightness of his cause; a ruthless military efficiency more reminiscent of modern Prussia than of mediaeval England. They might none the less have served to deal with the problem of the over-mighty subject and to re-establish the rule of law in England. For, as he showed in the mud of northern France on St. Crispin's Day in 1415, when he had got himself cut off from his bases by a French army five times the size of his own, he had the trick of capturing the loyalty of ordinary men. He might have used it to rally to the crown all the classes which found baronial anarchy intolerable. He preferred to beg the whole question by diverting the dangerous surplus of military strength abroad and uniting the political classes only temporarily behind him in the quest for glory and French loot. By adding Agincourt to the list of the English long bow's victories he completed the growth of English patriotism, but he committed the nation to an attempt to conquer France for which she had neither the money nor the man-power. He increased the military strength and efficiency of the nobles who raised and officered the contingents which made up his army—the very men whom it should have been his prime object to subdue. When he died prematurely, worn out by campaigning, in 1422, he bequeathed to the country an infant son and all the inevitable perils of a long minority, a bankrupt treasury, and a war still only half won.

All this time, from 1400 to 1422, the disruptive forces were merely piling up, awaiting the opportunity of weakness at the centre to break out into open anarchy. In the first six years of his reign Henry IV had had to deal with two great conspiracies, the second of which brought together the Mortimers and the Percies with Welsh and Scottish backing and cost 7,000 men killed at Shrewsbury, the greatest battle on English soil since Hastings. On the eve of sailing for the Agincourt campaign Henry V unearthed a conspiracy centred in his cousin, Richard of Cambridge, who had acquired through his Mortimer wife a very good claim to the throne. After that the diversion of baronial energy abroad was tolerably, though only precariously, successful, until the appearance of Joan of Arc in 1428 put an end to the tide of English victories in France, so throwing the problem back across the Channel. Henry VI grew up into quite the wrong sort of man for such a crisis. He hated war and hunting and turned in horror from the sight of the remains of a quartered traitor on Cripplegate, crying that he could not bear 'that any Christian man be so used'. He was nervous, affectionate and generous; his hobbies were architecture and Church history; and he was entirely without political sense. Plunged too early into an almost impossible inheritance in which he became the centre of venomous intrigues and rivalries, his reason ultimately gave way under the strain, and for two short but disastrous periods of his reign he was unfit even to make a figurehead for a government.

Thus from 1422 until 1461 there were the conditions of a prolonged minority: at the centre a scramble for power, office and wealth; in the country administrative breakdown, paralysis of law, and every form of local violence and anarchy. London and the greater cities mostly preserved their own order. Elsewhere the family with most retainers and the most powerful friends would dominate a whole county and the towns within it, compelling the appointment of their nominees as sheriffs, packing juries, interfering with Parliamentary elections, and intimidating law courts with their armed followers—the evil of 'maintenance'. Under cover of this there was land grabbing by trumped-up legal process, or even by naked force. Lord Moleyns brought 1,000 archers and gunners to seize the Pastons' manor of Gresham, and in 1469 the Duke of Norfolk, in the course of a private quarrel, settled down with cannon and an army of 3,000 men to the siege of Caister Castle. Lower down the scale anyone who wore a great man's livery could steal and murder in comparative safety. Lawyers dared not appear in court against the powerful and, when even royal judges could be bribed or browbeaten, it is not surprising that ordinary men feared to give honest evidence or an honest verdict.

It was these disorders, and not the occasional short bursts of vicious civil war, that constituted the evil of the times. There was very little devastation or large-scale misery; much petty tyranny, loss, and frustration. The Cornish coast, for example, from Plymouth to Land's End, was systematically organized for piracy on a joint-stock basis, with almost all the squires and justices holding shares in pirate ships. Thus when, in 1451, William Joyce of Bristol lost his ship, the *Kateryn of Bayonne*, with a cargo of wine, iron, saffron, and ivory, he had to lodge his first complaint before a justice named Richard Penpons who was half owner of the pirate ship concerned. It took Joyce eleven years of Chancery proceedings and applications to the King's Council to get an order to arrest some of the identified pirates and then, when he tried to execute it, he and his friends were chased ten miles from St. Ives to Redruth. He never got redress, and his case was one of many. That sort of episode was what the political breakdown meant to the ordinary man. It did not stop the total volume of English trade from being doubled during the same period. But it created an overwhelming public opinion of merchants and lawyers and small gentry who would give solid support to any strong government, however harsh, which would restore the rule of law.

This then was the all-important background to the struggles of rival gangs of nobles to get control of royal policy; struggles which, even when they culminated in war, the ordinary Englishman watched with more detachment and a good deal less enthusiasm that he would bring to-day to the fluctuating fortunes of football league clubs. While Henry VI's only competent uncle, John, Duke of Bedford, carried on in France, the groups round the king slowly crystallized into two factions, to which some semblance of political principle was given by the fact that one stood for carrying on the French war at all costs, and the other wanted an honourable peace, while it might still be possible to get one. Bedford's brother, Humphrey, Duke of Gloucester, though the real soldiers regarded him with contempt, led the war party. He was well educated and his library became the foundation of the Bodleian in Oxford. But he was shallow, vain, stupid, and immoral and he devoted what political talent he had to a vain attempt to get Parliament to recognize him officially as Regent. To him in due course rallied Richard, Duke of York, who might have claimed the throne by right of his mother, Anne Mortimer, and was fearful that the Beauforts would squeeze him out of the succession altogether. One of the main sources of the trouble throughout was the anomalous position of these Beauforts, John of Gaunt's second family by the mistress whom he belatedly married; they were legitimatized by Richard II, and cut out of any claim on the Crown by royal patent of Henry IV. Insecurity forced them to intrigue for power and so rouse the hostility of Gloucester and York. Round them—the immensely wealthy Cardinal Henry Beaufort and his two nephews, successive Dukes of Somerset—was grouped the peace party. The most important member of it, and the only one with a touch of real statesmanship and patriotism about him, was John de la Pole who, by becoming Duke of Suffolk, completed a remarkable climb to social eminence which had started when his great-grandfather, a Hull merchant, had lent Edward III £76,000 at a critical moment.

It was this group which won the struggle for power and which ultimately crystallized into the Lancastrian party. Three things made England hate them; their neglect of government in the whole-time scramble for power and profit; their championship of peace, which seemed to unthinking men an unpatriotic betrayal of the memory of Henry V; and finally their association with the queen whom they found for Henry in 1444, Margaret, 'the she-wolf of Anjou', who was cruel, vindictive, and above all things French. The result was a series of political crises. Bedford died and resistance to the French slowly crumbled in Normandy and Maine. Gloucester, refusing to face the facts, died of shock when he was impeached and arrested in 1447. Bishop Moleyns, the King's Secretary, was assassinated by mutinous seamen at Portsmouth. Suffolk himself was impeached and exiled, caught off Calais by pirates in the pay of his enemies and, after a day and a night to shrive himself, rowed out in a small boat to have his head hacked off on the gunwale with a rusty sword, by an Irishman who was reckoned 'the lewdest man in the ship'. By June the men of Kent were back in London, this time under a man called Jack Cade, who claimed to be a lost Mortimer heir, and they murdered the Bishop of Salisbury and Lord Saye, the Treasurer, before they were dispersed. Their grievances were the grievances of England and their enemies the racketeers who waxed fat on misgovernment. It was only in

Cornwall that Lancastrian government was popular because it was weak.

Two events precipitated the last phase of open war: the birth of a son to Henry VI, followed almost immediately by the King's madness. Faced with the prospect of a long regency controlled by Margaret, even the moderates began to waver. The Nevilles, Salisbury and Warwick, the most powerful landed nobles in England, swung over to York, who, to save his own head, was more or less forced into war. His victory at St. Albans in 1455 secured him the Regency, but Henry's recovery gave Margaret her chance in 1459 to drive him into exile. In a year he was back, this time claiming the Crown, and Margaret had the satisfaction of putting a paper crown on his head when she stuck it up on the gate of York after her victory at Wakefield. But she failed to get London which, with the industrial south-east, was always bitterly resentful of Lancastrian incompetence. At Towton in Yorkshire, on Palm Sunday of 1461, the nineteen-year-old Edward of York handsomely revenged his father. With their backs to a flooded river and a blizzard in their faces, the Lancastrians were annihilated in the bloodiest battle of the war.

It looked as if England was out of her troubles at last. Tall, good-looking, with captivating manners which made him easily popular at London city banquets, already proved to be a competent general and a brilliant organizer, Edward IV promised a revival of all the glories of Plantagenet tradition. The French war was at last over; trade was expanding; and there was no great Lancastrian family left to support Margaret's desultory warfare along the Scottish border. But his achievement was disappointing. Like Henry IV before him he owed too much to the nobles who had helped him to the throne, Warwick in particular, and he bitterly offended them by his marriage to a pretty, characterless widow of no birth, Elizabeth Woodville, whose many relations were rapidly ennobled and enriched. He formed a small, powerful Council, financed himself by forced loans, and set himself to restore order at least, by arbitrary and illegal methods if necessary. But his own monarchy was rooted in the tradition of violence and treachery which he had to destroy, and he made little progress. Even in his first energetic years he could not create a government much more efficient or less corrupt than that of the Lancastrians. In the end he did no more than hold his own. He fought Margaret of Anjou off in 1464, capturing poor Henry VI and lodging him in the Tower, and survived a much more formidable attack between 1469 and 1471, when Warwick and his own brother, Clarence, turned against him. For six months he was driven into exile, while Warwick earned the nickname of 'Kingmaker' by digging the pathetic, 'not cleanly kept' figure of Henry out of the Tower again. But Clarence changed sides once more. Warwick was killed in a confused fight in the fog at Barnet. At Tewkesbury the Lancastrian Prince of Wales, Henry's only son, was killed and Margaret captured; and on their return to London Richard of Gloucester, Edward's youngest brother, made assurance doubly sure by putting Henry VI out of his misery.

But, having destroyed the Lancastrian Plantagenets, the Yorkist branch now set about destroying itself. Too much eating and drinking and dalliance with City wives sapped Edward's superb constitution and killed him in 1483, at the early age of forty-two. Already he had been compelled to denounce his treacherous brother, Clarence, to Parliament as 'incorrigible', and to have him murdered in the Tower. Now he left a twelve-year-old heir at the mercy of an uncle of whom most men went in terror, and who had already grasped most of the essentials of royal power before the king died. The almost universal hatred of the Woodvilles made the rest easy, once he had got control of both his nephews and sent them to the Tower to be murdered. None of the many attempts which have been made to clear Richard III of that crime has yet succeeded; and indeed historians are still bewildered, as his contemporaries were, by the character of the last Plantagenet. Many of the contradictions can be traced easily to the formative influences of his youth: the high renaissance culture which produced not only the Italian masterpieces, but also the civilization of the Borgias; and the wolfishly brutal background of a world in which Queen Margaret would delightedly encourage her eight-year-old son to condemn Yorkist prisoners to death, and Tiptoft, the scholarly Earl of Worcester, amused himself by watching Lancastrians being impaled on spears.

Certainly Richard might, in other circumstances, have made a very good king. All that he did in his short two years suggested a thoroughly businesslike reorganization of the government. But there was too much blood, Yorkist as well as Lancastrian, crying out for revenge, and they were two years of ceaseless conspiracy and executions. Moderates of both parties could all unite at last against the king. They had a possible claimant to the throne in Henry Tudor, son of the last Beaufort heiress, who had been an exile in Brittany for the last twelve years. The plan to marry him to Elizabeth, daughter of Edward IV, won over all who longed to see the end of the dynastic feud, and in August of 1485 he landed in his native Wales. He had still only 5,000 men when he faced Richard three weeks later at Bosworth in Leicestershire. But treachery was to be the keynote of these wars to the very end. More than half Richard's army deserted by previous arrangement as the battle started, and he himself was pulled down and killed as he hacked his way towards Henry's standard furiously shouting 'Treason'. So, appropriately enough, ended the story of the Plantagenets.

Chapter Seven

RESTORATION OF GOVERNMENT AND REORGANIZATION IN A NEW WORLD

✳

It is very important for English history that what triumphed at Bosworth was not a new monarchy, but the old one. England did not, as did most European countries, surrender her mediaeval liberties in despair as the price of order, and substitute a despotism for the mediaeval state. She carried the old liberties and law and government forward into a new age, adjusting the one and reorganizing the other as necessary. Henry Tudor had himself crowned as Henry VII, rightful heir to the Plantagenets, before getting Parliament to recognize him as such, and before marrying Elizabeth of York to give his son a good Yorkist, as well as the best Lancastrian, claim to the throne. He picked up the problem of government where it had been left by Richard III—in its essentials the same problem as had been tackled by Henry II with his Assizes and centralized law courts—and he applied to it, like every king with strength and brains for the past four centuries, the old remedy of making the law prevail. Unlike his immediate predecessors, he was successful, for two main reasons: he seized the throne at a moment when the disruptive power of the great nobles was at least temporarily crippled by the recent wars; at a moment also when the power of the rising classes, the merchants, lawyers, and lesser gentry, was great enough to turn the scale in favour of law and order.

Though it is surprising how little they disturbed peaceful men, the Wars of the Roses had been murderously destructive of the nobility and gentry who took part in them. Within sixteen years the Beauforts lost a father and three sons, leaving Henry's mother as their sole heiress. The huge estates of the younger Nevilles passed to two sisters whose marriages to Clarence and Richard III brought them eventually in to the Crown. Death and forfeiture had thus given the king a private rent roll of £30,000 a year, while there was no subject left in 1485 who could behave with the sovereign independence of a Warwick. Power in any case was passing from those whose feudal holding of land gave them the nucleus of a feudal army, to those whose control of money gave them gunpowder, cannon, and mercenaries. Along the Scottish border military necessity had kept almost intact the power of the Percies and Dacres and Cliffords, and in the old marcher lands of the west there was still dangerous disorder. But a government which could mobilize the support of the moneyed men would eventually be able to deal even with these.

The men whom the Tudors were to use to govern the country and whose support kept them on the throne did not constitute a new class: it had been growing steadily in numbers and wealth for centuries. It was rooted in the first place in the growth and prosperity of London. The great city companies, round which so much of the social, charitable and educational activity of the City still revolves, were already turning it into one of the richest cities in the world before 1400. As Lombard Street and the three golden balls of the Medici coat of arms still remind us, fourteenth century England had often depended financially on Italian goldsmiths and bankers. By the end of the fifteenth an Italian counted fifty-two goldsmiths' shops in Cheapside alone whose contents, he reckoned, exceeded in value all those of Rome, Milan, Venice and Florence put together. All over Europe merchant companies which could only thrive in the hands of large capitalists had thrust into a sub-

4. 'The Thames from above Greenwich' by an unknown artist

(By kind permission of Capt. Sir Bruce Ingram, Bt.)

ordinate position the purely craft guilds—Carpenters, Coopers, and the like. In London their direct interest in the export of raw wool had given the Mercers a virtual supremacy even over the Grocers, Drapers, and Fishmongers, so that they supplied a quarter of the aldermen and nearly a third of the mayors of the fifteenth century. But the richer merchants were less and less specialized in their nominal trades, owning ships not only in London but in Continental ports, and exploiting dozens of profitable sidelines. They had not yet squeezed out the Italians; and the Germans of the Hanseatic League—the 'Easterlings'—still held their privileged premises in the Steelyard under government protection, and, it is said, left the pound sterling as their permanent memorial in the English vocabulary. But an increasing tide of wealth poured through the city as the new company of the Merchant Adventurers, formed mainly to deal with the growing export of cloth in competition with the weaving cities of Flanders, took the risks and the profits of forcing their way into new markets.

The men who made great fortunes and built princely London houses sooner or later sought a more permanent investment in land, and so founded the families—the Wottons, Knollys, and Boleyns, the Russells and Cecils, who were to be the so-called new aristocracy of the Tudors. Much of it was less newly aristocratic than appeared, for there was two-way traffic between manor and counting house, and the famous Dick Whittington, 'thrice Lord Mayor of London,' was the younger son of a Gloucestershire gentleman sent up, like many others, to make his fortune. County families with sheep runs would see to marketing their own wool and even apprentice their sons to London merchants. The older aristocracy had to adapt itself to these new ways or perish, and so the English ruling class kept its characteristic fluidity for centuries to come, continually depleted by financial casualties and recruited from City fortunes.

It was important for Henry VII and VIII that this was also an educated class. An expanding commerce put continually greater demands on the law, and the Inns of Court already formed learned groups outside Oxford and Cambridge and the control of the Church. Needing a knowledge of the law more and more to protect the titles to their lands and carry out their accumulating functions as justices, the country gentry were sending their sons to round off the education of grammar school and university with a spell at Lincoln's Inn or the Temple. Meanwhile there were already nearly 400 grammar schools by 1400 and very many more were founded by guilds and rich merchants during the fifteenth century. Originally intended to give a grounding of reading, writing, and Latin to would-be clerics, these schools were being used more and more by the ambitious laity, and also by the gentry who increasingly found the old method of sending their sons to the household of a great nobleman or to an Abbey unsatisfactory. William of Wykeham had made special provision for the sons of gentlemen in his foundation of Winchester in 1382, and so given it from the start a more than local influence, and Henry VI's Eton followed his example, becoming early a largely aristocratic preserve thanks to the high boarding fees payable to the Fellows in order to be within reach of the free education provided by the College.

Thus by Henry VII's time a grammar school education had become normal for all who did not need their sons as additional breadwinners at the earliest possible age. The growth of the college system, taken from Paris in the thirteenth century, but extended into a characteristic and almost exclusively English institution by Oxford and Cambridge, encouraged gentry and merchants to send their sons on for a year or two of further education in disciplined establishments where they were now protected from the riotous licentiousness of the mediaeval university. Apart from the standard, latinized education of the Middle Ages, there was a flood of new English literature and of translations available to such young men, since Caxton, that admirable merchant who retired with a fortune to devote himself to literature, had set up his printing press by Westminster Abbey in 1477. The educated layman now dominated local politics in town and country, and the existence of this numerous and powerful class, perfectly capable of appreciating intelligently the problems of reform and reorganization, was a major factor in the success of the early Tudors. These were the men who sat in their Parliaments and on the bench in every market town, who supplied their law courts with barristers and the expanding administration with its officials, gradually ousting the churchmen from control.

The actual task faced by the government was not to rebuild a nation shattered and devastated by a century of civil war, but to bring the political machinery up to date in a society which had been getting steadily richer and more civilized. In spite of Cornish pirates and of the local disorders for which the war occasionally provided an excuse, men and women travelled freely about on business. A Chancery clerk like William Marchall could arrange without difficulty the building of his country house down in Oxfordshire, writing and receiving letters, and sending down money by carrier to pay the workmen, only taking the precaution of packing it in a pound of powdered pepper or two pounds of rice. In the Calais which Warwick filled with red-coated soldiers wearing his badge of the bear and ragged staff while he planned the overthrow of a dynasty, twelve married merchants of the Staple merrily challenged twelve bachelors to a shooting match at thirteen score yards, 'for a dyner or a supper per XIId. a man'. Though the depopulation of the Black Death on one hand, and the growth of home weaving on the other had reduced the exports of wool by three-quarters, cloth exports were going steadily up; and even in decline the wool industry could send as many as forty shiploads out of the Thames in a single day at the height of the summer season. All that was needed was not a new set of laws, but the enforcement of the old. A machine which already existed in all essentials had to be made to function efficiently.

For this task Henry VII was the perfect man. He lacked the athletic, spectacular qualities which in all ages have endeared rulers to the masses. He was civilized and unheroic, enjoyed music and books as well as hunting, and detested violence and bloodshed. Those in close contact with him fell under his charm and served him with devotion. His family life was happy. He made his servants his friends and kept them for life. He even had the self-confidence to trust enemies, once he had won them over, giving Northumberland almost unrestricted power in the north, and, when he was told that 'all Ireland could not govern Kildare', sending Kildare to govern Ireland. There have been few more successful political gestures than the contemptuous tolerance with which he sent Lambert Simnel, taken in arms in 1487 masquerading with Yorkist support as the son of Clarence, to menial employment in the royal kitchens. The other Pretender, Perkin Warbeck, who announced himself as Richard of York, the younger of the Princes murdered in the Tower, and with Burgundian and Scottish support plagued Henry on and off for years, had equally no right to expect clemency after an unsuccessful invasion of the west country in 1497. But he too was merely held in the Tower, until he started plotting with Clarence's real son, Warwick, who was there too, and both were executed.

But Henry's mildness was deceptive. When Stanley, whose treachery to Richard III at Bosworth had largely won him his crown, betrayed him in turn ten years later, he was beheaded with all his friends. The long-standing laws against keeping liveried retainers and using them to terrorize law courts, Henry would have obeyed at all costs. On them ultimately depended all peaceful internal development, all commercial expansion, all possibility of a successful foreign policy. The other famous story of the king's visit to the Earl of Oxford, most loyal of Lancastrians, shows one of the reasons for his surprising success. For, when Oxford turned out a guard of honour for him wearing his private badge of the radiant star, Henry promptly fined him heavily, observing tersely that he loved not to see his laws broken in his own sight. The first fifteen years of his reign were full of troubles, but it is a commentary on the immediate efficiency of the new government that the Yorkist plots drew their support almost entirely from those areas which had thriven on disorder and had therefore in the old days preferred the weak government of the Lancastrians—the northern and Welsh marches, and Cornwall, which staged two major rebellions in one year.

Behind a façade of careful ceremonial Henry in fact worked tirelessly, attending his own Council meetings, going through accounts item by item, directly interested in all the expanding activities of his government. The instrument of all the early Tudor success was the King's Council, whether it sat as an overriding court of law in the Star Chamber, or in detachments of itself at York and Ludlow, or meeting the king after hunting and dinner to discuss Navigation Laws for the protection of English shipping against foreign competition or the despatch of the Genoese Cabot brothers to explore the coasts of North America. In 1523 Henry VIII formalized what had already been his father's practice by ordinances which established part of the Council permanently at Westminster, easily accessible for routine business, while part remained with the king where high policy could alone be formulated. Here were the germs out of which the civil service and the cabinet would much later develop; but meanwhile what was happening was the extension throughout the government of the basic English method of dealing with any corporate problem, whether in the village or in the state, by forming a committee which in turn would form sub-committees to deal with each separate and specialized problem. It has not always been the most logical or efficient way of dealing with government. But it grew out of the Norman adaptations of the Saxon village community, and, because it worked successfully, became a habit of mind which remains at the root of all our political thought and activity to this day.

So, gradually, the first Tudors achieved what the Normans and Plantagenets had begun: the extension of an even-handed royal justice based on the common law of England into every corner of the realm and every department of the national life. When Sir Robert Harcourt sent his servants to steal the nets and fishing boats of the monks of Eynsham and batter their way into the monastery, he now had to face the king's government directly in the Star Chamber, where judges were not to be browbeaten or bribed and there was no jury to threaten. The king's writs forced their way into the remaining feudal areas where nobles like Northumberland had hitherto kept an absolute jurisdiction. By tactful bargaining with the Papacy the rights of sanctuary were restricted and the worst exploitations of the leniency of ecclesiastical courts by all who could read a verse or two of Latin were stopped. Gradually the disorders subsided. After one brief invasion of France in 1492, remarkable because, by allowing the French to buy him off, Henry even made war show a profit, there was peace abroad. Advantageous commercial treaties protected our wool trade with the Netherlands. The northern border was temporarily settled by the marriage of Henry's daughter Margaret to James IV of Scotland. Something had even been done to establish law and order in Ireland. When Henry died in 1509 he left nearly a million pounds hoarded in his Treasury—in some ways a more remarkable memorial than the exquisite, fan-vaulted chapel which he had added to Westminster Abbey.

With the accession of his son, Henry VIII, it was as though the Renaissance stepped on to the throne. In fact, of course, the revival of English learning, the study of Greek and the far-reaching consequences of contact with the classical literature and art and outlook, were no more new and sudden changes than all the other apparently startling changes of the early Tudor age. The rebirth of letters went back along many threads, through Tiptoft and Duke Humphrey, Wycliffe and Chaucer, to the men like Walter Map and John of Salisbury who had made Henry II's court a centre of learning; beyond even them, to the despairing beginnings of King Alfred. The work of the Oxford scholars of international reputation, of Grocyn, Linacre and Colet, and of Sir Thomas More, the friend of Erasmus who was to serve Henry VIII as Chancellor, was only the climax of centuries of development, just as the chapel of King's College, Cambridge, crowned the glory of five centuries of English architecture. But, much more aggressively than his father, Henry VIII was the product of all these forces, educated by great scholars into the Renaissance world. While still a boy he could exchange learned little notes in Latin across the dinner table with Erasmus. He composed music some of which is still played, and wrote poetry. He was an outstanding athlete, good-looking, charming and adventurous, with the large appetites of healthy youth; and the streak of brutal cruelty which too much power was later to reveal was still, at the age of eighteen, held in the discipline of an exquisite civilization.

Henry VII's reign had ended on a note of sadness and decline. Prematurely aged by plots and disorders which sickened him, and by the deaths of his wife and eldest son and of all the old friends like Cardinal Morton, the amusing companion of his exile and trusted minister of his heyday, he died in a solitude in which careful prudence had turned to avarice, alienated by massive forced loans even from the classes whom his rule had most benefited. Henry VIII, 'the best dressed sovereign in the world', who started in a blaze of popularity by executing his father's most hated and grasping ministers, Empson and Dudley, burst through this atmosphere like sunshine, if only by setting himself to spend handsomely his father's accumulated wealth. His preoccupation with 'girls and hunting', his craving for spectacular intervention on the Continent, and his almost complete abandonment of affairs to Cardinal Wolsey, all pointed the contrast. Wolsey himself, Archbishop of York, Chancellor, and Papal Legate, had by 1518 achieved a magnificence which would not have been tolerated in the frugal days of Henry VII. His administration was a sound enough prolongation of the old, using the same instruments to the same ends. In the Church he carried forward a policy of moderate reform, suppressing over thirty insolvent or inefficient religious houses and using their revenues to found Ipswich Grammar School and Christ Church in Oxford. But he was, as his portraits clearly suggest, a gross man, and whole-hearted reform of the Church was impossible so long as he himself was the greatest scandal, with his wealth accumulated from benefices held in plurality, his palaces at Whitehall and Hampton Court, and the illegitimate children richly endowed with Church preferments. For fifteen years his supremacy lasted, until an unpopular war and the king's matrimonial difficulties combined to destroy it.

The war with France, in which Henry and Wolsey lightheartedly engaged in 1511, and which lasted off and on until 1526, had no valid national objective. High-sounding claims to the French throne were out of date and meaningless, and captured ports in northern France no longer had much commercial or strategic value. The Agincourt which was Henry's real ambition always eluded him and high war taxation alienated the very classes on which Tudor government most depended. Henry won his victory, at the Battle of the Spurs in 1513, but the French ran away so quickly that it was an unheroic affair. Ironically enough, it was the seventy-year-old Earl of Surrey, left behind as Treasurer to deal with the almost certain intervention of the Scots, who won the spectacular laurels of that year. For James IV, more loyal to the 'auld alliance' with France than to his brother-in-law, came over the border with the most formidable army the Scots had ever put into the field. At Flodden Surrey, by some risky but skilful manœuvring, forced the Scots to abandon the high ground and the defensive and outfought them in a desperate, evening battle until darkness saved the dwindling remnant who still held the ring round the dying Scottish king. The Scots lost the flower of their nobility and in all 10,000 men in this fight, which was both the end and the beginning of an age: for it was the last great triumph of the English long bow and the first big battle in which artillery played a decisive part.

By 1526, when renewed war had still brought no decisive result, when there was rioting everywhere against extortionate taxation, and Parliament openly resisted the government's demands, Wolsey faced the crisis of his career. Henry decided to divorce Catherine of Aragon, his elder brother's widow whom he had married under Papal dispensation at the beginning of his reign. Older than he was in the first place, and worn out by ill health and miscarriages, she had not given and clearly now would not give him the male heir for which his soul hungered, and his feeling that this showed God's curse on a doubtful marriage was probably genuine. In any case there was still too much Yorkist blood about to make it safe to leave so turbulent an inheritance to his only daughter, Mary, and there was every reason to expect the Pope to grant what was, by the standards of the time, a perfectly reasonable request, especially from a prince who had only recently earned the title Defender of the Faith for his spirited attack on the heretical writings of Luther.

But Wolsey was asked to produce the divorce at the moment when it had suddenly become quite impossible for the Pope to grant it. For Imperial troops held Rome and dominated all Italy and Clement VII dared not offend the Emperor Charles V, who was Queen Catherine's nephew, though he wept and wrung his hands as he listened to the increasingly emphatic English demands. For three years he dragged the negotiations out, until it was clear that Henry could only get his divorce by defying Rome. Since he was by now in love with Anne Boleyn, sister of his late mistress, Henry decided to take the risk, threw Wolsey overboard, and called Parliament together to mobilize support and share the responsibility, so releasing a chain of events which ultimately produced the English Reformation.

For an anti-Roman and anti-clerical policy, as distinct from an attack on the established religion, the king could count on a good deal of support. In an age of genuine piety educated men resented more than ever the scandals and abuses which had gone unremedied since the days of Chaucer and Langland and Wycliffe: the traffic in faked relics and money payments for absolution; the worldliness and greed of many of the higher clergy and the immorality and ignorance of the lower, which reduced worship to a magical mumbo-jumbo; the hair-splitting theological argument which overlaid the simple basic truths of the New Testament. Behind them were the still unremedied grievances of Piers Plowman and the unlettered masses, always responsive to a reforming movement which seemed to promise a return to the Gospel uncontaminated by a priesthood which had largely forfeited their respect. Finally, uniting all classes who could think politically at all, there was the long-standing resentment of the annual cost of allegiance to Rome: not only the large sums paid direct to the Pope, but the tithes and rents and offerings which went to support an unworthy clergy and decaying monasteries. Against this background the work of the would-be reformers—Colet's sermons at St. Paul's denouncing clerical wickedness, high and low, and More's book, *Utopia*, pleading for a genuinely Christian society—only succeeded in hardening English educated opinion against a Church which seemed incorrigible.

These converging forces combined to produce three distinct elements in the English Reformation. There was the desire of the king to bring under his complete and direct control the one remaining institution which eluded it, which paid money and owed allegiance to a power beyond his reach and jurisdiction, whose courts interfered with the pattern of his justice, and whose scandals and abuses he could not remedy. There was the long-standing resentment among most educated laymen of a hierarchy which every year did less to justify its wealth and its pretensions. Finally there were those whose main protest was against the actual doctrine of the Church as well as the clergy and institutions:

the descendants of the peasants who had followed John Ball and of the merchants whom fifteenth century persecution had forced to burn or conceal a Wycliffe bible, in whom the Lutheran appeal to the Scriptures and insistence on the importance of simple faith as opposed to religious observance woke an instant response. United these swept the king along courses which he had never foreseen and to consequences many of which he had neither foreseen nor desired.

Everything now turned on whether these accumulated grievances and the new sense of nationhood among the English would prevail over the ancient loyalties and enable Henry VIII to escape the humiliation which the attack on Becket had brought on Henry II. If the masses turned against him under competent leadership, he could not coerce them with a standing military force of four-score yeomen of the guard, and it was this which brought Parliament back into the forefront of politics. Hitherto he and his father had used it very little: when taxes had to be voted; or, occasionally, to rally support and establish unity of purpose between the government and the local administration of county and borough. For their main business of enforcing obedience to the law it was useless. From 1529 onwards Parliament met almost every year for the rest of the reign and step by step, sometimes enthusiastically, often reluctantly under the pressure of dire threats, collaborated in the piecemeal destruction of the Roman Church in England.

Item by item, from 1529 to 1533, all the Pope's English revenues were shorn away. Then, goaded by the annual disappointment of his expectation that Rome would give way, and by the knowledge that Anne Boleyn was with child by him, Henry found churchmen like Cranmer and Latimer who would shoulder responsibility for blessing his remarriage, and invested them with the necessary authority by himself assuming supreme headship of the Church in England under an Act of Supremacy, and so abolishing finally the power exercised by 'the Bishop of Rome, otherwise called the Pope'. It was a quite logical next step to use

123

this new authority to carry through a reform of the monasteries, whose slackness and mismanagement had, after all, been a scandal for centuries. But financial difficulties and a growing lust for power, as he found how far he could go with impunity, carried Henry much further than that. In 1536 all the smaller religious houses—those with an annual income of less than £200 a year—were dissolved, and in 1539 the remainder.

Thomas Cromwell, whom Henry used to carry all this through for him, was one of the least attractive characters who have ever held power in England. Coarse and brutal, a lawyer self-made largely by money-lending, with an Italianate education which had taught him to revere nothing but power in a prince, Cromwell now descended in person or by deputy as the King's Vicar General, on one after another of the 370 lesser monasteries to extract the evidence needed to justify their dissolution. The confessions secured from monks and nuns who were encouraged to denounce each other, and especially their own superiors, were valueless as serious evidence, but sufficient as propaganda. Even so, Cromwell got little to justify accusations of gross scandal or immorality. The true picture, as revealed by the ordinary visitations carried out half a century earlier, by Cardinal Morton at St. Albans, or by Bishop Fox in his diocese of Durham, was not in general one of licentiousness, but of an almost universal laxity, with a system of punishment so mild as to be quite useless. Services were not kept, and there were 'drinkings after Compline'. Monks went hawking and hunting and rode abroad in 'short and tight doublets', fought with each other in the cloister, or sat in taverns on market day. A canon who had pawned three library books was only condemned to say the seven penitential psalms. Abbots deposed for immoral behaviour were comfortably pensioned, and nuns more seriously accused, like those of Godstow who had got into trouble with Oxford undergraduates, were only directed to say the psalter through seven times, or fast for a week.

Shortage of numbers, mismanagement of revenues, and non-performance of duties all pointed to the fact that monasticism in England had lost all driving force. The greater houses of the north still fulfilled many useful social functions as hospitals, schools, safe-deposits and almshouses. Elsewhere most had neither the means nor the inclination to do so, and their revenues were better diverted to founding six new bishoprics. Had the whole of the remainder gone to founding schools, the wholesale dissolution might have been better justified; as it was the shortage of schools for the next few generations was acute. The bulk of the land confiscated, worth something like £135,000 a year, or some two millions of modern money, passed to the king; and he, when he had spent the great windfall of the plate and jewels of rich shrines like Canterbury and Walsingham, passed it on, mainly by sale, to gentry anxious to round off an estate, or to corporations for re-sale. An era of land-grabbing and profiteering by men whose self-interest was hardly yet tempered by a tradition of public responsibility, was one of the results. Another was that the gentry, all of whom, however Catholic and conservative, participated in the scramble, emerged even richer and more powerful, but committed irrevocably to support of the new régime. Deliberately or not, Henry created a vested interest which became the greatest obstacle to any restoration of Rome's authority in England, since too many men feared having to disgorge lands, often long coveted, and now absorbed into their estates.

By confining his attack to the financial and political institutions of the Church, Henry nearly got through without any open or serious opposition. A few honest men in high places, like More and Bishop Fisher of Rochester, lost their heads for refusing to subscribe to the Act of Supremacy; and a number of friars suffered martyrdom in the same cause. There were murmurs, and sometimes open opposition in Parliament, but Henry drove forward so fiercely that it was only the dissolution of the lesser monasteries and the clearly revealed threat to the greater that provoked nearly the whole of northern England into the revolt known as the Pilgrimage of Grace.

The grievances of the pilgrims and the story of their failure provide in themselves a summary of the problems and achievements of the first two Tudors. For this was essentially a conservative protest against not only the religious, but all the changes which were making a new world. The cloth workers of Lincolnshire and south Yorkshire rose against the loss of their civic rights to the richer merchant families in each town. The peasants, who actually started the movement by tearing down new sheep fences near the village of Dent, were out against enclosure which, though it made agriculture more prosperous and efficient, put small holders out of business. The Abbot of Barlings, who rode into York in full armour at the head of his monks and tenants, represented the protest, widespread in the still primitive north, against the loss of monasteries which were still the only sources of education and charity. Finally the surviving feudatories saw here their last chance of rallying popular support against the encroaching power represented by the King's Council at York, cutting into their liberties and destroying the still living allegiances of a land which 'knew no lord but a Percy'. They were all men who, whatever their grievances against each other, looked back to the good old days. Their clamour for the removal of Cromwell and the 'mean men' who governed about the king was the last expression of the mediaeval hatred of upstarts. To all, the dissolution seemed the last straw, and under the banner of the Five Wounds of Christ they merged their divergent interests. The defiantly liveried trumpeters who rode before Northumberland's brother, Sir Thomas Percy, into York to join the 40,000 already gathered there, were sounding the last defiance of the Middle Ages in England at Tudor government and all that it stood for.

Though he could not get enough men together under the Duke of Norfolk to crush the rebellion out of hand, Henry survived it with skill and surprising ease. He fetched its leader, Robert Aske, to London to discuss remedies, and spun out negotiations until dissension began to destroy the movement from within. Large promises sent most of the rebels home; the strategic points were seized; and the inevitable failure of the too honest Aske to control his own wilder followers gave the excuse for a vicious revenge. The heads of abbots and nobles appeared above the gates of Lincoln and York and Carlisle and local ringleaders swung from gallows in every considerable village of the north. Henry, for the first time in his life, had been badly frightened. One by one the Yorkist survivors, whose Plantagenet blood made them a permanent menace, went to the block under the new, tightened-up treason laws, until in 1541 even the aged Countess of Salisbury paid the penalty of being Clarence's daughter.

The vital importance of the Pilgrimage of Grace in English history was that it completed the destruction of the last effective feudally disruptive forces before religious dissension hardened to divide the solid support on which the king's reforms rested. Henry VII and VIII achieved what the kings in France and the emperors in Germany failed to do, and so saved England from half a century of religious civil war. The process was completed only just in time. In 1540, when the king suddenly turned on Cromwell and beheaded him for no better reason than his unpopularity, he undoubtedly thought that he had weathered the last storm. He had secured more real, personal power over Church and state than any ruler of England before or since. He had got rid of Anne Boleyn on a trumped-up charge of adultery, and his third marriage, to Jane Seymour, had at last produced a male heir. He had restored the alliance with the Spanish group of powers which, because it included the Netherlands, was commercially vital to England. But in destroying the authority and structure of the Roman Church he had irretrievably damaged the whole fabric of Roman belief. He had given England Cranmer's bible; and at the moment when he thought of the Reformation as complete, it was in fact only about to begin. For, with the removal of the agreed abuses, the third element of English anti-Romanism, the evangelical, always present but hitherto subordinate, was now to take charge. Henry, in fact, had reckoned without Protestantism.

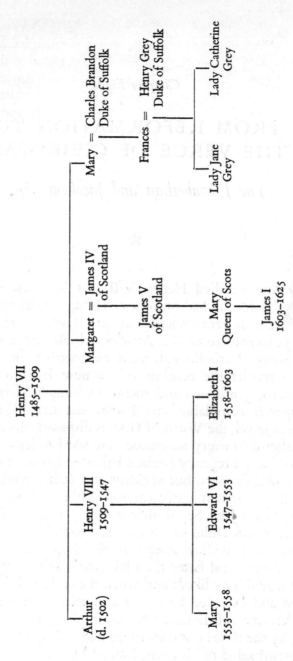

THE TUDORS

Henry VII
1485–1509

Arthur
(d. 1502)

Henry VIII
1509–1547

Margaret = James IV
of Scotland

Mary = Charles Brandon
Duke of Suffolk

Mary
1553–1558

Edward VI
1547–1553

Elizabeth I
1558–1603

James V
of Scotland

Mary
Queen of Scots

James I
1603–1625

Frances = Henry Grey
Duke of Suffolk

Lady Jane
Grey

Lady Catherine
Grey

Chapter Eight

FROM REFORMATION TO THE VERGE OF CIVIL WAR

The Elizabethan and Jacobean Ages

★

Befored he died Henry VIII was fully aware of the dangers he had unloosed. Though he burnt Protestants as remorselessly as any Catholic king in an attempt to enforce his Six Articles, which were a conservative, purely Catholic statement of doctrine, he tried too late to restrict the reading of his new English Bible to noblemen, gentlemen and merchant householders, and his last speech complained to Parliament that: 'That most precious jewel, the Word of God, is disputed, rhymed, sung and jangled in every ale-house.' He tried to leave his nine-year-old son a regency council balanced between conservatives and reformers, but accident and skilful intrigue put a strongly Protestant party on top within a fortnight. Encouraged by Jane Seymour's brother, who made himself Protector and Duke of Somerset, extremists like Hooper, Latimer and Ridley swept Archbishop Cranmer along much further and faster than his gentle and compromising spirit would have liked; and when the ruthless John Dudley ousted and executed Somerset and seized the regency the pace became still hotter. Moreover, the precocious young King by the time he was fourteen had a clear and extremely Protestant mind of his own, backed by a wholly Tudor intolerance of opposition. So the two Prayer Books of 1549 and 1552 progressively demolished all Catholic teaching, imposing on a bewildered and unready England Communion in both Kinds for the laity, clerical marriage, the repudiation of the Real Presence, the setting of the altar as a communion table in the middle of the church, and the abolition of vestments for the clergy.

The general result of this violent swing from extreme to extreme was an almost complete demoralization of the nation. The despair of men who could not live without faith in a world in which all authority for faith was suddenly undermined turned easily to hooliganism and excesses of all kinds. Sometimes the Host was rabbled as it was carried through the streets; sometimes the crowd would turn out to save their church windows and ornaments from destruction by enthusiasts. And while the new ideas gained ground fast in London and the south-east, and very slowly in the agricultural north and west, there was no uniformity or agreement, but everywhere chaos and disillusionment. The easy spoil of the monastic lands had whetted the appetite of a ruling class already debauched by the collapse of all the traditional mediaeval restraints on exploitation, and they plundered the commonwealth indiscriminately, seizing all they could of the remaining church wealth and stealing even the endowments of schools and hospitals, until Bishop Ridley cried out that Christ lay in the streets of London 'hungry, naked, and cold'. On top of all this the nation was near to bankruptcy, thanks to years of indeterminate, unsuccessful war with France and Scotland. The coinage was debased until the shilling was officially revalued at 6d.; gold and silver from Spanish America increased the inflation, until prices were up by 200 per cent and the real value of wages had dropped by more than half. To save themselves the landlords raised rents, did all they could to upset copyhold leases, and enclosed common lands on a scale which ruined numberless small holders, flooded the towns with a surplus of unskilled labour and the country with dangerous gangs of vagabonds.

Amidst the continuous disorder two great risings under-
lined the nation's grievances: the west country turned out in
defence of churches and a Latin Mass more comprehensible,
to Cornishman at least, than an English Prayer Book; and
Robert Kett assembled 20,000 men at Norwich in protest
against enclosures, whose slogans recalled the primitive
communism of the Peasants' Revolt. Christ, they said, had
died to make men free. With foreign mercenaries Dudley
broke both risings, rewarded himself with the dukedom of
Northumberland, beheaded Somerset, and set out on the
wild gamble of extreme Protestantism, secured for the
future, since the king was already consumptive, by an improvised Protestant succession. For Mary, daughter of
Catherine and heiress to the throne by Henry's will and Act
of Parliament, had been reared in bitter seclusion to a rigid,
Spanish Catholicism. Northumberland tried to make
England accept instead her cousin, the luckless Lady Jane
Grey, whom he married to his own son; but the whole
scheme was miscalculated. The country was loyal to the
Tudors, detested Northumberland, and was not nearly
ready for the extremes of the new Prayer Book. Within a
fortnight of Edward's death in 1553 Mary was proclaimed
Queen and Northumberland, his family, and his few friends
were in the Tower.

Mary had many of the Tudor qualities which might have
made a great queen, but her overmastering desire to restore
England to Papal obedience at all speed and at all costs made
her reign a five-year tragedy. England was prepared for a
reaction, and a more cautious approach could at least have
secured a return to the position left by Henry. In the wild-
ness and anarchy of Northumberland's rule the vociferous,
irreconcilable minority had forfeited public support and,
provided it was not reinforced by persecution, might with
patience be eliminated. In time even Rome's authority
might have been accepted, provided there was no question
of restoring Church lands. Sound government, peace
abroad, and a trade recovery were prerequisites. Yet another

violent swing from one extreme to another must be avoided at all costs.

Every one of these political considerations which governed a possible restoration of Catholicism Mary ignored. By marrying Philip of Spain she ensured a renewal of French and Scottish war for which we had neither a fleet nor an army, in which we had nothing to gain, and Calais ruinous, undermanned, and permeated with French influence, to lose. At the same time she gave her religious opponents the support of an intolerant patriotism which brought Sir Thomas Wyatt and the men of Kent to Charing Cross to shout against the Spanish match. Deceived by the popular upheaval which had set her on the throne and by the ease with which Parliament restored the Six Articles, far too soon she brought her cousin, Cardinal Pole, from Rome to negotiate reconciliation; and as opposition sullenly mounted and her marriage proved a failure and the crowds shouted 'Liar' and 'Papist' at her priests who celebrated Mass, she embarked on a decisively fatal persecution. She only burnt some 300 people—by French and Dutch standards a trivial number. But the vast majority were ordinary citizens and artisans of London and the densely populated south-east; and it was they, rather than Cranmer, Ridley, Latimer and Hooper, who lit the candle which, as Latimer said, by God's grace should never be put out. A still brutal generation, which made an execution the excuse for a picnic, was moved to compassion, and still more to anger. In the end Mary had nothing left: Philip had gone and the baby she wanted so passionately was never born; Calais was lost; Cardinal Pole was dying; and even she could not blind herself to the hatred she had roused for all that she loved. Five years after her triumphant accession England was lighting bonfires to celebrate her death.

The young woman who emerged from the seclusion of Hatfield to mount the throne as Elizabeth I was largely an unknown quantity. At one stage in Henry's matrimonial muddles she, too, had been proclaimed a bastard, and had only been reinstated in the line of succession by his will. As the inevitable centre of plots against Mary she had been in the Tower and had all but lost her head. Now, though she had a fine brain and was exceptionally well educated, even for that age, talking and writing Latin and most European languages with fluent ease, she was without experience of government, and she had to take over an almost impossible inheritance in an age which did not believe a woman capable of government, except through a competent husband—a belief only too recently strengthened by Mary's failure. But the political world had not realized how much she was her father's child. She had the same bluff, cheerful, rather coarse way with people at large: could bandy words with a waterman or a Lord Mayor, rebuke a schoolmaster for a false quantity in a Latin address, and always make a crowd laugh. Her rages, like his, were terrifying, because she retained her dignity even when she slapped a Councillor's face. Though she lost her heart often, she never, like her cousin, Mary Stuart, lost her head, drawing back at the critical moment from a fatal mésalliance with Leicester, and even in her infatuated old age dismissing and executing Essex when familiarity bred contempt and treason. Vain, meaner about money even than her grandfather, and sometimes exasperatingly capricious, she was every inch what she liked to call herself, 'A Prince', and never for an instant lost confidence in her people or in herself. 'If I were turned out of the realm in my petticoat,' she told her Commons, 'I were able to live in any place in Christendom.'

So she held the throne, dangerously but magnificently, for forty-five years of prosperity and glory which seemed unthinkable in 1558. For behind the religious bitterness and the social and economic miseries bequeathed her by Edward and Mary there was a nation uniquely fitted to respond to the sort of leadership she gave. The late but splendid English renaissance reached its climax in her reign and gave her a wealth of talent from which to choose her servants: poets who were also men of action, who would die on the field of battle, like Sidney, or on the block after a lifetime of tempestuous adventure, like Raleigh; free-booters with centuries of Cornish piracy behind them, like Drake, Hawkins, Grenville, Gilbert and Frobisher, redeemed from mere brutality by a deep-rooted, simple, Protestant faith and a breadth of vision which would carry them round the world; polished courtiers who could competently command armies and fleets and had the taste and discrimination to be the patrons of Marlowe and Shakespeare. This was the stuff of which Elizabethan England was made. But the harvest of all this glory must have been lost in religious war and political and social ruin without the statesmanship of Elizabeth herself, backed by the long-headed, conscientious William Cecil, Lord Burghley, who was her trusted minister and friend for forty years, and the more selfish and disapprovingly Puritan Walsingham, who none the less spent his life overworking to save her from Catholic plots.

Obviously the biggest danger in 1558 was a permanent religious division between two extremes. The solution which saved the nation, the Elizabethan Church Settlement, was largely imposed by the Queen herself on a Parliament which would have liked something much more Protestant. Broadly it was the most conservative solution which England could be induced to accept. Elizabeth kept the supreme governorship of the Church. She took the Prayer Book of 1552 as her basic model, but inserted in it bits of that of 1549, notably two sentences which gave a loophole to those who clung to the doctrine of the Real Presence at Communion. She kept surplices, and put the Communion Table back at the east end of the church, though it might be moved when needed. The Thirty-nine Articles gave England a form of service still on the pattern of the old Catholic ritual; bishops and priests who, though married, still claimed apostolic succession from St. Peter; and an authoritarian Church ruled by the Crown through the two houses of Convocation, with Archdeacon's Courts to enforce discipline in each diocese, and the Court of High Commission as a sort of ecclesisatical Star Chamber. Everybody had to go to church on Sunday or pay a shilling fine.

At the same time there was an impressive effort to remedy the social and economic disasters which had flowed from the Reformation and to save the labouring class from the irresponsible exploitation which had all but ruined them. By 1561 the silver coinage had been revalued, government credit restored, and a system of tariffs and bounties started to protect rising home industries, exploit new sources of tin, copper, and zinc, save the remaining forests for ship-building, and in general to make England independent of essential imports in wartime. Paternal, authoritarian government set itself to replace on a national scale the services and controls once found locally from Church and guild re-sources. Regulations slowed down, though they could not stop, enclosures. The Statute of Labourers of 1563 extended London's seven-year apprentice system throughout the country, overhauled conditions of employment, ordered J.P.s to adjust wage rates annually in relation to local prices, and decreed compulsory land work for the able-bodied unemployed. At the same time the Poor Law authorized for the first time a compulsory local rate for the relief of genuine distress.

These and innumerable lesser administrative controls, combined with the Church Settlement, made up Elizabeth's and Cecil's long-term programme. Time alone could enable them to produce a new social system: a new relationship between capital and labour, producer and consumer, government and people. A new generation must grow up which knew no other formal worship but that of the Prayer Book; which, never having known the Roman Church in its hey-day, found a monthly fine merely for the privilege of stay-ing away from Church irksome and increasingly pointless. The Church itself must have time to create its own tradi-tional orthodoxy and scholarship. For an invasion by the Counter Reformation powers, France or Spain, in 1559 would have found in England a vast fifth column—perhaps a third of the population—whose religious duty would have been to side with the invaders. Mary Stuart, Queen of Scotland, Queen-consort of France, and next in succession to Elizabeth anyway, was also, in the eyes of all who held Henry VIII's divorce invalid, already rightful Queen of England. The danger was not remote and academic, but urgent and terrifying. In the Peace of Câteau Cambrésis, signed between France and Spain in 1559, there was a secret clause arranging for a joint crusade to restore England to obedience to Rome.

The next thirty years thus constituted the first of the three great crises of modern English history, when national existence in any acceptable form depended absolutely on diplomatic skill and military courage. The Elizabethan flowering of English civilization grew on a knife edge of incessant risk, and derived from that fact much of its colour and character; and the tremendous personal prestige of the Queen, which held the nation together in the last fifteen years of the reign, was built up in these first thirty, when hers was the decisive intelligence threading a tortuous way, with hesitations which maddened her ministers, towards the final triumphant defeat of the Spanish Armada in 1588.

The Franco-Scottish threat embodied in Mary Stuart was the immediate danger. The possible assets were Philip of Spain's desire to keep open his Channel communications with the Netherlands, still closely linked to England commercially; his intense dislike of the idea of Mary, three-quarters French by breeding and wholly by education, sitting on the thrones of England and Scotland; and his conviction that Elizabeth, with whom he had got on well when he was in England, would in the end overcome her maidenly hesitations and marry him, so bringing England back to Rome without French interference or the expense of war. Playing brilliantly on all these, Elizabeth tided over the first years, until three events put into her hand the cards for a much more decisive game: the French slowly collapsed into religious civil war; the Protestant Netherlands rose against

Spain and Catholicism; and factious Scottish nobles, in the name of Protestantism, drove Mary to take refuge in England. So long as judicious help in money, munitions, and occasionally men, kept the Protestants fighting in France and Holland and precariously on top in Scotland, Drake, Hawkins, Grenville and Raleigh could be loosed to prey on Spanish colonies and trade without much fear of reprisals. Philip still hesitated to intervene on behalf of Mary, and his sea communications with the Netherlands were more vital to him than ever.

It took Philip fifteen years to accept the challenge of the undeclared war fought by the English seamen and by English volunteers in the Netherlands. Even Elizabeth's knighting of Drake in 1578, when he returned from rounding the world with £800,000 of Spanish treasure in the hold of the *Golden Hind*, only provoked Philip to a slightly less half-hearted support of the Catholic plots to kill her and put Mary on the throne. It was this which made it worth while to keep Mary alive for nineteen years in spite of the rising of the northern Earls in 1569, and the Ridolfi, Throckmorton, and Babington conspiracies all centred on her, until she, in despair, signed in 1586 a will making Philip her heir, and so untied his hands. From that moment events moved fast. Mary, having become merely a menace, was executed at Fotheringay Castle in February 1587, and that summer Drake sailed into Cadiz harbour to destroy thirty-seven of the ships which Philip was at last fitting out for invasion—the exploit he himself described as 'singeing the King of Spain's beard'.

Drake, probably rightly, would have played the same game in 1588, but for once Elizabeth lost her nerve and kept him on the defensive at Plymouth until the 19th of July, when the news that the Armada was off The Lizard interrupted his celebrated game of bowls. The response of England to the news, carried by a chain of beacon fires to every corner of the land, was a complete justification of the cautious playing for time of the past thirty years. A truculent patriotism united the whole nation behind the Elizabethan Settlement in all its aspects with an enthusiasm inconceivable in 1558, though it was probably as well that the Queen never had to lead into action the somewhat amateur force of 70,000 men which she reviewed at Tilbury against the 50,000 crack troops Medina Sidonia and Parma planned to land. With ships more heavily armed, faster, and infinitely easier to handle than the Spaniards', the seamen did the job by themselves, herding the Armada up the Channel in a week of continuous fighting, 'plucking its feathers', as the Admiral, Howard of Effingham, put it, dislodging it from Calais with fire ships on July 28th, and finally forcing it out into the North Sea. Southerly gales and Medina Sidonia's decision to get home by rounding Scotland and Ireland completed the work, and only fifty-three ships out of the original one hundred and thirty got back to Spain. 'God blew', ran the Latin inscription round the medal Elizabeth struck for the occasion, 'and they were scattered.' But it had not been all luck. The Spaniards had been fairly outfought in every phase of the battle.

After that, inevitably, the reign closed on a note of anti-climax. With better ships and tactics and a well-planned convoy system, the Spaniards could prevent the English plundering expeditions from capturing enough to pay dividends, and by subsidizing Irish rebels Philip in the end forced Elizabeth to spend a million pounds on a full-scale conquest of Ireland. Moreover, she could no longer find servants of the old calibre. The hunch-backed Sir Robert Cecil carried on his father's administration competently enough. But the last great favourite of the reign, Essex, having disgraced himself in Ireland, tried to recover power by armed rebellion and was beheaded in 1601. Though solid gains were being made, with the foundation of the East India Company and Raleigh's first colonial experiments in Virginia, the relaxation everywhere of the sense of emergency brought Tudor monarchy face to face with a problem of its own creation which had been blanketed by

the almost continuous crisis since 1526: the rising power of
the Parliamentary class, coupled with the growth of a strong
Protestant opposition to the conservative, Catholic-minded
religious settlement of 1559. At the same time the government found itself under the steady pressure of a long-
deferred financial crisis. The struggle for power between
the Crown and the House of Commons, which is generally
thought of as essentially a feature of the Stuart government
of the next century, was in fact rooted in these two problems and began seriously the moment it was clear that the
main danger from Spain was over. Puritans no longer felt
that the 1559 settlement alone stood between them and the
fires of the Inquisition, and saw no further necessity for the
large concessions which had been made to a potentially
treacherous Catholic minority.

So they began to question the Queen's right to impose
ceremonies and rubrics, harked back to the severe Protestantism of 1552 on the issues of the Communion service,
vestments, and the altar, and clamoured for a more rigid
observance of the Sabbath. Even many of the clergy and
some of the bishops, including for a time Archbishop
Grindal, opposed the official policy; and, since Convocation
and the ecclesiastical courts were a government-controlled
machine, inevitably brought their grievances to Parliament.
As early as 1571 a Mr. Strickland was in trouble for tabling
a Bill to amend the Prayer Book. There was bickering in
1572 and 1581 and another row over the Prayer Book in
1587, which landed four members of the Commons in the
Tower for defying the Queen's prohibition to debate
ecclesiastical affairs. By 1597 Elizabeth had to give way and
allow debate, and when James VI of Scotland crossed the
border in 1603 to take up his mother, Mary's, English inheritance, a Puritan petition for reform with 1,000 signatures confronted him at once as the culmination of years of
agitation.

Similarly in finance James I faced a difficulty which had
been accumulating for half a century. Like all the Tudors,

Elizabeth hated the unpopularity of direct taxation through Parliament. But in a world of rising prices the Crown, with the largest fixed income in the land, was the greatest sufferer, and the permanent royal income from rents, feudal dues, and the customs duties known as Tunnage and Poundage, was increasingly inadequate. Some of the deficit Elizabeth met by selling Crown lands, and so mortgaging the future; some by expedients such as the sale of Monopolies, which produced the first major struggle in 1601. Monopolies served a dual purpose, as patents to protect inventors and the founders of new industries, and, as Elizabeth herself said, as rewards for 'ancient servants who had deserved well', in the absence of any proper salary and pension scales. But in the scramble for money to pay for the Irish wars the system was shockingly abused. When the list of existing patents was read over in the Commons in 1601, Mr. Hakewill of Lincoln's Inn was heard demanding: 'Is not bread there?' And he went on to say stoutly: 'If order be not taken on these, bread will be there before the next Parliament.'

Out of these two main grievances—religion and finance—grew the so-called constitutional question: who in such a dispute had the last, sovereign word, Crown or Parliament? Always within the framework of the law, the Tudors had, in fact, done much as they pleased. The large emergency power to make and enforce law, necessary anyway to the government in an age of rare and short parliamentary sessions, needed no justification in a century of continuous and genuine emergency. But, as the crisis passed, the House of Commons, nursed to a great sense of its own importance by successive monarchs in need of its support, began to assert claims to a share of authority for which cloudy precedents could be found from the days when Lancastrian kings sought to bolster up a weak title by parliamentary approval. The religious dispute had produced from Mr. Peter Wentworth—always a difficult man—a string of propositions in 1587 tending to show that no authority could 'add to, or diminish from the laws of the realm, but

only this Council of Parliament'. Mr. Francis Moore put the
matter even more clearly and testily in the hot-tempered
Monopoly debate of 1601. 'To what purpose is it,' he asked,
'to do anything by Act of Parliament, when the Queen will
undo the same by her prerogative?'

In this atmosphere of frayed tempers the accession of
James I in 1603 was a disaster. Though he hated the Presbyterianism in which he had grown up, he had a hard,
pragmatical, Scots mind, logical and incapable of compromise. Elizabeth had ably defended, without ever defining,
her prerogative. James asserted it as Divine Right which it
was treason to question. Ignorant of the delicate balances on
which English politics had rested for nearly a century, he
lectured the Commons on the limitation of their rights by
his good pleasure, so provoking the extreme counter-
statement of their claims which Elizabeth had successfully
avoided. She had surrendered over Monopolies in a speech
which brilliantly turned grievance into gratitude and made
capital out of defeat. Without her accumulated prestige or
the dignity and charm to make surrender graceful, James
was yet not strong enough to bluster successfully. His
shambling walk and ungainly seat on a horse, his quilted
coats to guard against assassins, and his habit of tasteless
ostentation in dress and entertainment all helped to make
him a slightly ridiculous public figure. His virtues—easy,
homely manners, a sense of humour, and, in small matters, a
devastating common sense—were such as could only be
appreciated in private by the greedy courtiers and the circle
of attractive, rowdy young men with whom he loved to
surround himself. In consequence the atmosphere of politics
continuously deteriorated throughout his reign, and a
disastrous rift gradually opened up between Court and
Country which was to dominate English history for a
century.

In spite of the efforts of Robert Cecil, now Earl of Salisbury, to maintain Elizabethan standards of government, by
1610 both religious and financial differences had hardened

into clear-cut disputes. The Hampton Court Conference, called to discuss Puritan grievances in 1604, though it put in hand the Authorized Version of the Bible which remains the finest achievement of English prose, did nothing else but affirm the old settlement without any concession to an opposition which was rapidly becoming a majority of the House of Commons and a respectable minority in the Church itself. Standing firmly on his dictum of 'No Bishop, no King', and persisting in tolerating Catholics even after their attempt, through Guy Fawkes, to blow sky high King, Lords, and Commons in 1605, James lost the sympathy of the very classes to whom he had to apply for unprecedentedly large taxes in the House of Commons. Basically these demands were justified by the continuing problem of meeting rising costs out of a fixed income, intensified by the legacy of a deficit of £400,000 from Elizabeth. But the irresponsible extravagance of the Court and a lax administration which allowed a growing corruption, especially in the Treasury and Admiralty, made this case difficult to present convincingly to Parliament. The expedients, some old and some new, to which the government resorted to raise the non-parliamentary revenue made matters worse. The decision of the judges in Bate's case in 1606, that the Crown had an absolute power to impose extra customs duties, faced men with the possibility that the Crown might really be able to free itself from the control of law and govern arbitrarily, by Divine Right. It was fear of this which inspired the claim that sovereignty lay in 'the King in Parliament' and prepared the House of Commons to fight to the last for its own right to an unrestricted control over taxation.

From 1610 to 1621, with one short, quarrelsome interlude, James tried to govern without Parliament; successfully, so long as he remained at peace, though always on the edge of bankruptcy, and at the price of a growing clamour against monopolies, impositions of extra duties, forced loans, and the indiscriminate sale of peerages and baronetcies and trading privileges to anybody who would pay. The outbreak of the Thirty Years' War in Europe put an end to the experiment. For one of its first consequences was that the Elector Palatine was driven out of his dominions; and, since he had married Princess Elizabeth, the only widely popular member of the royal family, King and Commons were for once agreed on diplomatic and, if necessary, military action to help him. No financial trickery would pay for that, and a Parliament became inevitable.

Moreover, enthusiastic sympathy for the Electress would not carry the Commons so far as to grant money which they were reasonably sure would be misspent; for they trusted neither James nor his ministers. The Elizabethan tradition of government died with Salisbury and policy was thereafter handled more and more through the young men of Court and Bedchamber who had before been only the companions of the King's leisure. The first all-powerful favourite, Robert Carr, Earl of Somerset, crashed in 1615, when his wife confessed to having poisoned Sir Thomas Overbury in order to make sure of a trumped-up divorce from her first husband. The scandals revealed by the enquiry into this divorce and murder did much to sicken sober men of all classes with court and government. The impression of crime and corruption in high places was strengthened by a series of financial scandals, involving the disgrace of a Lord Treasurer and his wife for bribery and embezzlement and of the Lord High Admiral, Nottingham, whose ageing incompetence had allowed the Admiralty and dockyard administration to become riddled with corrupt practices. It was perhaps bad luck that the greatest genius of the age, Francis Bacon, should have been incidentally involved and convicted of taking bribes while Lord Chancellor, since it was proved that the bribes had not influenced his decisions. But it all helped to increase the resentment and hostility with which the Commons watched a diplomatic and military crisis being handled by the King's new favourite, George Villiers.

Villiers had more ability than might have been expected

in a penniless younger son from Leicestershire, whose looks
and charm alone had carried him to the dukedom of
Buckingham and supreme power, but not enough to enable
him to play at international politics when the pace was
being set by the French Cardinal Richelieu. Even the most
provincial of country squires could see the futility of a
'statecraft' which sent Buckingham and Prince Charles, the
heir to the throne, to Madrid, thinly disguised as John and
Tom Smith, to woo a Spanish princess in the hope that
Spain, in gratitude for the marriage, would persuade her
allies to disgorge the Palatinate. James died in 1625, popular
for the first time in his reign because he had at last declared
war on Spain. But Charles's hero-worship of Buckingham
was to be even more disastrous than James's paternal infatua-
tion, and there was no change in the conduct of affairs. The
only army we put into the field, 'raw and poor rascals' conscripted by counties, disintegrated amidst flies and disease at
Flushing. The naval expedition against Cadiz in 1625, ill
found and ill led, in ships some of which had not been re-
fitted since they fought against the Armada, was a spectacular failure. Charles started by marrying Henrietta Maria
of France, but changed sides within two years. Buckingham
himself led another untrained, badly victualled fleet and army
to help the rebellious French Protestants of La Rochelle and
failed miserably; and only his assassination at Portsmouth
on the eve of embarkation prevented him from repeating
this costly disaster in 1628.

Against this background the tide of Parliamentary discontent steadily rose. In 1622 the Commons, forbidden to
meddle in foreign affairs, had asserted their 'birthright' of
free debate so sharply that James, before dissolving them,
himself tore from their journals the page recording their
protest. There were Lords as well as Commons who found
themselves in prison for carrying opposition too far, while
Charles I's harassed government conscripted troops, sub-
jected them to martial law, and billeted them without payment on private householders. A Chief Justice was dis-

missed for refusing to countenance a Forced Loan, and five knights were gaoled, without trial or bail, for refusing to pay it. But opposition could not be silenced. 'Our honour is lost,' Sir John Eliot thundered in the Commons when the remnants of the Cadiz expedition returned, 'our ships are sunk, our men are perished . . . not by the sword, but by those we trust'. Seeking a hold on policy, they refused to vote Tunnage and Poundage for more than a year at a time, and three times impeached Buckingham for treason and corruption. To save his friend Charles dissolved three Parliaments, and he continued to levy his customs duties un-voted, by virtue of his 'prerogative royal'. But in the end financial stringency forced him to accept the Petition of Right which embodied all Parliament's claims and griev-ances in statutory form, asserting their absolute control of taxation, abolishing martial law and billeting, and depriving the king of the right to imprison his subjects without trial.

So the Tudor system of government by King in Parlia-ment broke down. Its basic assumption had been that the king could be trusted to govern competently and legally, and with due regard for properly expressed public opinion. His prerogative to act for the best in emergency without consulting anybody was unquestioned, and Parliament's claims were new and unprecedented, provoked not by Stuart tyranny, but by Stuart incompetence. Such tyranny as there was was defensive and could find ample Tudor precedent. But precedent and legal theories were alike valueless in an unprecedented situation which demanded a fresh definition of sovereignty, one way or the other. The Petition of Right showed one general direction which re-form might take. By dissolving Parliament in 1629 and ruling without it for eleven years, accepting his Judges' ruling that his emergency prerogative allowed him to ig-nore the Petition, Charles set himself to explore the oppo-site alternative.

Chapter Nine

CIVIL WAR, RESTORATION, AND REVOLUTION

★

Buckingham alone had been able to penetrate the stiff reserve—the almost intolerable sense of Kingship—with which Charles I hedged about his personal shyness. Henceforth he trusted nobody save the Queen, charming, but feather-headed and quite without understanding of the English situation. He never really gave his confidence to his chief ministers, Thomas Wentworth, later Earl of Strafford, who tried to make the King's government in reality what its enemies have called it, an 'Eleven Years' Tyranny', or Laud, Archbishop of Canterbury, who fought to stem the Puritan revolt by discipline and a harsh enforcement of uniformity. The government muddled along, just avoiding bankruptcy by a series of inadequate expedients: a new form of Monopolies, granted to corporations instead of to individuals, and much more damaging to trade; new revivals of out-of-date feudal dues; the reintroduction of Ship Money, traditionally levied on maritime counties in wartime, but now used in peace, and after 1635 extended throughout the country. It was a period of great activity by the Privy Council—the last serious attempt by the old monarchy to save the labouring classes and the poor from flagrant exploitation at the hands of gentry and employers by enforcing poor laws and price and wage controls. But only in the north and in Ireland, where Strafford was personally in charge, was there any real control over local administration.

147

Meanwhile the country prospered. Men with a little money to invest were finding land increasingly hard to buy, and so began that export of surplus population and capital which was in time to build up a world empire. Between 1630 and 1643 more than £600,000 was spent in settling some 60,000 people in different parts of America, and only about a third of these were the New England refugees from Laud's religious persecution. The political classes grumbled at government mismanagement and evaded taxes, but Hampden's famous stand against the levy of Ship Money in Buckinghamshire was an almost isolated protest. Only another Parliament could focus financial and religious grievance, and this, by scrupulously refraining from foreign entanglements, Charles just managed to avoid for eleven years. But then Laud's rash attempt to force an English Prayer Book on the Scottish Kirk produced a fierce and well-trained Scots army on the Border which Charles, with his conscript levies, was quite unable to meet in battle. Inevitably the so-called 'Bishops' War' left him bankrupt and so face to face, in the Long Parliament, with all the accumulated grievances of half a century; and within two years the attempt to remedy them was to bring England to civil war.

It is a mistake to see the Civil War as a straight fight between two single theories. It was not just a struggle between those who wanted a strong autocracy and those who were groping their way towards constitutional government, nor simply an attempt by the new governing class to break through the last controls by which Tudors and Stuarts had tried to check the exploitation of their wealth and power. It was not merely a religious struggle, though it seemed so to many who fought in it—the struggle, long delayed by the skilful Elizabethan compromise, between freedom and authority in the Church. It was all these things tangled together, with the intentions of both sides inextricably confused, and with both sides claiming with some justice to stand for 'the liberties of the people'. The motives of individuals who fought were often very simple, but they combined to produce patterns of baffling complexity on both sides.

With the King would be found the men, few but influential, who saw salvation in strong, centralized government, using law as a set of regulations to enforce the King's will. This was what Bacon had meant when he called judges 'Lions under the throne' and was Strafford's policy of 'Thorough', which drove him, quite logically, to attack Buckingham and then himself earn in the King's service the nickname of 'Black Tom Tyrant'. Many more of the Cavaliers were simply aware of their Church in danger and, though most disliked Laud's cantankerous severity, rallied to save bishops and Prayer Book. Edward Hyde, first Earl of Clarendon, represented yet another type: the conservatives who looked back to a golden age in Church and State, when Queen and Commons had happily collaborated, and who would oppose whichever side seemed most to threaten the old, undefined balance of King in Parliament. Thus Hyde led the opposition against unparliamentary taxation, but swung over finally to the King when extremists attacked the very basis of the royal prerogative. And then, of course, there were the merely self-interested: Catholics who sheltered under royal tolerance; racketeers whose monopolies and perquisites would be destroyed by Parliamentary reforms, and careerists whose fortunes were made at court. Finally, and perhaps in a majority, there were the simpler souls who scarcely understood the issues involved at all, for whom the instruction carved on the walls of so many manor houses to 'Fear God and Honour the King' was beyond the reach of political theory.

The men on the other side were equally divided on the nature of the tyranny which they all denounced. Disinterested men like Pym and Hampden, sharing Hyde's views on the abuse of the prerogative, unlike him sought a remedy which by implication was almost republican. To the Puritans 'tyranny' was Laud and the Court of High Commission which had sawn off John Bastwick's ears, fined him

£5,000, and imprisoned him for life for calling the Bishops anti-Christ. To Sir John Savile and his Yorkshire friends it meant Strafford's high-handed enforcement of the Eliza-bethan apprentice regulations in their clothing industry. There was not even a clear-cut demand for religious free-dom, for most of the opposition members in the Commons would have substituted for Laud's Church the even harsher discipline of the Scottish Kirk, disregarding the cry of Milton and his fellow Puritans that 'new Presbyter is but old Priest writ large'.

Moreover, up to the brink of hostilities the leaders on both sides were a single party united in Parliament to oppose the King. United they impeached Strafford and, when they could not prove treason, carried a Bill of Attainder against him and loosed a city mob to howl for two days and nights round Whitehall until Charles, without military protection and terrified for his wife and children, sacrificed the only efficient minister he had. United they abolished Monopolies, Impositions, Ship Money and the rest, and forced Charles to agree that he had no right to Tunnage and Poundage unless they had voted it. They destroyed the prerogative courts, Star Chamber and the provincial Councils and Laud's Court of High Commission—all the machinery, in fact, by which a policy of 'Thorough' might interfere with the Common Law. Against all this Charles, penniless and unsupported, save for a handful of terrified courtiers and officials, could do nothing. It was this fundamental unity which made the English Civil War unique in history, in that it was fought with as little barbarity and hatred as a war could well be. For when the division into parties came, it was between men of the same stamp, class, and even family, who found that they had reached a point where they could no longer com-promise over religious or political principle.

Two things created a party to fight for the King. The opposition extremists demanded that a Presbyterian form of Church government should displace the Bishops; and, terrified that the Irish rebellion of the summer of 1641 would give the King an excuse for raising an army which might then be used against themselves, they tried to deprive him of the most ancient and unquestionable of his prerogatives, the command of the militia. When these and other even more revolutionary projects were embodied in the Grand Remonstrance the opposition majority melted away. After impassioned debate far into the night the Remonstrance was indeed carried, but only by eleven votes, and any last chance of a compromise disappeared when Charles tried to arrest his five leading enemies on the very floor of the House of Commons.

When the King set up his standard at Nottingham in August of 1642 he could probably have won the war. He could appeal to more primitive loyalties and he had a simple objective, the capture of London. His nephew, Prince Rupert, reared among the battlefields of the Thirty Years' War, trained his hard-riding squires and grooms into a cavalry force which could have decided the issue in the first two years, had he ever been able to control it after a successful charge. It was this impetuosity which robbed him of decisive victory in the first battle at Edgehill, and it was to be a main cause of the last two great Royalist defeats at Marston Moor and Naseby. The Royalists, in fact, failed to learn from their mistakes in time to win a quick victory; and Parliament had all the assets which must prevail in a long war. Controlling London and the south and east of England, they drew on a larger and more easily available man-power. The fleet, unpaid in spite of Ship Money, joined them, and with it the great, strongly Protestant ports of Hull, Plymouth, and Bristol, deep in the heart of the Royalist recruiting grounds, so hampering any effective movement against London. Thus Parliament also had the large, regular customs revenue which, backed by the City's credit, made them financially inexhaustible, whereas Charles depended precariously on cavalier rents and the melted-down plate of country houses and colleges. Furthermore, by promising a Presbyterian Church Settlement in England, they brought the well-trained Scottish army in on their side; and when Oliver Cromwell, the one man of military genius thrown up by the war, produced for them the army of the Eastern Association, the issue was really settled. For Cromwell's 'Ironsides', a cavalry force drawn from his plain, russet-coated, Bible-reading, Puritan yeomen neighbours in the Eastern Counties, could not only outfight Rupert's squires, but keep formation and discipline after a successful charge. At Marston Moor in 1644 a combination of Scots and the Eastern Association won the whole of the north from the King, and in the following year, having reorganized the whole of their forces in the New Model Army under Fairfax and Cromwell, the Parliamentarians settled the matter finally at Naseby. A gallant attempt by the Marquis of Montrose failed, after four brilliant victories, to turn the tide in Scotland; Oxford, the King's Headquarters since 1642, surrendered; and Charles gave himself up to the Scots.

But the situation at the end of the war was more bewildering than ever to honest men. The survivors of the Long Parliament were anxious to preserve monarchy, but uncertain how to bind the King any faster than they already had by the statutes of 1641. The Scots would side with anyone who would pay their expenses and guarantee to establish Presbyterianism in England. Most important of all, the New Model Army, its pay some forty weeks in arrears, was seething with strange new sects and doctrines, but united in demanding freedom of worship from Bishop or Presbyter. The King tried to play these off: 'to draw', as he put it, 'the Presbyterians or the Independents to side with me for extirpating one another, that I shall really be a King again'. But Parliament, King, and Scottish Presbytery were all to go down because they failed to realize that political power had passed to an army which could think and act for itself and which Parliament could not afford to pay off. Free religious debate in the comradeship of military service had produced for the first time in England a large body of opinion which approached political questions with abstract logic, seeking authority from absolute principles, whether political or religious, instead of from custom and precedent in the traditional English way. Among the junior

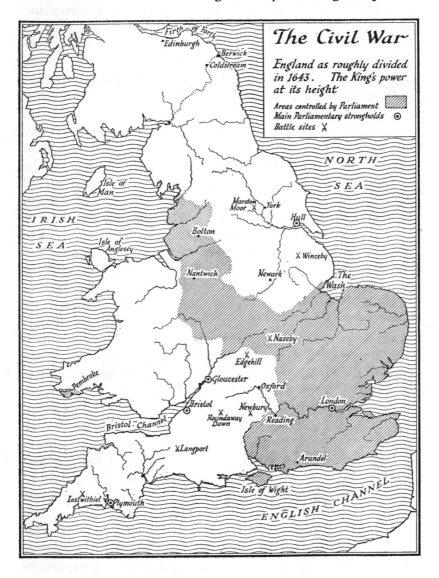

The Civil War

England as roughly divided in 1643. The King's power at its height

Areas controlled by Parliament
Main Parliamentary strongholds ⊙
Battle sites ✗

officers and the rank and file, Levellers were putting forward the wholly novel proposition that 'the poorest he that is in England hath a right to live as well as the greatest he'. Even the more senior and conservative were demanding a rational redistribution of Parliamentary seats, biennial elections, and a wide franchise based on a property qualification.

Thus from 1646 to 1649 it was decisive military action which cut, strand by strand, through the tangled web of political intrigue. Charles's attempt to play off Parliament against the Scots was abruptly ended when Cornet Joyce, in June 1647, seized him as the Army's prisoner. His next attempt, to play off the Scots against the Army, which brought a Scottish force down through Carlisle, and a second brief flare up of civil war, was ended by Cromwell's easy victory at Preston in August 1648. And when Cromwell returned to find Parliament and King again negotiating, Colonel Pride with a file of musketeers purged from the remnant of the House of Commons all who would oppose the Army's final decision to bring 'that man of blood, Charles Stuart', to trial for 'traitorously' making war on the People. In the teeth of an almost solid public opinion, powerless in face of the Army's pikes and muskets, Charles, steadfastly refusing to admit the competence of any Court to try him, was condemned to death and on 30th January, 1649, beheaded under the windows of Whitehall. The groan which went up from the great crowd when his head fell represented the country's real feelings. For only a few hundred Englishmen were genuinely convinced of Cromwell's 'cruel necessity', though he himself never wavered, then or later.

Even his enemies have had to admit that Oliver Cromwell was one of the greatest Englishmen that have ever lived. Intensely religious and yet prepared to tolerate all shades of Christian belief save Roman Catholicism, a visionary whose dreams were rooted in the hard sense needed by a lifetime of farming and land-drainage in the fens, he had the trick of leadership and a passionate desire to give England a govern-

154

ment which was both representative and 'Godly'. In fact he gave her perhaps the most efficient government she has ever had. For, though at the outset the 'Rump' of survivors of the Long Parliament nominally ruled, from 1649 to 1658 it was Cromwell who governed. It was he who suppressed the mutiny of the Army's Levellers in 1649 and then, with a brutal efficiency which has never been forgotten or forgiven, ended the last of the Civil War in Ireland. His victories at Dunbar and Worcester defeated Charles II's hope of re-covering his kingdoms by accepting Presbyterianism and sent the young man abroad to a demoralizing nine years of exile. He built up the Ship Money fleet into a powerful Navy which under Blake, the first of the long line of great English admirals, temporarily smashed the sea-power of the Dutch and captured Jamaica from the Spaniards, while the New Model Army showed its red coats in Flanders, and at the capture of Dunkirk proved itself at least the equal of the Continental professionals.

But none of this could make his rule fundamentally acceptable to the mass of Englishmen, whose feelings had been shown clearly enough by the crowds which lined the roads to be touched for the King's Evil when Charles I came south in 1647, and by the bells which rang all over the country for his last birthday. This did not imply approval of Charles I's methods. But it did mean that Englishmen clung obstinately to habits of thought rooted in the past and valued historic continuity more highly than logic in their political institutions. One by one, Cromwell's experimental constitutions broke down and were rejected: the Barebones Parliament of 1653, a distinguished body nominated by the Officers' Council; and the two Protectorate Parliaments elected under the Instrument of Government in 1654 and 1656. In the end it had to be openly admitted that the basis of the whole Protectorate was military force, and eleven military districts, each governed by a Major-General, were superimposed on the old local government of England. A régime of Godliness and toleration which could only be maintained by armed forces, press censorship, and inordinately heavy taxes, had already become universally unpopular by Cromwell's death in 1658. Without his personal prestige, efficiency, and command of the Army's loyalty, it then collapsed swiftly in a chaos in which more and more voices were raised to demand the return of King and Parliament and the good old days.

In the end, thanks to General Monck the commander in Scotland, who hated 'the intolerable slavery of sword government', it was the Army itself which put an end to its own tyranny. When Monck declared for a free Parliament and marched south all opposition melted before him, and the Parliament which was then duly elected forthwith arranged for the return of the King. On the 28th of May 1660, his thirtieth birthday, Charles II rode into London past the ranks of the Army which had killed his father, amid scenes of rejoicing never surpassed in English history.

So, in the eleventh year of his reign, cheerful, cynical and easy-going, sadly debauched by the years of impoverished idleness abroad, but immensely able when a crisis forced him to bestir himself, Charles II sought to pick up the threads dropped in 1642. With him came Clarendon, old now and embittered by years of preaching moderation to hotheads, opinionated and unattractively self-righteous, but still vowed to the causes which he had defended in the Long Parliament just as firmly as to the Royalism for which he had suffered privation and exile. It was mainly thanks to him that the Restoration was a careful, conservative compromise which insisted that neither side had won the Civil War. As far as possible the last eighteen years were wiped out of English history. The Act of Indemnity and Oblivion, a wise amnesty for all save the Regicides who had actually signed Charles I's death warrant, checked at once the temptation to a Royalist revenge; and, though Cavaliers raged that Restoration meant 'Indemnity for the King's enemies and oblivion for the King's friends', it was essential that the inevitable grievances and hardships should be shared by both sides. The same impartiality was shown over the vexed question of cavalier estates and Church and Crown lands confiscated by Parliament, so that, in general, extremist Parliamentary veterans felt that they had been robbed of the fruits of their victory; Royalists that they were being denied the triumphs of Restoration.

In the same spirit the financial settlement aimed, in the light of past mistakes and quarrels, at removing as many causes of future friction as possible. The King was deprived of all his old permanent, non-parliamentary revenue, but voted an income calculated to bring him in £1,200,000, which would cover his normal peacetime needs, but force him to apply to Parliament for a Subsidy in any emergency. The army was paid off and peacefully disbanded and the first election produced a Parliament so enthusiastically loyal that Charles kept it for eighteen years, though he was soon quarrelling with it as heartily as ever his father and grandfather had with theirs.

Only over religion did this spirit of compromise break down. In the country at large the Restoration had been on the whole just what Clarendon had hoped for—a peaceful resumption of the old ways—and in many parish churches there had been the same quiet, unostentatious change-over. 'May 12th, 1660,' one parish register reads, 'on which day I, Stephen Hogg, began again to use the Book of Common Prayer.' But religious passion still ran too high to allow Charles and Clarendon to put through the policy of toleration and 'Comprehension' by which they hoped to widen the basis of the Anglican Church and readmit all but extreme sectaries. Between 1661 and 1665, in the teeth of King and minister, Parliament passed a series of Acts known, very unfairly, as the Clarendon Code, which tightened up the Act of Uniformity and drove 2,000 Puritan clergy from their livings to become the founders of Nonconformity. Religious meetings other than Anglican were banned, and Nonconformist ministers and teachers were forbidden to come within five miles of any corporate town,

Apart from this persecuting intolerance in religion, 1660 established a perfectly workable system of government, and one which did in fact work so long as there sat on the throne a clever, if lazy, politician, who was 'determined never to go on his travels again'. Yet right from the start all the old grievances and squabbles reappeared in new forms. Thanks to a trade slump Charles never before 1670 got from the customs duties anything like the sum Parliament believed itself to have voted him. This was never really understood, and the Commons attributed to extravagance and peculation deficits which were, partly at any rate, unavoidable. The Plague of 1665, which killed 68,000 people in London alone, brought trade to a standstill; and the Great Fire a year later completed the ruin. The Fire did nothing to stop the recurrence of Plague in London, for it did not touch the densely populated slum areas outside the City walls, and it was the gradual disappearance of the Plague-bearing black rat which made 1665 the last great outbreak of the epidemic. But the loss in four days of nearly ten million pounds' worth of business property destroyed the very sources of taxation, besides making men mutter of God's curses on a licentious court and a city which had reopened the theatres and coffee-houses closed by Oliver. Though, by good fortune, the genius of Sir Christopher Wren was available to replace St. Paul's and the eighty-odd churches which had perished, there was no immediate remedy for the bankruptcy of the government. The war with the Dutch had been resumed in 1664, and Parliament had enthusiastically voted for it an extra four millions. But in two years six millions had been spent on the war alone. Penniless, and with peace already half negotiated, the government took the desperate step of laying up the battle fleet in the summer of 1667 and so provoked a final disaster. The Dutch broke into the Thames estuary and up the Medway, destroyed Sheerness and half the battleships at Chatham, and towed away the fleet flagship, the *Royal Charles*, as a prize.

This, the worst humiliation of British naval history,

brought Clarendon down, and with him the attempt to achieve any sincere collaboration of King and Parliament. The old situation of Court versus Country, with a solid majority of the Commons clamouring against extravagance and corruption, reappeared for fourteen chaotic years which all but ended in a fresh civil war. The situation abroad was one fundamental cause. For the Dutch, and indeed all Protestants, were beginning to see in the Catholic, over-mighty France of Louis XIV a greater threat to civil and religious liberty than even Spain had been. With a fair share of Dutch trade and empire already secure—New Amsterdam had been captured in 1664 and renamed New York—merchants and squires were more and more conscious of their duty to fellow Protestants, anti-Catholic and anti-French. They saw a Court permeated with Catholic and French influences: a Catholic Queen, a Catholic heir to the throne in Charles's brother, James, Duke of York, and his favourite sister, Henrietta, married to the Duc d'Orleans and second lady of France. They suspected an extravagance and debauchery far exceeding the reality, and their committees of investigation eventually proved that at least one and a half millions had been embezzled by government officials in the first nine years of the reign. It is not surprising that they were unreasonable and unco-operative.

Charles on his side was equally sick of the effort to work with a Parliament which, it seemed to him, involved him in war and then refused to pay for it. Though there were far too many of them, his mistresses and illegitimate children were no great charge on the Exchequer, while he had paid in, over and above what Parliament had voted, his wife's dowry and the purchase price of Dunkirk, which he had sold to the French, in all well over a million. He admired and envied the ordered despotism of Louis XIV, resented Parliament's attempts to disband the few thousand guards he maintained for protection against the City mob, and always leant personally towards Catholicism. So he signed with France the Secret Treaties of Dover, promising to help

France against the Dutch and, forcibly if necessary, reconvert England to Rome, in return for French subsidies which would make him partially independent of Parliament, and promises of French military help if needed.

Such arrangements could not be kept really secret. Charles's only tentative attempt to implement his promises, the Declaration of Indulgence of 1672, giving Nonconformists freedom to worship in public and Catholics in private, provoked such a storm that he not only had to withdraw it, but accept a Test Act which put both Catholics and Nonconformists out of public life altogether. Furthermore, he gave an almost fatal opening to the extremist opposition group led by Lord Shaftesbury, a Presbyterian who had been in office and been hoodwinked at the time of the Secret Treaty. Inordinately ambitious and burning for revenge, Shaftesbury certainly planned to get himself and his friends into supreme power, possibly by substituting an aristocratic republic for the monarchy. As a step to this he set himself to get the Duke of York excluded from the succession and to substitute as heir the pliable Duke of Monmouth, a son of Charles II who was to be legitimatized. To this end he organized from among the rich peers, the city bankers, and Dissenters and old Cromwellian soldiers throughout the country, a powerful group which was in due course to grow into the Whig party. They had a central office at the Green Ribbon Club, an army of pamphleteers for propaganda, and a well-drilled City mob for demonstrations. By means of a trumped-up Popish Plot, of which a villainous informer named Titus Oates professed to give full details, they stampeded the country into believing in a widespread Catholic conspiracy to murder all good Protestants and seize power with French help. Memories of the Armada and Guy Fawkes and the all too true rumours of the arrangements by which Charles drew subsidies from Louis XIV, made the story credible to the nation, and in the resulting panic a number of innocent Catholics were judicially murdered while Shaftesbury all but pushed through his Exclusion scheme. Indeed men said openly that 'forty-two is come again', and Charles only saved his throne by giving his enemies so much rope that their excesses opened the eyes of all moderate men and swung back to the King's side a loyal body in which may be seen the first rudiments of the Tory party. By 1681 Charles was able to dissolve the last Parliament in which Shaftesbury had a majority and in a declaration read from every pulpit of a loyal Church to expose the Plot for what it was. Shaftesbury fled abroad to die, and a wild Whig plot, the Rye House Plot to kidnap Charles and James, only served to raise the flooding tide of royalist enthusiasm. It was in this atmosphere of calm after the storm, with the country at peace and every year more prosperous, that Charles II, still penurious, but saved from bankruptcy by regular sums from France, died, leaving his brother to destroy, in three lunatic years, what he had so narrowly saved for him.

For a few months the Sabbath calm of the royalist reaction carried over into the new reign. Parliament voted generous supplies. Good churchmen closed their eyes to the spectacle of their King, with honest courage but little tact, publicly attending Mass; and Monmouth, landing in the south-west with grossly inadequate preparation in a last bid for the Crown, found the country solidly against him except for the half-armed rabble of west country dissenters who followed him to disaster at Sedgemoor. Deceived by all this, James thought that he could safely revert to the policy of Dover which had so nearly brought Charles down. He had always thought that a show of force and severer measures would have paid better dividends than his brother's patient manœuvres against Exclusion. He believed that the Church was powerless to oppose him because it preached a doctrine of 'Non-Resistance' to royal authority; and he reverted to Charles II's delusion of 1672 that Dissenters, if granted toleration, would in gratitude support toleration for Catholics.

So he kept under arms the troops gathered for Sedgemoor:

a standing army which camped each summer on Hounslow Heath, largely composed of, and very soon largely officered by, Irish Catholics, which seemed to Londoners who strolled out to watch the Masses in the tents on Sunday a permanent threat to life and liberty. In the bad old Stuart way he stretched the Crown's power to dispense individuals from particular statutes in cases of accidental hardship into a general right to dispense whom he pleased from the Test Act and the penal laws against Catholics. He tampered with the independence of the Judges to get this confirmed and then, logically but fatally, extended it still further into a claim to suspend laws altogether by royal prerogative. He began to fill Oxford colleges with Catholic fellows and even appointed Catholics as Dean of Christ Church and Bishop of Oxford. He had Catholics, and even a Jesuit priest, on his Privy Council. And he sought to legalize all this by two Declarations of Indulgence, the second of which was to be read aloud from every pulpit in the kingdom. Seven bishops who protested against this attempt to make the Church collaborate in her own destruction were tried for seditious libel and James would not be warned even by the universal rejoicing which greeted their acquittal. Men had been reluctant to risk another civil war and for two years Tory and Cavalier loyalty had held. Men gritted their teeth to see James out, trusting for the future to the Protestant daughters of his earlier marriage, Mary, married to William of Orange and the Princess Anne. In June 1688, the birth of son to James's new queen who would be brought up as a Catholic ended even this hope, and that same month an invitation, signed by seven of the leading men in both parties, was sent to William of Orange, asking him to come over with a Dutch army to save the liberties of Church and State in England.

So the old monarchy perished in the Revolution of 1688, and England was fairly launched on paths of constitutional development widely different from those of Continental Europe. William was only too glad to add England to the

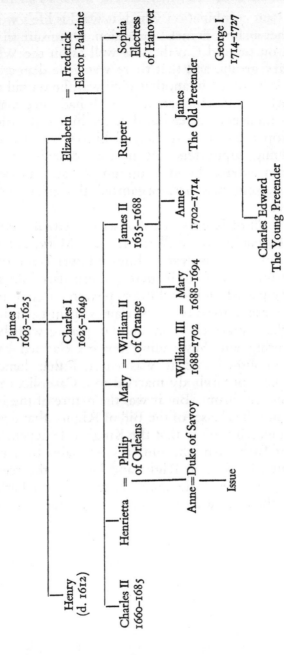

THE STUARTS AND THE HANOVERIAN SUCCESSION

James I
1603–1625

Charles I
1625–1649

Elizabeth = Frederick
Elector Palatine

Henry
(d. 1612)

Charles II
1660–1685

Mary = William II
of Orange

Henrietta = Philip
of Orleans

James II
1635–1688

Rupert

Sophia
Electress
of Hanover

George I
1714–1727

Anne=Duke of Savoy

William III = Mary
1688–1702   1688–1694

Anne
1702–1714

James
The Old Pretender

Issue

Charles Edward
The Young Pretender

Protestant combination which it was his life's work to hold together against French aggression. Once sure that he could count on the old Cavaliers as well as on the Whig parliamentary group, and that there was little danger of finding himself involved in another civil war, he set sail and landed in Torbay. The competence which had once made James a successful fleet commander deserted him at the end. He took no proper measures to defend himself until even his few remaining supporters left him in despair. In December William entered London unopposed and, to be rid of an embarrassing prisoner, organized the escape of James to France.

The Bill of Rights of 1689, which settled the basis of the new monarchy of William III and Mary, ruling as joint sovereigns, was as near as England ever came to a written constitution. Most of it merely summarized the restrictions already placed on the arbitrary powers of government during the previous sixty years: clauses against standing armies, unparliamentary taxation, and tampering with Judges. The Dispensing and Suspending powers claimed by James II were abolished and it was enacted that henceforth no Catholic, nor anybody married to a Catholic, might sit on the English throne. But it was the nature of the Revolution itself, not the clauses of the Bill of Rights, that destroyed the old monarchy. Now that the King's title depended itself on Act of Parliament the old, mystic claim to a prerogative inherited by Divine Right and beyond the reach of law, could never be made again. Henceforward Parliament, of which the King was only a part, was unquestioned sovereign in England.

Chapter Ten

POLITICAL STABILITY ACHIEVED

Conquest and Loss of Empire
Agrarian and Industrial Revolution

★

The reigns of William and Mary and Queen Anne, who died in 1714, form a transitional interlude: the change-over from Stuart to Georgian England. This was something much more profound than a mere change of dynasty, or even the surmounting of a great political and constitutional crisis. In Wren's work, in Georgian architecture, furniture, and landscape gardening, and in the diversion of much intellectual effort from theology to scientific enquiry, the late English renaissance was reaching a splendid climax; and at the same time commercial and colonial expansion were leading towards an agrarian and industrial revolution which between them were to transform the face of England and the whole fabric of English society. It was a new world in which the wealthy landed and commercial families who had been nursed to power and usefulness by the Tudors and who had fought the Stuarts for political predominance were to come into their inheritance. But, thanks to the Whig fiction that James's son had been illegitimate, smuggled into the Queen's apartment in a warming-pan, Tory England could still pretend that Mary and William were the rightful rulers of England and, while Queen Anne still touched for the King's Evil, could believe, in defiance of the Bill of Rights, that the old monarchy still lived.

It was three years before the Revolution was finally complete. There was a moment of danger in Scotland until Dundee, the only man who could rally the Highland clans, was killed in his own victorious charge at Killiecrankie; and more than momentary danger in Ireland, where James II, with 7,000 French troops, got control of the entire country save Enniskillen and Londonderry, where loyalist Protestants held out heroically. It was a year before William's victory at the Boyne saved the situation, and another year before the last resistance was stamped out and power handed over exclusively to the Anglo-Irish Protestant minority. But in 1692 the French Channel fleet was decisively defeated at La Hogue, so that there could be no more foreign support for Scottish or Irish rebels, though Jacobite plots on behalf of James II continued to be hatched in all three kingdoms throughout William's reign.

William was thus free to concentrate on his main interest, the war with France, which, in different ways, was to dominate English history until 1714. Though a luckless commander, he was a great leader, whose dogged courage at last halted French aggression, it seemed finally, at the Peace of Ryswick in 1697. But in 1700 Louis XIV could not resist the temptation to accept the offer of the Spanish throne for his grandson, in flagrant breach of his promises; and in 1701 he broke another promise on the death of James II by recognizing his son, the Old Pretender, as James III of England. Moreover it was commercially necessary to keep open English markets on the Continent. So another alliance, in which the Austrian Emperor, the Dutch and the English were the main partners, entered on the ten years' War of the Spanish Succession. But by the time it started William's horse had stumbled over a molehill and he was dead, leaving Jacobites to console themselves with the toast of 'the little gentleman in black velvet'. He left his throne to Anne and his Continental lifework to John Churchill, Duke of Marlborough, who was not only one of the greatest military commanders of all time, but alone had the intelligence, charm and patience needed to hold together the difficult band of allies.

Between 1705 and 1710 Marlborough won spectacular victories at Blenheim, Ramillies, Oudenarde, and Malplaquet, and by the Treaties of Utrecht of 1713, apart from the negative success of keeping the French out of the Netherlands, England acquired Newfoundland and Nova Scotia, Gibraltar and Minorca, and a monopoly of the profitable slave trade with Spanish America. But the importance of these two wars lay much more in their indirect political and financial effects. Our effort was on a vaster scale than ever before. William had an English army of 90,000 men and spent £40 millions of English money on the war alone. Even with the new Land Tax at 4s. in the pound and budgets four times as large as those of Charles II, much of this vast sum had to be found by borrowing; and out of the new experimental machinery which the City evolved to meet this need there emerged the Bank of England and the National Debt. Gradually the Stuart haphazard credit arrangements with goldsmiths and individual rich merchants were taken over and modernized until in 1709 the Bank had ousted its competitors and achieved a monopoly. The National Debt was already beyond the reach of immediate redemption at £20 millions in 1697. By 1713 it stood at £54 millions, guaranteeing the support of the moneyed classes for the Revolution Settlement in the same way that monastery lands had guaranteed Henry VIII's Reformation. For no one could be sure that restored Stuarts would not repudiate the debts of a usurping government.

Such a tremendous expansion of effort could only have come from a country in which wealth was increasing very fast. Some of it came from an expanding industry, cloth still being the staple export, though soon to be rivalled by nascent cotton and silk manufactures. Increasingly controlled by small capitalists, who leased looms and raw materials to scattered cottagers and rode round with trains of pack

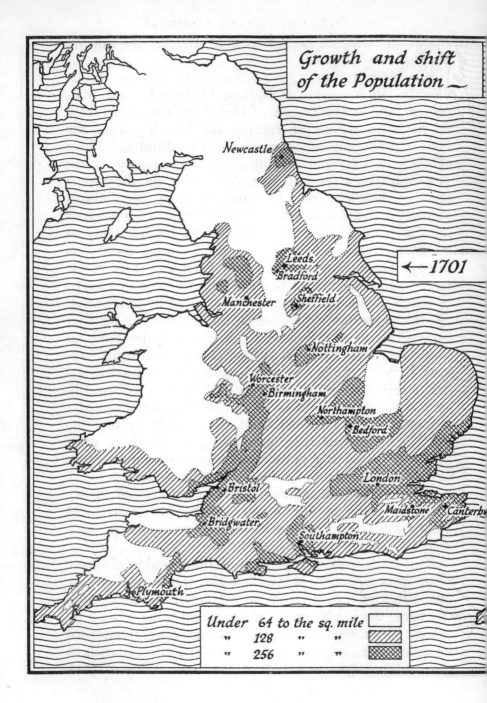

Growth and shift of the Population —

← 1701

Newcastle

Leeds
Bradford
Sheffield

Manchester

Nottingham

Worcester
Birmingham

Northampton

Bedford

London

Bristol

Maidstone   Canterb

Bridgwater

Southampton

Plymouth

Under   64 to the sq. mile
  ,,   128   ,,   ,,
  ,,   256   ,,   ,,

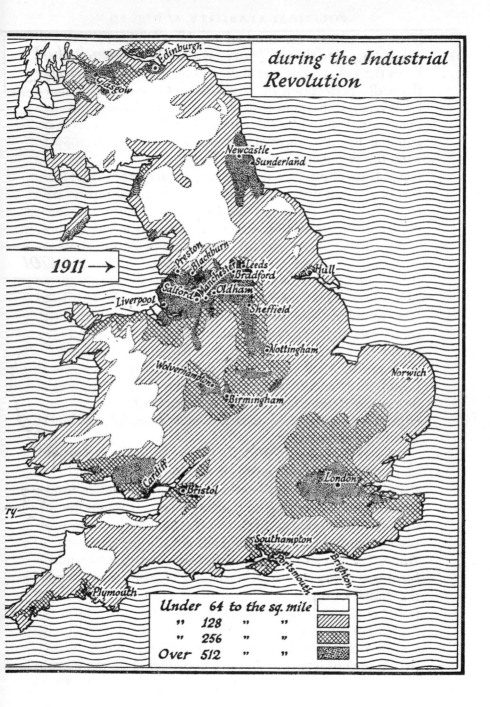

during the *Industrial Revolution*

1911 →

Edinburgh
Glasgow

Newcastle
Sunderland

Preston
Blackburn
Leeds
Bradford
Hull
Salford Manchester Oldham
Liverpool
Sheffield

Nottingham

Wolverhampton
Norwich

Birmingham

Cardiff
London

Bristol

Southampton
Brighton
Portsmouth

Plymouth

Under 64 to the sq. mile		
" 128 " "		
" 256 " "		
Over 512 " "		

horses to collect the finished products, industry was still expanding very slowly, partly because the stimulus derived from the influx of 30,000 skilled Huguenot workers fleeing from the persecution of Louis XIV was counter-balanced by severe competition from France itself. The big increases in industrial output would come later with the first machinery and the first big increases of man-power. From 1689 to 1760 the population rose only from 5¼ millions to 6¾, and it was from commerce that the big profits were made: from the 55 per cent dividends which the African Company paid in peak years; from the wealth derived from the sugar plantations tentatively founded in Barbados in 1625, whose exports by 1700 exceeded in value those of all the rest of the American colonies put together; from Newfoundland fisheries and the Hudson Bay Company's furs and all the rich mixed cargoes of luxuries brought in by the East India Company. As the wealth seeped down from the rich merchants and landowners who traded on this grand scale to the humbler tradesmen and craftsmen who catered for their needs, small savings and the small capitalist grew in importance; and it was largely to cater for them, and to divert small investments into government stock or new commercial enterprise, that the new financial machinery was being devised.

Thus if the reign of William III seems more an aftermath of the Stuart period, with all the old squabbles between King and Commons still embittering politics and an insular squirearchy clamouring against high taxes, foreign favourites, and corruption in high places, something of the prosperous calm of Georgian England already pervaded that of Anne. The houses that survive in town and country and the furniture testify to a society already elegant, which sipped the India Company's China tea and discussed the latest political satire of Swift or Defoe, the essays of Addison and Steele. For out of the party warfare of the reign were emerging the first newspapers and a wide reading public, emancipating men of letters from utter dependence on the patronage of great men. But if English civilization was moving forward into the rationalist, tolerant Georgian age, the politics of Anne's reign were a faction fight, with all the bitterness hung over from the Exclusion debates envenomed by a growing sense of crisis.

A crisis had been implicit in the political situation ever since Anne's last surviving child had died in 1701. The Act of Settlement was immediately passed fixing the Protestant succession on Sophia, Electress of Hanover, daughter of Elizabeth of Bohemia and grand-daughter of James I. But Sophia was ageing and in practice men had to look forward to her son, George, an exceptionally unattractive German prince who made no secret of his dislike of England and the English. The Tories, however much it had been forced on them, could not escape the fact that they had betrayed the loyalty that gave their party meaning only to make a Whig revolution. They had paid heavily in Land Tax for what they felt to be a Whig war, out of which Whig moneyed men made money by lending profitably to the government, while Whig politicians basked in the reflected glory of their general, Marlborough. Now they faced a future under what would be indisputably a Whig king. The standing reproach to their inconsistency was further emphasized by the Non-Jurors—the six bishops and 400 lower clergy who had forfeited their benefices rather than take a new oath of allegiance; and by 1714 almost all of them would have welcomed a Stuart restoration, if only the Pretender would give up his Catholicism, which he steadfastly and honourably refused to do. They had by then ousted the Whigs and made their peace, the Treaties of Utrecht; and Bolingbroke, the wildest of their leaders, who would probably have had the Pretender, Catholicism and all, had manœuvred himself into supreme power. But within five days of that, before he had time to win the Queen over definitely and make detailed plans, Anne died of the gout which had plagued her all her reign, and a combination of Whig and non-party magnates, anxious to avoid another civil war, peacefully proclaimed the Hanoverian Elector as George I. So the crisis passed away, except in Scotland, where Jacobitism joined hands with hatred of England.

The Act of Union of 1707 had made a single kingdom of England and Scotland, so that there was no longer a danger of Scotland choosing a different king. But there had been great opposition on both sides of the Border and the benefits of English free trade had not yet had time to reconcile the majority of Scots to their loss of independence and prestige or to being governed from London. The Earl of Mar's rebellion of 'fifteen might therefore have roused dangerously widespread support, had it been better managed. Indecision, the failure to concert action with the English Jacobites on the Border, and the fact that Tory England, though bitter at the savage exploitation of their triumph by the Whigs, made no move, doomed it from the start. The Border Jacobites were rounded up at Preston, and, after an indecisive battle at Sheriffmuir, the Pretender landed himself in Scotland to put an end to the movement by his gloom and lack of inspiration.

In the country at large the Hanoverian succession made little change. English life, still essentially rural and parochial, went peacefully forward along lines already clearly indicated by the time of Charles II. The same magnates, whether groups of local squires or single great landowners, dominated local affairs both in county and borough. The legal and administrative machinery set up by the Tudors functioned unchanged under the same magistracy, though with less and less efficiency even before large increases and displacements of the population made it altogether inadequate. A steady increase of the scale of coal-mining operations on Tyneside and a gradual enlargement of workshops until they were becoming small factories indicated the trend of industry, but had not really begun to revolutionize it. The process of enclosure of the still numerous and wasteful common fields went forward, but now mostly by agreement and without protest; and export trade continued to expand. In fact executive government continued along the old lines, the only difference being that it was responsible to a Parliamentary majority instead of to the King. In time this fact in itself—that the J.P.s on whose decision wage and price levels and poor law administration all turned were the same class and often the same men who sat in Parliament, and so were now responsible only to themselves—would lead to slackness and abuses of power. For the time being it worked reasonably well.

But at the centre of politics the changes were decisive. With George I housed in a few rooms in St. James's along with his two unattractive German mistresses, 'the Elephant and the Maypole', the Court as the nerve centre of the governmental, social, literary and artistic life of the nation disappeared for good; and the King, knowing no English, ceased to preside over his own Council or function as the real head of the executive. Though Anne's ill health had prepared governing circles for the change, there were seven confused years, both in home and foreign affairs, before the Whig leaders succeeded in adapting to the government of the country principles formulated almost exclusively in opposition. Out of the alarms of the 'fifteen emerged the Septennial Act, prolonging the life of a Parliament to seven years instead of the three laid down in William III's time. Otherwise home politics were merely a series of squabbles between selfish groups and factions without principle or meaning, while abroad difficulties in interpreting the Utrecht treaties all but involved more large-scale war, and did result in the sinking of the Spanish Mediterranean fleet off Cape Passaro by Admiral Byng in 1719. A wave of futile speculation brought this era to an end in 1721. At the core of this was an attempt to salvage the heavily over-capitalized South Sea Company by letting it carry through a large conversion operation to reduce the cost of the National Debt. Inexperience and fraud combined to produce a grotesque rise of the price of the company's shares within four months from £130 to £1,050. Numberless other companies, all worthless and mostly fraudulent—one was for 'importing jack-asses from Spain', and another for 'a certain design which will hereafter be promulgated'—simultaneously launched into the market to catch the investments of a wholly unwary public. Inevitably the 'Bubble' burst, and amid widespread ruin and suicides in high places, the one prominent Whig leader who had advised against the scheme, Sir Robert Walpole, took office.

Walpole stayed in office for twenty-one years and in that time the pattern of Georgian England was established. For more than half a century the Tories, tainted with Jacobitism and without a positive creed, could construct neither a majority nor a government. They maintained, however, the tradition of cantankerous, almost non-party opposition on the old Country versus Court lines, with a Whig cabinet of ministers substituted now for the old Court. The Whig leaders, large landowners mostly, with ramifying family, dependent, and City connections, succeeded now in doing what Stuart kings had always failed to do: partly by straight bribery, by the skilful use of patronage in the Church, the army, and the public service, and by the local territorial influence of their magnates, and also because they adapted their policies to suit the interests of those who controlled votes, they created a government majority in the House of Commons.

In this art of manipulating a majority Walpole showed himself a master. But though in this respect he easily accepted the worst standards of his age, in many ways he was one of the best representatives of his landlord class, an outstanding debater and a very shrewd business man, tolerant of everything save disagreement in his own government. His ruthless enforcement of discipline on his colleagues laid the first foundations of that cabinet solidarity which was to become the basic principle of Parliamentary government. It also introduced for the first time into politics the title of 'Prime Minister', though only as a term of abuse hurled at him by opponents. As might be expected from a man whose favourite motto was 'Let sleeping dogs lie', his term of office was not on the surface eventful and he evaded where possible dangerous issues. He refused to repeal the Test Act, but annually arranged for legislation to indemnify those who had ignored it. By abolishing export duties and customs on raw materials he helped to double the volume of export trade between 1720 and 1740; but when his excise reforms came up against severe opposition from vested interests he abandoned them. Similarly he allowed his efforts partially to free colonial trade to be blocked by the powerful sugar interest, and by the Molasses Act of 1733 clamped high sugar prices not only on England, but, ominously, on the American colonies, He did nothing for the poor; indeed he retained a tax on salt to reduce the squire's Land Tax. But twenty years of peace, sound finance, and still sounder trade policy produced a rising tide of prosperity in which almost all his countrymen to some extent shared.

It was a characteristic of the Hanoverians always to quarrel with their sons, and the household of the Prince of Wales was normally the headquarters of the Parliamentary opposition. When George II, a peppery martinet, but a better king than his father in that he at least talked English and was honest and loyal to his friends, succeeded in 1727, Walpole's administration only survived through his personal friendship with the new Queen, Caroline of Anshach, a remarkable woman who had her husband completely under her thumb. Her death in 1737 and the enmity in turn of her son were the first important factors in weakening his position. In 1739 public opinion forced him against his judgement to declare war on Spain, and his half-hearted, incompetent conduct of the war enabled a combination of Tory enemies and disaffected Whigs to bring him down in 1742.

With the fall of Walpole an era of peace was followed by more than twenty years of almost continuous fighting; and government under the general direction of one man gave way to the opposite conception, more popular among politicians at the time, of 'Broad Bottomed' administration, which was in effect government by a committee of influential leaders, each separately responsible for his department, and each contributing his personal following to make up a majority in the House of Commons. This system brought to the top men like the inept Duke of Newcastle with a talent for manipulating corrupt elections, and proved itself quite inadequate to conduct a major war, in which decisions had to be reached in three vital theatres. English merchants were determined, in defiance of treaty obligations, to break Spain's monopoly of the South American market. In North America the French were trying to join up their two small but compact colonies in Canada and Louisiana by a chain of forts and Indian alliances along the Mississippi and Ohio, which would stop all further expansion by the million and a half English colonists scattered in thirteen disunited provinces along the coast. Finally, the degeneration of India into a condition of warring anarchy made it necessary for both English and French merchants to intervene from their forts and trading stations, and so created a situation which amounted to permanent war, whether the home governments recognized it or not. Europe meanwhile was devastated by a series of great wars—barefaced struggles for territory which interested England not at all, but in which Hanover inevitably got involved, and which at least diverted French strength from the vital points overseas.

The proper allocation of the English effort between the three theatres, colonial, naval, and Continental, required statesmanship of the highest order, and for a long time too much strength was expended in European fighting which only served to demonstrate the qualities of British infantry and to give George II the distinction of being, at Dettingen in 1743, the last English king to lead his troops personally in battle. More important was the unexpectedly successful French counterstroke in 1745, when James II's grandson, Charles Edward the Young Pretender, landed in Scotland

5. Georgian prosperity. An artists' club by Gawen Hamilton, 1735
(By kind permission of the Director of the National Portrait Gallery)

on a forlorn Jacobite hope. In the teeth of the best advice he raised the Highlands, captured Edinburgh, defeated the English at Prestonpans, and reached Derby with 5,000 clansmen before his nerve failed him. Though the government and the City were thrown into panic, he had little chance of ultimate success. The Lowlands were sullen and England, grown comfortable and prosperous under Walpole, fearful for its dividends and terrified of his Highlanders, made no response to his appeals. But once on the retreat he was doomed. In April 1746, the Duke of Cumberland destroyed the remnant of his army at Culloden and went on to earn his nickname of 'Butcher' by his revenge on the Highlands, while Prince Charles, after a series of escapes which gave Scotland the greatest of all her romantic legends, got back to Europe to drink himself into obscurity.

The general peace of 1748 made little difference to the muddled, indecisive fighting in America and India. There were costly failures against the French forts on the Ohio—one of them commanded by a certain Colonel Washington—and only the genius for leadership of an obscure clerk of the East India Company named Robert Clive saved the English from being driven out of India altogether. But in 1757, at the worst of the crisis produced by a renewal of the general war, when a second Admiral Byng had lost Minorca, for which he was quite unjustly shot, and Cumberland had been forced to evacuate Hanover, when the Nabob of Bengal had massacred 123 Britons in the Black Hole of Calcutta, and two vital forts had been lost in America, England at last found a statesman. Within two years William Pitt had provided the co-ordination needed, and by 1759 victories in every theatre on sea and land had secured all the essential objectives. Canada was won and the French had lost all chance of developing political power in India.

It was a tragedy that Pitt's gouty, overbearing temper provoked a combination of his colleagues with the new king, George III, to thrust him from office in 1761, for there were problems in the next twenty years requiring even

M

greater statesmanship. George III, young and aggressively English, virtuous and pleasant, but deplorably stupid, was bent on reasserting the influence of the Crown in politics. He did so, not by reviving old prerogatives, but by turning the Whigs' machine against themselves, using the vast resources of patronage and influence still vested in the Crown to create in the Commons a majority of 'King's Friends'. There was nothing new in this: it was what Charles II had constantly attempted. Nor was it strictly unconstitutional. But the effect was disastrous. For the men whom the King manœuvred into power were incapable of dealing with a situation in which the political machine set up by the Revolution was at last beginning to show itself antiquated and inadequate.

In the first place a House of Commons filled with friends, nominees, and dependents of the Whig leaders was no longer as effective a check on ministers as a hostile and suspicious Parliament had been on Stuart ministers a century before; and, unless checked, ministers will always and everywhere be tempted in the name of efficiency or convenience to interfere with liberty and ignore the law. At the same time the House of Commons was extraordinarily reluctant to concede to the American colonists the rights of representation and self-government which its ancestors had won from the Stuarts. Behind this again there was a wider and more dangerous breakdown of the whole administrative machine, designed, with its unpaid county magistrates and village constables, for a rural population which stayed within its parish boundaries, when the first beginnings of industrialization began to create new, massive communities for which there was no machinery at all.

The claim to arbitrary powers which would put ministers above the law was mainly defeated by a disreputable aristocrat named Wilkes who had the trick of popularity with crowds and used the London mob against the Whigs as they had once used it against Charles II. For the government, seeking to convict Wilkes of seditious libel for a scurrilous newspaper attack on the King's Speech, used arbitrary powers of arrest and search under general warrants which constituted a real threat to the liberty of the individual. In the course of a ten-year legal battle Wilkes was elected as member for Middlesex, and the Commons, having refused to let him sit, when he was re-elected for the fourth time went further, and declared his opponent elected. This was as bad as anything the Stuarts had ever done, and it brought mobs into the streets to the cry of 'Wilkes and Liberty', and Pitt, now Earl of Chatham, out of retirement to protest. In the end Wilkes won all along the line, incidentally frightening government and judges from any further attempt to interpret the law of libel so as to stifle legitimate criticism of policy, and also securing the right of the press to report debates of the House of Commons.

The attempt to bully the American colonists, against which Chatham also protested, almost literally with his dying breath, in the House of Lords, was utterly disastrous. Most of the trouble sprang from the accepted theory of the age that colonies should be wholly dependent on the mother country and obliged to trade exclusively for her benefit. London trade monopolies and attempts to prevent smuggling were at the bottom of at least half the colonists' grievances, for they seldom remembered their own profitable monopoly, for example, of supplying England's tobacco. Their cry of 'No taxation without representation' was harder to meet, since it turned against the English the very principles on which their own constitution rested. The government case, that the colonies should make some contribution to the Exchequer for the military and naval protection supplied by Britain, was not in itself unreasonable. But it was unreasonably asserted, though equally unreasonably resisted. There was no statesmanlike attempt to explain the case or deal with the whole vexed question of relations between Parliament and the provincial Assemblies; no allowance made for the fact that the colonists descended from highly individualist stock which had emigrated specifically for the sake of religious or political freedom. The government neither made effective concessions nor effectively suppressed colonial riots, and so in 1775 allowed the situation to drift into war.

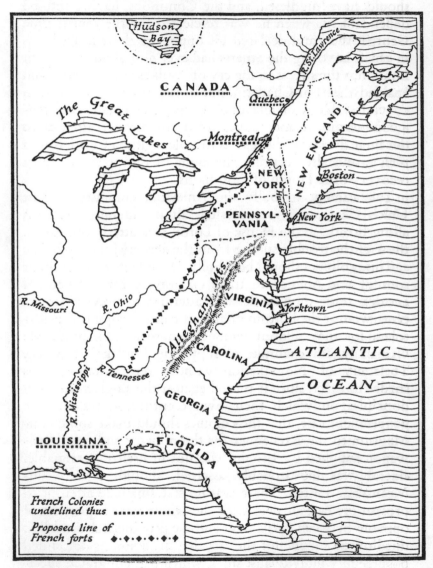

Having blundered into war, the government of 'King's Friends' was, equally inexcusably, incapable of winning it. Even red-coated Hessians and Hanoverians, in insufficient numbers, and with tactics quite unsuited to the country, should have made short work of the insubordinate, undependable volunteers who made up the forces which George Washington controlled as American commander-in-chief. Lack of policy, however, and confused orders from London, rather than bad tactics and leadership on the spot, enabled the colonists just to hold their own, and even, in 1777, to surround and capture General Burgoyne with 4,000 men at Saratoga. This was decisive. For it encouraged the French to join the Americans and bad naval strategy in turn gave them temporary command of the seas. Rodney's recovery of naval initiative at the great victory of the Saints in 1782 came too late, and in 1783 the Independence of the United States of America was recognized, loyalists being allowed to migrate north to form a new colony alongside the French in Canada.

Though it took England many years to learn all the lessons of the American failure, the immediate shock was enough to disrupt the self-satisfied calm of the past half century. In the villages the old system was still working tolerably well. Except over certain things, such as the Game Laws, the eighteenth century squire was on the whole a tolerant and benevolent landlord. Where the unit was still small enough, Poor Law overseers could still manage outdoor relief and the apprenticeship of poor children without pauperization or throwing an undue burden on the rates. Magistrates' assessments still held a fair balance between wages and prices, and local custom often kept wages considerably higher than the theoretical 'subsistence' level. Meanwhile agrarian reform was producing a steadily rising prosperity. At the base of this was the discovery and development of root crops which not only avoided leaving a third of the cultivated land fallow every year, but made it possible to winter fat as well as breeding stock and so at last made fresh meat plentiful in winter. Progressive farming, drainage, experimental crop rotations, and scientific breeding of stock produced startling increases of quality and quantity: the size of sheep trebled and that of cattle doubled during the century, and the total output was five times what it had been. The new methods also produced the wholesale enclosure of most of the remaining seven million acres of open field and common by improving landlords. Between 1702 and 1760 Parliament passed 200 private bills authorizing enclosure; between 1760 and 1780 over 4,000. This certainly resulted in a fresh wave of unemployed smallholders, who could not live without their common grazing, thronging the towns with unskilled labour. It also meant that the small farmer, and even the small squire, were squeezed out by the competition of the great estate with unlimited capital behind it. Though the triumph of more efficient methods was inevitable, the loss of the independent yeoman farmer was socially a disaster.

But in more and more areas a growing population was creating problems which, by their mere magnitude, defeated the old system. The mechanical inventions which were to transform industry had hardly yet begun to have decisive effects. Kay's fly-shuttle and the Spinning jenny had enormously speeded up the processes of the cotton industry, but left it in the cottages still, so that, though the population of Yorkshire and Lancashire doubled and imports of raw cotton rose in value from three to twenty-eight million pounds in forty years, it was still a rural population. In 1770 Manchester had only 30,000 inhabitants and Leeds fewer still. Arkwright's water-driven frame of 1769 did indeed concentrate spinners in mills; but these, dotted along the river beds, did not produce any great concentrations of population. The exploitation of Watt's steam engine, invented the same year, which would produce the large agglomerations of people round the coal and iron fields, could not take place on any large scale until transport improved; and until 1760 the mediaeval system by which each parish maintained its own roads continued, quite inadequately, to function. In areas out of reach of seaports or navigable rivers coal was unobtainable and, the forests having gone to smelt iron, there was real hardship from the shortage of domestic fuel, and certainly no margin for industrial development. Brindley's canals and Macadam's turnpike roads did not effectively remedy this until towards the end of the century. Until then industry was perforce still largely ruralized.

The final proof of the overall prosperity of Georgian England was a rising population due, not to a rising birth rate, but to a falling death rate produced by improved medicine, better building, and a higher standard of living. Prices were stable, wages tending to rise, and the consumption of meat, tea, and wheat bread was steadily increasing. Against this background of contentment the conditions of misery, squalor, and degradation of the poor in London, and elsewhere where early industrialization had produced great concentrations of people, presented an indescribable, almost incredible contrast. Hogarth's England, brutal, vicious, gin-sodden, and starving, was the London which already held a tenth of the population huddled in cellars and single rooms, ravaged by typhus and gaol fever: an unpoliced world of cruel sports and unpunished crime, where infant mortality was 74 per cent and there were three deaths to every two births. A steady rise in the number of capital offences shows both the increase of crime and the panic of a governing class which disposed of no effective police force. The surviving Tudor welfare machinery was either useless or actively harmful. The apprenticing of poor children in great droves to manufacturers who would sweat all but the toughest few to death in Spitalfields silk factories or northern mills was the only way in which harassed Poor Law overseers could relieve the rates of an appalling burden. The able-bodied employed struggled on on starvation wages; the unemployed died amid dirt, poverty, vice and disease in the unsupervised workhouses.

By the middle of the century individual philanthropy was doing much to alleviate such conditions. Five of the great modern London Hospitals were founded between 1719 and 1752. Some provision was made for foundlings and an Act of 1757 sent pauper children thenceforth to the country with proper board and lodging allowances. Though the Church of England as a whole was torpid, over-rationalistic, and lacking in spiritual force, its Evangelical wing was never more vitally alive. From it sprang the Wesleys and their battle to bring religion and morals and some element of hope into lives of otherwise unmitigated despair, and the Charity schools with which the S.P.C.K. began the task of restoring primary education to the masses. Perhaps the most important of all to London was the high duty on spirits clapped on by Parliament in 1751 which stopped the flow of cheap gin. Cumulatively all these measures did much to palliate the greatest evils, and London's death rate fell spectacularly from 1750 onwards. But in the country as a whole the problem was to spread and multiply faster than haphazard charity and a totally out-of-date administrative machine could remedy it. Only political reform and new state machinery could enable England to survive the really large-scale industrialization which was only beginning when, out of the parliamentary confusion following the loss of America, Chatham's gifted younger son, the second William Pitt, came into power at Christmas, 1783.

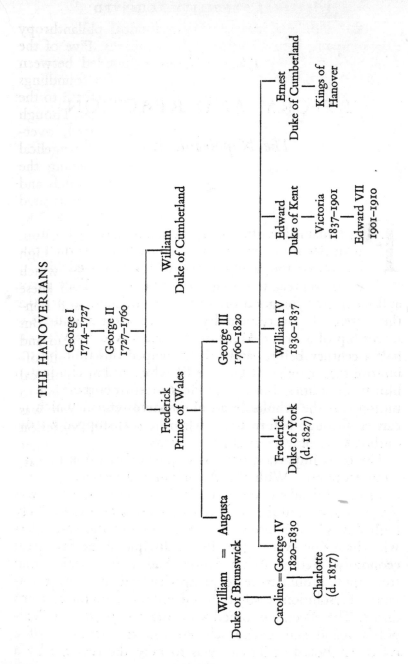

THE HANOVERIANS

George I
1714–1727

George II
1727–1760

Frederick
Prince of Wales

William
Duke of Cumberland

William = Augusta
Duke of Brunswick

George III
1760–1820

Caroline = George IV
1820–1830

Frederick
Duke of York
(d. 1827)

William IV
1830–1837

Edward
Duke of Kent

Ernest
Duke of Cumberland

Charlotte
(d. 1817)

Victoria
1837–1901

Kings of
Hanover

Edward VII
1901–1910

Chapter Eleven

REFORM AND REACTION

The Napoleonic Wars

★

itt remained in office almost uninterruptedly for more than twenty years. During that period he turned that section of the Whig party which followed him in Parliament—a precarious majority—into a new Tory party, and he riveted for good on English constitutional practice the system of government by a united cabinet under the leadership of a Prime Minister, foreshadowed by Walpole half a century before, and greatly helped this time by the intermittent insanity of George III which at last eliminated him from politics. But by far Pitt's most important contribution was the wholesale administrative reform which he carried through before 1792, when he was stopped by the outbreak of a new series of French wars.

The most important matters requiring attention in 1784 were economic. With the American colonies had gone a third of England's overseas trade. The National Debt was £238 millions and the tariff system a chaos of prohibitively high duties which profited nobody except the smugglers who throve on every coast. Pitt, a disciple of the first great economist, George Adam Smith, had a clear notion that freer trade would recreate prosperity and in many thousands of resolutions vastly reduced and tidied up the customs duties. The effect, combined with the completion of Walpole's abandoned Excise scheme and the activities of a reformed Board of Trade, was to raise the revenue by a third within ten years and more than restore the volume of trade lost with America, in spite of the fact that at the same time the fleet was being completely rebuilt. A modern system of budgeting and a regular audit of government accounts, commissions of enquiry into expenditure of every department of the state, and the practice of putting government loans out to tender instead of using them to mobilize votes—all these helped to restore confidence and prosperity and reduce the corruption which had so paralysed eighteenth century government. A sinking fund was established to pay off the National Debt, which indeed by 1813 it successfully did, though by then another far greater debt had been accumulated by the war. He abolished the worst of the ancient sinecures—those offices which carried emoluments without responsibility which had been a mainstay of political jobbers; and wherever possible he substituted regular salaries for the old wasteful and unequal fees and perquisites.

All this amounted to a wholesale modernization of the administration. Left to himself Pitt would have gone much further, for many of his ideas were startlingly modern. But on matters which required sweeping legislation for reform he was rarely strong enough to defeat the vested interests which controlled so many votes in the Commons. He imposed death duties, but was not allowed to apply them to land. He tried to free trade with Ireland and was prevented by big business interests, which also forced him to postpone the abolition of the Slave Trade, so strongly advocated by his Evangelical friend, Wilberforce. Most important of all, his bill to reform Parliament itself, transferring some thirty-six seats from rotten boroughs, where scarcely a voter remained, to new centres of population, and giving the vote to copy-holders, was defeated by seventy-four votes, half his own cabinet voting against him. His one great legislative achievement was the India Act which at last brought the political activities of the East India Company under parliamentary control and ended the anomalous system by which a body of chartered merchants could involve the nation in war and conquest without reference to the government. That, and the grant of a large measure of self-government to the two provinces of Canada with the promise of more for the future, laid the main foundation for a new empire and showed that some lessons had been learnt from the loss of the old. Much still remained to be done when, as a result of the French Revolution of 1789, war broke out again in 1793, and the tide of reform was checked. But there had been enough to stave off an English revolution and to give the country the strength for a twenty-year struggle which was to be the second of the great crises of English national history.

It did not at first strike the political classes in England that the French attempt to reform and modernize their absolutist constitution to the watchwords of 'Liberty, Equality, and Fraternity' was fundamentally different from what the English had done in their Revolution 100 years earlier. Only the extremists on both sides immediately saw that this appeal to universal and fundamental rights of man must threaten the established order everywhere and not only in France, and that it bore no resemblance to the severely practical English constitutional adjustments of 1688. Radicals like Tom Paine, who had supported the American Declaration of Rights, hailed the fall of the Bastille in Paris as the beginning of emancipation for all mankind. Tories, and also the most profound and conservative-minded of the Whig thinkers, Edmund Burke, saw at once the inherent threat to an order he valued more than any theoretical equality. But within three years the declaration of the French that they would help all peoples struggling for freedom, their massacres of suspected reactionaries, and finally the execution of their King and Queen and the overflow of their armies into Belgium made it impossible for English politicians to continue as what Pitt called 'spectators'. Out of this decision, for or against, forced on them by the French, emerged the English two-party system. Toryism, for a century little but a collection of grievances—against high taxes, and the monopoly of power by the Whig moneyed interests—was suddenly provided with a principle and a faith; and out of the fusion of the old Tories with the more conservative Whigs who followed Pitt emerged the new Tory Party. The courageous handful, who under the leadership of that dissipated, charming genius, Charles James Fox, still saw something more in the Whig Revolution than an assertion of the privileges of a propertied class, evolved in the course of time a theory and programme of political reform from which was to spring nineteenth century Liberalism.

This French war was, as Pitt complained, a war against 'armed opinion'—war, in fact, as the Elizabethans had known it and as twentieth century England was to know it again. In such a war political opposition is inevitably branded as unpatriotic. Foxites and extreme Radicals invited this accusation by friendly correspondence with the French revolutionary leaders, by forming 'Revolutionary Societies', and by conniving at riots by discontented workers even when extremist leaders of the Jacobin Club were in control in France and it was clear that this was not Liberty and Equality, but the rule of the mob—what Burke called 'that strange nameless wild enthusiastic thing'—in Paris. This unnecessary courting of unpopularity when the nation was settling down grimly to the immediate business of winning the war reduced the parliamentary opposition to a handful which, it was mockingly said, could have ridden in a couple of hackney coaches. But they survived and so ensured that after the war politics would cease to be the eighteenth century scramble between groups and factions, but a conflict, if not of principle, of points of view which transcended class and local interests.

Even during the war it was invaluable to have voices raised in Parliament against the suspension of Habeas Corpus in 1794, and against the 'Gagging Acts' of 1795 which forbade meetings of more than fifty people without the permission and presence of a magistrate. For, though similar safeguards are a commonplace of modern war, and Pitt was fully justified by the subversive activities of revolutionary societies and the mobs which stoned the King's carriage and shouted for bread and peace, the panic of the government and of the governing classes everywhere was exaggerated. War psychosis and the Reign of Terror in France made employers, magistrates, and members of Parliament see a threat of social revolution in every protest against wicked factory conditions, low wages or high prices, so that even long after the war the reformer who denounced the most scandalous abuse was liable to be denounced as Jacobinical. Fortunately the venerable safeguards of the Common Law still functioned to prevent the worst effects of government panic. When two Radicals, the shoemaker, Thomas Hardy, and Parson Horne Tooke, whose worst crime was to advocate through a Corresponding Society the establishment of universal suffrage, were prosecuted in 1794 for High Treason, the London juries stoutly acquitted them. By maintaining in Parliament through the darkest days the cry not so much for 'Liberty', as for 'English liberties', Fox and his successors preserved an upper-class leadership for reform agitation and so prevented a class war and an English Revolution from becoming the inevitable sequel to victory over the French.

Unfortunately Pitt lacked his father's genius as a war minister. He could weave together great coalitions of subsidized European powers against France, but he never concentrated the British effort on clear or obtainable objectives. He had not Chatham's unerring judgment in picking leaders, nor the ruthless intolerance of administrative incompetence needed to galvanize a British War Office into efficiency at the outset of a great war. Moreover the War Department itself had done nothing to remedy its shortcomings at the end of the American war. The army as a whole was untrained and scandalously under-equipped. Expeditions of raw recruits went out without greatcoats to face a Dutch winter; without boots to fight in the fever-haunted tropics; short of transport and medical supplies; short even of ammunition. There was little strategic planning, and the tactical leadership of commanders picked by seniority or influence was shocking.

The first phase of the war, from 1793 to the Peace of Amiens of 1802, though redeemed by some brilliant naval successes, was disastrous. The wild enthusiasm of the ragged volunteers of the Revolutionary armies defeated the European coalition and won for France in three years what Louis XIV had dreamt of in vain, the Rhine frontier. The second of Pitt's coalitions collapsed before the rising genius of Napoleon Bonaparte, leaving the French by 1800 supreme in Europe and in occupation of most of Italy. Moreover Britain's extreme interpretation of her rights of search for contraband in neutral ships had ranged most of Europe in a semi-hostile Armed Neutrality. The direct British military contribution, except for the destruction of a French expedition in Egypt and the defeat of a reviving French power in southern India, had been ignominious: scattered and disastrous coastal raids ill co-ordinated with French royalists; a five-year campaign in the West Indies which captured Martinique and Sta Lucia at the price of 100,000 men dead or permanently disabled; and two major expeditions to the Low Countries under the King's second son, whose activities were adequately summed up in the popular nursery rhyme of the noble Duke of York who had 10,000 men;

> He marched them up to the top of the hill,
> And he marched them down again.

The Navy, meanwhile, did little more than maintain a precariously successful defensive. In spite of Lord Howe's victory of the Glorious First of June, we could not effectively blockade the French Channel ports, and only luck and contrary winds prevented the enemy from landing 15,000 men in Ireland in 1796. The following year, when Britain stood alone against France, Holland, and Spain, Jervis crippled the Spanish fleet off Cape St. Vincent, thanks to the initiative of a certain Captain Nelson, and Duncan beat the Dutch at Camperdown. But the Admiralty, too, was having to pay for the maladministration of the past, and these victories were won in the midst of mutinies provoked by bad pay, bad food, and a too harsh discipline. Nelson's first two great victories, at the Nile in 1798, when he ended Napoleon's dream of opening a land route through Egypt to reinforce the French effort in India, and at Copenhagen, when he smashed the Danes and kept the Baltic open in defiance of the Armed Neutrality, lightened the general gloom. But by 1802 an exhausted England was only too glad to make peace. £290 millions had been added to the National Debt; and Pitt had fallen from power, defeated on the Irish question by the obstinacy of a temporarily sane George III.

For England was at last beginning to pay for centuries of mismanagement, cruelty and treachery in Ireland. The deliberate impoverishment of the country, the vicious penal laws against Catholics who had not even a vote, and the trade restrictions which alienated the Ulster Presbyterians meant that English rule was no more than a hostile garrison, and government a manipulation of votes in the indescribably corrupt Irish Parliament. The implications of the American war, above all the necessary withdrawal of all troops, had led to half-measures of concession. The Irish Protestant Parliament was given its independence. Some modest free trade measures merely served to emphasize the greater grievances which the English Parliament would not allow Pitt to remedy. 1789 brought the illogicality of all this home to roost and faced the government with the United Irishmen, banding together Catholic voters, who would use French help to expel the English, and Presbyterian Ulstermen who would adopt the principles of the Revolution against their own landed aristocracy. Pitt was probably right to see the only solution in Union with England

6. Eighteenth century philanthropy. 'Mr. Howard offering relief to prisoners' by E. Wheatley

(By kind permission of the Earl of Harrowby)

coupled with full emancipation for Catholics. For, though the Irish rebellion of 1798 was but a feeble affair, the constant threat kept 45,000 much needed troops out of the war. By exceptionally scandalous bribery the Irish Parliament was induced to vote the Union and its own dissolution, but on the clear understanding that Catholic Emancipation would follow. This George III, taking his stand on his Anglican coronation oath and abetted by faction and prejudice in Parliament, absolutely refused to allow. Pitt, feeling himself personally dishonoured, resigned, and Ireland was left, momentarily cowed, but with one more great betrayal added to the long list of grievances.

So England faced one of the greatest crises of her history with a feeble, disunited government reminiscent of the days of the King's Friends, determined on peace when it was increasingly clear that no peace was to be had. For only a fanatic could fail to see that the nature of the enemy had changed. Napoleon, First Consul now, and soon to be Emperor, stood not for the emancipation of peoples from tyranny, but for a permanent French tyranny in Europe. He was the prototype of the modern dictator, alternating blustering threats with veiled offers of a shared world power, and using peace only as cover for further aggression. Between him and his dreams of Egypt and India and world empire there seemed to be only England and her fleet. With them unsubdued he could not even establish with any hope of permanence his dynasty in France or French hegemony in Europe. There was no longer any question of 'armed opinion' which might find sympathizers this side of the Channel. The next ten years were to be a grim, uninterrupted fight to a finish.

From May, 1803, to August of 1805 England went through the unaccustomed experience of preparing for invasion. The whole European coastline from Gibraltar to Hamburg was under enemy control. Antwerp had become a vast, fortified base, and massed round Boulogne could be seen on a clear day the tents of the Army of England: 160,000 veterans of the finest army Europe had ever seen, who rehearsed their landing operations while the flat-bottomed boats gathered in every creek and estuary. It is not a difficult feat of imagination for modern English people to conjure up the atmosphere of those two years: the hasty organization and drilling of volunteers, the panic measures to move the Bank and the Arsenal, the observers in the Martello towers all along the coast—all the amateurish, slightly incredulous preparation of an incurably civilian nation for war on its own doorstep. Had Napoleon got ashore with any substantial force there is little doubt that he would have made short work of English military resistance. But he had demanded from his admirals the uninterrupted use of the Channel for three days; and this their Lordships at the Admiralty and the fleet commanders at sea were imperturbably convinced he could never have.

Years of continuous blockade at sea in all weathers and the battle experience of the nineties had completed the work of the brilliant young officers who had begun the tactical reform of the Navy at the end of the American war. In its own sphere it was as incomparable as the Grand Army, and the veteran Lord Barham at the Admiralty moved fleets and squadrons to counter the French attempts to break out of their ports and concentrate, with the same confidence that Napoleon moved his armies about the Continent. When Admiral Villeneuve broke from Toulon in January 1805, all his manœuvres to join the fleets at Brest and Rochefort were countered by long-prepared moves which had defeated him before Nelson got back from chasing him to the West Indies. Napoleon saw this clearly enough then and gave his orders to move the Grand Army against Austria and Russia the moment that Villeneuve took refuge in Cadiz. Pitt was back in office and another coalition was on the move. Foiled of his invasion, Napoleon would seek in the east a back door to English power and immunity; and it was to co-operate in this eastward move by returning into the Mediterranean that Villeneuve sailed from Cadiz to meet Nelson at Trafalgar. The invasion threat had already been defeated.

No commander has ever captured the imagination and affection of England as Nelson did. It was not his spectacular personal courage nor his tactical genius which made him England's darling, but a quality which was both lovable and inspiring, which dwarfed his faults of character, made his captains a 'band of brothers' and every seaman in a fleet he led a hero. The details of his last great victory at Trafalgar, the famous signal, and the scene in the cockpit of the *Victory* as he died, are the most familiar of all episodes of English history; and although Trafalgar ended for good the possibility of invasion and defeat, the predominant feeling in England at the news was a sense of loss. His last words, 'Thank God I have done my duty', were true in every possible sense. From then on an unchallengeable sea power faced a land power which within a year seemed equally unchallengeable. For Napoleon smashed Austria and Prussia, secured alliance with Russia, and answered the British blockade with the Continental System which sought to close every port in Europe to British merchandise.

In 1806 Pitt died, worn out by overwork and disappointment, leaving this apparent deadlock first to a coalition of 'All the Talents', which gave Fox before he died the chance to put through the one positive achievement of his life, the abolition of the Slave Trade; thereafter to a group of Tories who sought as best they could to carry on Pitt's life work. The deadlock was more apparent than real. Napoleon's counter- blockade hit England hard and caused widespread economic ruin, bankruptcy, and defeatism, and the British attempt to supervise all Europe's seaborne trade exasperated the U.S.A. into declaring war on her in 1812. But the exasperation of a Europe deprived of every overseas luxury undermined Napoleon's power far more rapidly. It forced him to invade Spain and Portugal to close leaks in his system, giving England her chance to open the Peninsular War which he himself deplored as a 'running sore';

and it led directly to his quarrel with Russia, whose Baltic trade was vital to her, and so to the invasion and retreat from Moscow in 1812 which ruined him.

Portuguese geography and Spanish national resistance gave Britain the perfect opportunity to exploit the advantages of amphibious power. The brief campaign of 1808, when Sir John Moore's small force, cutting across northern Spain, disrupted the operations of 200,000 men under the Emperor himself before slipping back to embark at Corunna showed the advantage in mobility sea power could give an army. Sir Arthur Wellesley, in due course Duke of Wellington, entrenched behind his famous Lines of Torres Vedras above Lisbon and supplied from the sea, could starve out, wear down, and harry into defeat French forces far outnumbering his own. He was very half-heartedly supported at home: the War Office still hankered after a Belgian campaign and in 1809 sent another 40,000 men to rot, knee deep in water, on the Isle of Walcheren for an attack on Antwerp which never materialized; and no tents went out to the Peninsula for four years. But Wellington had learnt to improvise supply in India. If not a genius, he was a fine tactician; and he trained his infantry to meet the shock tactics of the French column in line with fire power. The result was a string of victories: Talavera in 1809, Busaco in 1810, Salamanca in 1812, and finally Vittoria which cleared the French out of Spain. When the war ended he was fighting at Toulouse, deep in France.

It was Lord Castlereagh, one of the ablest of Pitt's disciples, who more than anyone held together the last of the great coalitions, which rolled the French armies back within their frontiers, replaced Napoleon with the Bourbon Louis XVIII, and set itself at the Congress of Vienna to reconstruct Europe. Britain's main war aim had been won when Napoleon fell. Her only material gains to balance twenty years of effort and £600 millions of new debt were strategic points such as Malta and the Dutch Cape Colony, which she paid for. She also secured the general abandonment of the Slave Trade. With the settlement of Europe, and especially with the embryo international system known as the Concert of Europe, Castlereagh and his successor as Foreign Secretary, George Canning, were increasingly out of sympathy. For the Congress established everywhere an unenlightened conservatism and the statesmen began to use congresses not to prevent frictions, but to organize the suppression of revolutions wherever they might occur. Britain would have nothing to do with meddling in other nations' internal affairs and non-intervention became the accepted British policy. Castlereagh's 'peace and a just equilibrium' were all that Britain wanted in Europe, from whose politics she held herself more and more aloof.

But before anything had been settled, while the Congress of Vienna was still sitting, Napoleon's return from exile brought the British army back into the field for a final effort. At Waterloo, just south of Brussels, Wellington had to meet the first shock with a mixed allied army of 67,000, of whom only 21,000 were British and those mostly untried, since the bulk of the Peninsular veterans had gone to America. It was one of the fiercest battles of the war. From 11.30 in the morning until 8 at night Wellington's troops held off the assaults of some 74,000 French, losing a quarter of their number in killed and wounded. Marshal Blücher's Prussians, who had promised to be in on Wellington's left by noon, arrived at 4.30 and did not effectively relieve the pressure on the British for two hours after that. It was indeed, as Wellington said, 'the nearest run thing you ever saw in your life'. When the French broke, carrying Napoleon with them in the rout, all chance of his restoration had gone. So badly had he frightened Europe and England that this time he was relegated to the lonely island of St. Helena in the South Atlantic, where he was treated with some discourtesy, though it is hard to see that he deserved much better.

With the war at last finally won the government now faced an almost equally critical situation at home. Pitt's reforms had been halted by the war, but the problems had gone on multiplying at an alarming rate. There was scarcely an institution in England in 1815 which was not wholly out of date and unequal to its task. Respect for all that was venerable, legal, and customary, which had served England well by preserving the Common Law and its safeguards through a period when the rest of Europe was losing its liberties, had preserved a great deal of useless lumber as well. The older towns were governed by charters never revised since Charles II's time; the new towns had generally no statutory authority at all. The universities, the grammar schools, almshouses, and many of the hospitals were clamped fast in statutes and conditions of bequest related to conditions in the Middle Ages, administered by unsupervised governors and trustees, some of them corrupt and most of them idle. In any case the shifts of population from south to north and from country to town left what charitable and educational effort there was concentrated in areas where it was least needed. The criminal code was out of date. The unpaid, elected constable in the villages and the antiquated town Watch were still all the police force in the country. Bow Street runners had done little to combat crime in London; the densest areas elsewhere were unpoliced.

Above all this were a Monarchy which had lost all respect and a Parliament itself in crying need of reform. The King had been blind and quite mad since 1811. The Regent, who was to succeed as George IV in 1820, had been, through his debts, extravagance, disreputability, and factious opposition to his father, a public scandal for the past thirty years, and was now a bloated parody of the elegance and charm which had once enabled flatterers to call him the First Gentleman of Europe. He was about to embark on a squalid divorce suit, and his only daughter, Charlotte, on whom the nation's hopes had been pinned, died childless in 1817. His brothers were an ageing, equally disreputable string who were only now belatedly putting aside their mistresses and seeking legitimate families to secure a vacant succession. As for Parliament, it was no longer possible to pretend that, in spite of illogicalities and inequities, it generally fairly reflected public opinion. The county vote was still restricted to the 40s. freeholders to whom it had been given in 1434, though the typical farmer was now the prosperous tenant of a great estate. Apart from corrupt and rotten boroughs, the fact that sparsely populated Cornwall returned forty-four members, London and the surrounding areas only ten, and Manchester, Leeds and Birmingham none at all, meant that the House of Commons was out of touch with, and even unaware of some of the most crying needs of the country.

The problem of 1815, essentially unchanged since Pitt's time, was whether this cumbrous governmental machine could reform and modernize itself to meet the economic and social needs of the people created by progressively more rapid industrialization in time to avert revolution. The economists of the time were probably right in arguing that, given enough time, the situation would right itself without interference. For the country as a whole was still moving on a rising tide of prosperity. The birth rate had ceased to rise—was indeed falling slightly after 1790. It was a continued startling fall in the death rate which sent the population up to 11 millions by 1801—the first census—and from that to 16½ millions by 1831; and over the whole period industrial wages were rising faster than the cost of living. In spite of the war British exports rose in value from about £25 millions in 1790 to £70 millions in 1830; and though a scandalously disproportionate amount of this new wealth went to the already rich landowners beneath whose estates the coal and iron lay, and to create a new rich class of industrial employers, the total effect was to enrich rather than to impoverish the labouring masses. But the economists' solution could only be applied at the price of appalling destitution and discontent for a very large minority—the inevitable casualties of changing economic circumstance.

Every advance of industry created unemployment. As one by one the processes were mechanized, in spinning and weaving, in metal and steel working, fresh droves of skilled labourers found themselves first ground down by the competition of machines and then forced out of employment altogether; a defenceless mass of labour unskilled in the new terms, at the mercy of conscienceless employers. The differences in the pace of mechanization within an industry made matters worse. The first spinning machinery made hand loom weaving prosper as never before, attracting large numbers at high wages to keep pace with the output of yarn, so that when the mechanized loom came it plunged into destitution an artificially swollen population. Despairing stockingers of Nottinghamshire or weavers in Yorkshire might smash up the frames and looms which were destroying their livelihood; they could do nothing to arrest the processes which were, in the blanketing modern phrase, rendering them redundant.

Apart from their defencelessness in a labour market whose wage structure had entirely escaped from the rough and ready supervision of county magistrates, every other circumstance combined to make the lives of these people intolerable. They were massed most thickly in areas where even the rudimentary state machinery of the age could not reach them. Manchester's population rose from its 30,000 of 1770 to 187,000 in 1821 and Lancashire and Yorkshire redoubled their population. In the new towns thus suddenly created there were not even the surviving mediaeval charities to alleviate misery, no local authority to control development, no churches and no schools. Houses went up in rows, back to back, along unpaved streets through the surface of which sewage drained into cellars each of which housed a family. Apprenticeship, designed to relieve distress, now meant the herding of small children into unventilated, ill-lit factories to mind machines or sort needles and buttons for fifteen hours a day. No ancient Common Law could be invoked to compel a mine owner to safety precautions or to enforce minimum standards of sanitation on employers and urban landlords.

Against evil on such a scale private charity and the occa-

sional conscientious employer could do little. The very concentration of these ills in a few black areas at a time made
them to a large extent remote from the lives of the well to
do. Regency society, in all the ridiculous foppery of its
beaux and bucks, could move on its orbit of London, Bath
and Brighton almost unaware of the cruelties which went
to make the wealth it spent so carelessly. Moreover, the
fashionable economic theories of *laissez-faire* made many
whose consciences were not dead believe that interference
would do more harm than good. The eighteenth century
had seen life essentially in rational, mathematical, mechanical terms. Their classically inspired literature, their great
Palladian country houses, their carefully planned parks and
landscapes, all testify to the love of a regulation and sym-
metry which they believed they found in the natural order
itself. Addison's satellites rolling in solemn silence 'round
the great celestial ball' stood for a universe which was a
machine, with God relegated to the role of the mechanic
who made and ran it, while Nature was a system of checks
and safety valves which maintained species and populations
in nice balance with each other and the supplies of food
available. Therefore wages and prices—and this was the
ugly derivation from the freedom preached so profitably on
the commercial side by Adam Smith—must be left to open
competition and the laws of supply and demand. Malthus
in his Essay on Population seemed to prove that numbers
would always rise to the subsistence level, where they
would be checked only by war, famine, or disease, and so
took all the heart out of philanthropy and reform.

It was in pursuance of these ideas that Parliament, in 1799,
finally made illegal all combinations to alter wages or conditions of employment, while the fear of fixing minimum
wages destroyed the bare protection hitherto given by the
magistrates' assessments to the agricultural labourer. From
1798 onwards the so-called Speenhamland decision of the
Berkshire magistrates resulted in wages, when they fell
below an agreed subsistence level, being supplemented by

relief from the rates. Over all the southern counties farmers seized the chance to get part of their wage bill footed by the parish, while labourers were tempted to take the subsistence in comparative idleness rather than work harder for a slight extra gain. Thus by the end of the war the total spent annually on poor relief had risen from £2 millions to £7 millions.

It would not be true, of course, to say that this slightly de-humanized rationalism was universally dominant, even in the eighteenth century. The Evangelical movement loosed great spiritual forces both within and without the Church, and brought comfort especially to many thousands of the poor. But it did so by fixing their eyes on a salvation which lay beyond the material world, and so contributed little to the alleviation of material ills. Moreover, by 1815 the rationalist world was fast breaking up. The poets of the romantic movement, Wordsworth who had been in revolutionary Paris, Shelley and Byron whose vicious attacks on Castlereagh have so blackened his name for later generations, Coleridge reasserting forgotten Christian standards, were leading the assault on complacency which was to bring in a new age. But the politicians lagged behind, and in 1815 everything depended on them.

Chapter Twelve

THE ERA OF REFORM

★

The government of 1815, for which public opinion and history have largely held Castlereagh responsible though he was only its Foreign Secretary, found no positive answer to the problem of industrial discontent. While armed bands smashed machines and men drilled on the moors by moonlight with strange improvised weapons, ministers could only suspend Habeas Corpus once again and send out spies and agents provocateurs who provoked revolt if they could not detect it, so that dragoons might make an example by riding down some despairing mob. A landlord Parliament saved agriculture from a disastrous post-war slump by the Corn Laws which aimed to peg the price of wheat at its war level, and so added dear bread to the other burdens of the poor. Between 1817 and 1819 the cost of living was higher in relation to wages than it was ever to be again. The business world struggled back to prosperity in spite of the difficulties left by a depreciated paper currency, the sudden loss of war markets, a flood of unemployed soldiers and sailors, and the loss between 1812 and 1815 of much merchant shipping to American privateers, while radical leaders tried to focus discontent on its real and remediable causes. A modest measure to restrict the hours of children working in factories was the only recognition of the social problem.

The years 1819 to 1821 were both the climax and the end of this disastrous period. The magistrates grossly mishandled a great meeting of 80,000 people in St. Peter's Fields at Manchester, and when the cavalry went in to disperse it eleven people were killed and many more injured. Feeling themselves bound to support magistrates whom they knew to be in the wrong, the government countered with the Six Acts, forbidding the organization and drilling of private armies and open-air mass meetings except under magistrate's licence, and by a high stamp duty on newspapers, seeking to prevent the ventilation of artisan grievances in a cheap press. The restrictions were not all unreasonable and some of them remain law to-day. Unaccompanied by reform, however, they roused bitter opposition, and the discovery of a genuine plot—the Cato Street conspiracy—to assassinate the government in 1820 seemed to indicate a real possibility of crisis, and probably only a trade revival and a fall in the cost of living averted one.

Then, in 1822, worn out by overwork and nervous strain, Lord Castlereagh went mad and killed himself. The cheers of the crowd as his coffin was carried into Westminster Abbey were not a fair commentary on a great career of public service. But the fact remains that his death brought in a new age in which first the Tories and then the Whigs were to carry through what amounted to a peaceful revolution. Between 1821 and 1846 bit by bit all that was essential of basic reform was accomplished, in the teeth of die-hard Tory opinion solidly entrenched in the House of Lords behind the Duke of Wellington and on the back benches of the Commons. It was achieved by the force of the massive discontent of the industrial labouring class, unenfranchised and inarticulate, incapable of understanding the causes of its own sufferings, and with mob violence as the only direct method of political action available to it, but which none the less represented a pressure and a public opinion which even an unreformed Parliament could not ignore or resist. The men who used and led it, and who carried the reforms they taught it to demand, did not any of them see the whole problem; but as discontent was focused first on one aspect of the problem and then another, piece by piece it was, partially at any rate, solved.

The cabinet reshuffle which followed Castlereagh's death brought in new and younger men who followed Pitt's party because of his reforming policy of pre-war days. Canning, whose foreign policy was, indeed, but a logical development of Castlereagh's, led and inspired an enlightened group among whom Huskisson at the Board of Trade, Robinson the Chancellor of the Exchequer, and Sir Robert Peel at the Home Office achieved most. Huskisson and Robinson working together set themselves to free trade from the mass of customs and navigation restrictions still left over by Pitt. All the remaining duties impeding home trade and trade with Ireland were abolished and a consolidated list of import duties, low on raw materials and approximately 20 per cent on manufactured articles, immensely simplified and stimulated foreign trade. At the same time a series of advantageous commercial treaties was concluded on a basis of reciprocal concessions, though high preferences for colonial goods were retained. The results of their labours were seen in steadily rising revenue and falling taxation. At the Home Office meanwhile, Peel got through a mass of overdue administrative reforms of which two were of outstanding importance. He overhauled the criminal code, abolishing more than 100 capital offences for crimes such as shop-lifting on which juries had for years simply refused to convict; and he created the Metropolitan Police on which in due course every modern, unarmed police force was to be modelled.

Though all these measures and the prosperity they engendered did much to alleviate misery and discontent, they still did not touch the roots of the main evils. Much more important was the almost inadvertent repeal of the Combination Laws, slipped through by the skilful Parliamentary lobbying of Francis Place, the retired tailor who, from a second-hand bookshop in the Charing Cross Road, largely directed the democratic Westminster constituency and had made himself a master of the art of agitating causes in Parliament. Of all the social injustices created by *laissez-faire*, the laws forbidding workmen to combine were the least defensible. Not only was there no real equality of bargaining power between a workman with only his labour to offer, and a family to starve if he was out of work for a week, and an employer with capital reserves and plenty of cheap labour available anyway. *Laissez-faire* was not even true to its own principles, since employers could not be prevented from combining to keep wages down, which they could do undetected round a dinner-table, so that there was not even the free competition demanded by the fashionable economists.

The immediate effects of the repeal, however, were disastrous. Hundreds of small unions, hastily formed on too narrow a basis to be effective, struck without waiting to accumulate the reserve funds, the organization, and the experience which could alone make strike action successful, irritating employers without forcing substantial concessions from them and discrediting the whole movement. Led by inexperienced agitators to expect far too much too quickly from combined action, the mass of workers was by 1832 disillusioned, though in fact great progress had been made. Hepburn's great Tyneside mining strike of that year, in which, in spite of low funds and a cholera epidemic, he kept 8,000 men out for twenty-three weeks without serious disorder, though it failed, taught lessons on which was to be built in the next twenty years a formidable trade union movement. Largely without striking and beneath the surface, as it were, of history, this was to achieve more improvement in working conditions than any legislative or administrative reform, turning industrial discontent from revolutionary paths to practical negotiations for specific concessions. The temporary disillusionment with the effect of industrial action, however, had two important effects. It threw the mass of artisan discontent behind the campaign for Parliamentary reform, so making possible the Whig triumph of 1830 and the following years; and when that in turn produced disappointment and disillusion, provided the driving power behind Chartism and the Anti-Corn-Law League. The two parties had by no means as yet settled into their modern shape. Only the extreme Tories, who really believed that the existing constitution was perfect and immutable and that the business of government was merely to govern, were a solid and unchanging group. Those who saw the necessity for change—Radicals, philanthropists, old Whigs, and the Canningites who were called 'young' Tories —still shifted their groupings bewilderingly often on the old basis of personal loyalties. Toryism proper was doomed. For two muddled years after Canning's death in 1827 Wellington tried to govern without accepting the necessity for reform and failed. Except for Peel, who followed him loyally, even the younger Tories who revered the ancient constitution and disliked the Whig formulas of reform accepted the ancient Whig doctrine that government must in the long run rest on the consent of the governed and shied away from the Duke's military notions of his function. The newly rich and growing industrial class, controlling the new resources of power and wealth, whose opposition had been largely damped down by patriotism until 1815, had now come out into the open against a Parliament in which they were often unrepresented. Behind them were the gangs of agricultural workers who marched about burning ricks and smashing threshing machines, the northern strikers, and the mobs who burnt down Lancashire mills, voicing grievances not directly remediable by parliamentary reform, but none the less convinced that only a reformed Parliament would remedy them, as Cobbett's wildly radical Political Register, selling 50,000 copies at 2d. each week, assured them it would.

So Wellington, after an ineffectual attempt to steal his enemies' thunder by passing the long overdue Catholic Emancipation, which only divided his own party more hoplessly against itself, was forced to resign, and in 1830 Lord Grey, a seventy-year-old disciple of Fox, formed a government of convinced reformers. There was nothing democratic about Lord Grey, his cabinet or, when it was produced, his Reform Bill. He himself regarded it as a necessary concession to the wishes of the country. His Home Secretary, Lord Melbourne, was to say of the savage sentences of hanging and transportation passed on agricultural labourers who had technically offended the old treason laws by banding themselves together with an oath, that 'the law had been most properly applied'. And the Bill which Lord John Russell read over to the Commons in March 1831, while it was thorough in its redistribution of seats, was firmly based on the rights of property. One hundred and forty-three seats were taken from the rotten boroughs and towns too small to be entitled to separate representation and given to the more thickly populated counties and the new industrial cities. The more substantial tenant farmers were added to the 40s. freehold voters in the counties, and in the towns all the old distinctions were swept away and the vote went to every occupier of a house worth £10 a year.

By democratic standards this was a modest measure. It would add to the existing 435,000 voters only another 250,000. But to the older Tories it appeared the rankest revolution and they prepared to use their majority in the Lords to defeat it. Grey therefore had a very difficult time, and everything turned on his handling of King William IV, an eccentric and unbalanced sailor who had succeeded his brother, George, in 1830. The King's good will was reasonably sure if only because his hated brother, Cumberland, very improperly made himself the mainstay of the opposition in the Lords. But he was easily alarmed, and as Grey fought his way, first through the Commons who forced him to another election on the specific issue of Reform, and then through the Lords, the mounting disorder in the country began to look like the beginnings of revolution. Crowds everywhere shouted for 'The Bill, the whole Bill, and nothing but the Bill'; showers of stones

7. The English scene at the end of the Napoleonic Wars. 'Punch and Judy' by
Benjamin Haydon

(By courtesy of the Trustees of the Tate Gallery)

greeted the King's coach and smashed the windows of the Duke's house; there were movements to stop payment of taxes, wildcat schemes for armed marches on London, and the Bristol mob, badly mishandled by magistrates and military, burnt down the whole centre of the city. But the King promised at last to create if necessary the fifty or so Whig peers required to swamp the Tory votes, and on the strength of this Wellington was able to induce his more sensible followers to withdraw before they pushed the country into civil war. So, in June 1832, amid wild rejoicing, the Bill passed.

It is easy to belittle the Reform Bill for its attachment of political power exclusively to the well-to-do, and to criticize the Whigs for using working-class agitation to force through a measure which gave not one worker the vote. Even so, it was a remarkable achievement of the political common-sense built up in England over the past four centuries to make so unrepresentative a Parliament conform to the national will and a ruling class give up its exclusive hold on power. Men still argue as to whether the Bill was rightly conceived; but the fact remains that it worked. It averted revolution and it produced between 1832 and 1840 governments, first under Grey and then Melbourne, to complete the much-needed process of reform. Municipal Councils elected by all ratepayers replaced in the towns the corrupt chartered corporations which had everywhere usurped power at the end of the Middle Ages. The Factory Act of 1833, though it disappointed the Radicals, further improved hours and conditions for children in factories and, most important of all, appointed government inspectors to see that it, unlike its predecessors, was really enforced. And the Tory Evangelical, Lord Shaftesbury, who sponsored it, was able to push through two more bills which by 1847 fixed a ten-hour day for women and children; moreover, since many mills could not run without their labour, this meant in practice a ten-hour day for most men as well.

The thorniest of all problems which remained was the

Poor Law. The Act of 1834 dealt effectively with the rise in rates and the demoralization of the idle who were subsidized at the expense of the honest worker, but with appalling ruthlessness. Outdoor relief for the aged and sick was, in accordance with Elizabethan principle, continued. But the able-bodied unemployed were now faced with the choice of starvation or life in one of the new workhouses, deliberately made as unpleasant as possible, with wives separated from husbands, no tobacco or comforts, and with 'old and young, infirm and able-bodied, imbeciles and epileptics' indiscriminately herded together. The problem was solved: the rates came down and employers could no longer use relief as an excuse for not paying a living wage. But the cost in human suffering was fearful, especially among those unemployed during a slump through no fault of their own. No measure has ever roused so bitterly the hostility of the poor or left a more enduring memory of resentment.

Along with these large-scale measures went a host of smaller reforms, completing the work of the Tories in the twenties: more capital offences, among them horse-stealing, were abolished; game laws were modified; legal procedure was simplified and cheapened; the stamp duty on newspapers was reduced; and prepaid penny postage, thanks to the patient championship of Rowland Hill, replaced the old expensive, slow postal system. Church endowments were overhauled and to some extent equalized by the Ecclesiastical Commission, and both the banking system and the East India Company's administration were brought up to date. Finally, affecting England directly hardly at all, but in the history of humanity most important of all, slavery was abolished throughout the British Empire.

The steady modernization of the state to keep up with a rapidly changing world did not stop when the Whigs were displaced in 1840 by a Tory party revived and reorganized by Peel, pledged to work within the reformed constitution, and beginning to call itself Conservative. Throughout the century the Conservatives preferred, in the tradition of the twenties, to leave the more sweeping changes to Liberal politicians and to concentrate when in power themselves on the minor adjustments needed to make the existing machine work better. Most of Peel's constructive work was done through his budgets, which carried on the process of lowering duties, recovering the lost revenue by the income tax first used by Pitt in the Napoleonic wars. This combined with a trade boom and a series of good harvests to make life easier and cheaper for the working man. The 'hungry forties' was not a fair description of his period of office. Apart from the famine year of 1847, the astronomical rise in industrial production and export trade continued, while the great railway boom—the 500 miles of railway of 1838 had become 5,000 by 1848—brought the cost of living further down by cheap transport, so that by 1848 it had fallen to the level of 1780 while wages had steadily risen. Destitution and poverty were concentrated in the dying industries, among the stockingers and the last of the hand-loom weavers, for whom there was no remedy but poor relief.

At the same time a stroke of immense good fortune had saved the Monarchy from the universal discredit to which George III's rash intrusion into politics and the grotesque antics and scandals of his sons had brought it. It was, of course, the great length of her reign that chiefly enabled Queen Victoria to establish herself and the throne so deeply in the affections and political institutions of England. For the first few years after her accession, at the age of eighteen in 1837, she was often headstrong and excitable and only saved from dangerous and unpopular courses by the careful guidance of old Lord Melbourne; and her marriage to her German cousin, Prince Albert, brought an alien influence into the public life of the nation which was never really popular. The Prince Consort was too earnest and intellectual for English taste, and too much wedded to Prussian, bureaucratic, and authoritarian methods of government. Moreover, between them the Queen and he had family contacts all over Europe in an age when most kings still ruled as well as reigned, which enabled them to interfere more than was proper in the conduct of foreign affairs. But, even allowing for the early mistakes and difficulties, Victoria's youth and her conscientious acceptance of responsibility and duty altered the whole atmosphere surrounding the throne and changed the Monarchy from an ancient piece of political lumber of declining usefulness into the greatest stabilizing force in the country: a permanent assertion of the unity of all Englishmen whatever the clashes of political or social beliefs. Incidentally, thanks to the operation of the Salic Law, Hanover went to her impossible uncle, Cumberland, thereby ridding the country of two nuisances at once.

Amid all the disorders, the riots and rick-burnings, strikes and mass protests which were the inevitable background to this period of upheaval, two great movements gathered and fused most of the remaining discontent with the government's achievements: Chartism, and the Anti-Corn-Law League. Chartism was basically the protest of all those who had expected the Reform Bill to give them a new world and found that it had not even given them the vote. The People's Charter, behind which all the diverse elements of discontent rallied between 1832 and 1838, was in itself a sensible programme of further political reform, demanding manhood suffrage, a secret ballot, and other measures all of which, except for the foolish demand for annual general elections, have since become law. But the movement attached to itself every crank and political adventurer, and many more whose thought was too far ahead of their times to give them any immediate political value.

Thus the Charter covered a multitude of divergent aims. Physical Forcists, radicals, currency reformers and early socialists, teetotallers and Bible evangelists, all competed for a share of the leadership, while the rank and file who made up the mass meetings and demonstrations and affixed their signatures to monster petitions to Parliament were the minority untouched by rising prosperity, who were really protesting against want and neglect. The business world, which might have given the Chartists the funds and the intelligent leadership they needed, had been satisfied itself by the Reform Bill and was, selfishly but naturally, opposed to any further extension of the franchise. Thus the Chartists fell into the hands of their own worst leader, Feargus O'Connor, a brilliant speaker and journalist, but a muddled thinker and a coward. Conscious that the propertied classes were enrolling as special constables, as they had refused to do in 1830, and that all the stable elements were behind them, the government could afford to ignore the Chartist petition, and very quickly the movement disintegrated in scattered riots and internal quarrels, while the masses turned to support the more hopeful agitation of the Anti-Corn-Law League.

The one important commodity which had not cheapened with the general fall in the cost of living was bread. The price of wheat remained so high that in a year of bad harvests the poorest classes, agricultural labourers and those in depressed industries, might have to spend two-thirds of their incomes on bread alone. For this the Corn Laws were blamed, since they aimed, by a sliding scale of duties on foreign corn, to keep the price of wheat at 56s. a quarter; and that was in fact the average price throughout the 1840s. The real cause was the failure of world wheat supplies to keep pace with a rising demand, and in fact the repeal of the Corn Laws did nothing to reduce the price of wheat in England, which still averaged 53s. 5d. fifteen years later. But the attack on the Corn Laws which could be represented as filling the landlords' pockets by starving the poor presented an irresistible appeal to every class prejudice in the land, offering the poor a simple solution to all their troubles and manufacturers what seemed an opportunity to increase the purchasing power of the masses without raising their wages.

Thus the Anti-Corn-Law League, formed in 1839, had all the advantages Chartism lacked in business brains, money, and leadership. In the House of Commons Richard Cobden, a Manchester calico printer with a passion for free trade, remorselessly demolished Peel's protectionist arguments, the more easily because Peel had got himself, as leader of a party still largely represented by the squires, into the position of supporting free trade in everything except corn. In the country at large the more powerful evangelical eloquence of the Quaker mill-owner, John Bright, rallied the masses to the cause. Financed by the Manchester Chamber of Commerce, they carried through the first great modern propaganda campaign, employing 800 whole-time organizers, spending £200,000 and issuing nine million tracts in one year; and in 1846, under the pressure of a bad harvest and an Irish potato famine, Peel gave way and passed the Repeal, splitting his party and ruining his own career in the process. He did not even relieve the starving Irish by producing cheap wheat for them; for throughout the horrors of the famine Ireland continued to export her own grain and butter.

None the less the successful agitation did probably provide a valuable safety-valve for English discontent over a number of difficult years while the worst evils of the industrial revolution were abating and the full advantages of the rise in material prosperity only beginning to be felt. 1848 was the year which demonstrated the total value of what had been achieved since 1821. In that year there were revolutions all over Europe—the result of the accumulated miseries of a land-hungry peasantry combined with the frustration of urban middle classes who were denied a share in government. The barricades were across the streets in every capital and there was hardly a government save the Russian which did not for a time lose all control of events. London, for years the refuge of foreign liberals and leaders of Continental lost causes, now filled up instead with the fallen royalties and ministers of reaction. But there the only demand made on Wellington, the aged Commander-in-Chief, was so to dispose his troops round Kennington

Common that a monster meeting of the temporarily revived Chartists should not be able to march to the Houses of
Parliament to present the Petition on which they had collected 5½ million signatures. The wisdom of admitting the
new industrial middle class to a share of power in 1832 was
clearly demonstrated by the 170,000 who enrolled themselves as special constables in 1848. There was still much
social injustice to be remedied, and more scandalous poverty
would be created before the process of industrializing
England was completed. But, as Karl Marx and his socialist
disciple, Engels, experts in such matters, found when they
investigated conditions in England in the forties, there was
not the hopelessness which drives men to revolution.

The period of great legislative change was over in England
for the time being. Universal free education had still to
come. There were to be more reforms of Parliament, giving
the vote to more and more men and ultimately, in 1918
and 1928, to women as well; but these were only the logical
conclusion of 1832. Indeed the activities of the political
leaders of the reform years made a pattern which English
development was to follow for nearly 100 years, during
which more was to be achieved by the men who applied
science to industry, who explored and colonized a new
empire, and who organized and directed the growing trade
unions than by legislators in Parliament. The material progress of civilization has always depended on the enterprise
and initiative of comparatively few men, and one of the
perpetual problems of a civilized society has been to prevent
these men from selfishly exploiting their gains to the detri-
ment of the mass of the people: to protect in fact the poor
and the powerless from the powerful or the rich. The
Middle Ages sought to do so by Christian charity operating
through monasteries and guilds. The Tudors had used a
rudimentary state machine to control prices and wages and
poor relief and labour conditions in such a way that life
should not become intolerable for ordinary people. This
was the system which broke down in the eighteenth century

under the impact of *laissez-faire*. Nineteenth century England, mistrustful of state interference, was able to hand the main problems over to organized labour itself, bargaining and negotiating ceaselessly with employers for better conditions and a bigger share of the growing profits of industry, and this was where the most vital progress was made after 1850. But, finally, it was to the Tudor conception of state action to provide social security that twentieth century England, in vastly different circumstances, was to return.

Chapter Thirteen

VICTORIAN ENGLAND

Triumph and Disaster

★

In 1845 a rising young Conservative politician named Benjamin Disraeli had written in his novel, *Sybil*, of 'two worlds' living side by side in England: the rich, comfortable, still predominantly agricultural England, and the England of the black areas where all the joy was being crushed out of men's lives by machines. To a very slight extent was this still true of the golden age of Victorian England, which lasted in its full tide of prosperity perhaps only from 1850 to 1880. The continued expansion of commerce and industry was not offset by a disastrous decline of agriculture. About half the population were still countrymen, though a fast rising birth rate combined with a still falling death rate was soon to push the population up to 35 millions and to produce a dangerous preponderance of industry in ever more densely populated areas. Meanwhile, with occasional—very few—set-backs, production of steel and iron, coal, cotton and woollen goods went up and up. The 5,000 miles of railway of 1850 lengthened again to 18,000 by 1880. A third of the world's shipping was British, and by 1874 the total foreign trade of Great Britain and her colonies equalled that of France, Italy, Germany, and the U.S.A. put together.

In such a world, where there were few black spots and profits everywhere were steadily rising, the growing trade unions did not find it difficult to secure a steadily improved share of wages and leisure. Led by the powerful Amalgamated Engineering Union, they achieved most of what they wanted by negotiation. They established an almost universal working week in industry of 56½ hours, and sometimes 54, with a Saturday half-holiday. With such a plenty to share, there was no need felt for state action to secure a fair share for everybody. And this suited the political philosophy of the age which still preached the utilitarianism made popular at the beginning of the century by Jeremy Bentham: believing that, if every citizen pursued his own interest in the most enlightened way, the ideal of the greatest happiness of the greatest number would be obtained. To the Victorian Liberal mind the Trades Union Congress, founded in 1868, and the first Labour M.P.s of 1874 were but fulfilling this same essential duty, of enabling the industrial classes by fair bargaining to secure their own best interest. Taxes were low—startlingly so by modern standards— since there was so little state welfare activity, and even those things which we think of as essentially public utilities, such as gas-lighting, were provided by private enterprise.

This immense gain of material prosperity in England was not, perhaps oddly, accompanied by any widespread substitution of materialism for faith, as has happened in so many modern societies. For, in spite of the coming battle between religion and science, as evolutionary biologists like Charles Darwin and archaeologists and geologists combined to destroy belief in the literal truth of the Bible story of the Creation and the Flood, the Victorian age was essentially one of faith. The more rational and ordered the physical universe appeared to be, the more impressed were most non-academic Victorians with the wisdom of the God who had created it; and there was a seriousness of purpose about even their intellectual agnosticism which almost turned it into a faith. Gladstone's rugged Liberalism, his passion for individual and corporate freedom, was deeply rooted in High Church faith and principles, so that English constitutional progress appeared to him one more aspect of the working out of an all-wise divine plan. Something of the same feeling showed in Macaulay's *History*, and it pervaded the poetry in which Lord Tennyson glorified:

> *A land of settled government,*
> *A land of old and just renown,*
> *Where Freedom slowly broadens down*
> *From precedent to precedent.*

It was a view of life which was hotly challenged by a very different set of beliefs no less characteristic of the age: the revived claims for the Church as a historic, living, sacramental force not heard since the days of Laud, which the Oxford Movement brought to supplement the still undimmed missionary zeal of the Evangelicals. The fact that the movement coincided with a revival of Roman Catholicism and the return of a Catholic hierarchy to England made it doubly suspect to the more conservative; and it was, perhaps, dangerously over-ritualistic for English taste. But it gave the impulse which produced many of the new churches in areas where vast populations were growing up in irreligion, and which as much as anything broke up the idle complacency into which the Established Church had been lulled. Royal Commissions in the universities, and enquiring into Church revenues, charities, and benefices, set new life flowing everywhere, however contentiously, and made this much more than the merely church-going age which scoffing generations later depicted. The daily family prayers of innumerable households signified something genuine, and not just conformity to a convention.

Much, indeed, of the Victorian achievement deserved the sneers of posterity—the sentimentalized art and the architecture of Gothic revival and faked baronial country seats. But these, too, testified not to a materialistic, but to an essentially romantic outlook. And no sneers can destroy the immortality of the literature which included, among much else that was excellent, the poetry of Tennyson and Browning and the novels in which Dickens and Thackeray from their different standpoints satirized and castigated the society in which they lived. Romanticism and a tremendous individualism, not only preached but practised, were dominant characteristics in every phase of Victorian life; and nowhere, perhaps, more noticeably than in the spreading colonial empire and in India.

For, thanks to missionaries and traders and explorers all over the world, to philanthropists who saw in colonization a remedy for unemployment and poverty at home, and to business men in search of expanded markets and supplies of raw materials, a scattered British Empire had come into existence almost haphazard, unplanned by governments which were content down to 1854 with a single Secretary of State for War and the Colonies. Canada, after a disastrous period of unrest among the original French colonists, had settled down to the two processes of working out self-government on lines laid down by Lord Durham in his celebrated Report of 1839, and a steady expansion westwards to the Pacific, not without a good deal of friction with the U.S.A. By the middle of the century this great Dominion had absorbed already 1½ million British emigrants and had set a pattern in self-government which was being emulated by the men who were turning a convict settlement into the Commonwealth of Australia and by Gibbon Wakefield's more 'systematic' and deliberate colonizers in New Zealand. There was rapid, but ominously confused development going on among the complexities of Dutch settlements and native wars in South Africa, and an expansion of territory in the far east, in and beyond Malaya. Above all, a series of small wars and annexations had resulted in the acquisition of sovereignty over most of India by the East India Company and virtual control over the native rulers of the remainder.

Victorian England was to pour into this Empire an enormous energy and derive from it a fabulous wealth. The large families of a prosperous middle class provided a seemingly endless supply of younger sons who must make their own way in the world or starve and who, as colonial administrators, as soldiers, missionaries and traders, led and organized this tremendous overflow of wealth and vitality into the undeveloped regions of the world. If sometimes narrow in outlook and prejudice, they were educated to a remarkably high standard of probity and devotion to duty by the Public Schools, new and old, which from 1840 onwards increasingly modelled themselves on the reformed Rugby created by Dr. Arnold. His insistence on the greater importance of character-building education than of academic learning exactly matched the need of his times and gave England a governing class unique in history for size and quality; and, though nationalist and racial prejudice have since belittled their achievement and often stultified their plans and hopes, their service in giving peace and orderly government and a rising standard of life to huge primitive populations which had never known these blessings was not invalidated by the big dividends England often reaped from their activity and deserved no sneers from posterity. For with their many faults, of insularity, arrogance, and insensibility, they carried with them the peculiarly English sense of justice and freedom to tracts of the world which without them would not have begun civilized development.

This mass of communities of diverse race, religion, and civilization, so variously linked to the Crown, created one dilemma which perplexes English statesmen still. Geography has made England part of Europe; perhaps even more important, her culture is and always has been part of that western civilization which looks back to origins in Rome and Greece. History has made her part, politically and commercially, of an empire in every way remote from Europe. For a century or more the reconciliation of these two interests and responsibilities has been the basic problem of English foreign policy. A distaste for foreign autocrats who meddled in the internal affairs of their neighbours, interrupting peace and trade, had led Castlereagh and Canning to a doctrine of non-intervention which tended more and more to isolate England from the Continent, and this trend was largely followed by Lord Palmerston, who more than any man laid down the pattern of English policy abroad in the nineteenth century.

Palmerston was Foreign Secretary in the Whig governments of 1830-40; he was back on Peel's fall in 1847; and, after an eclipse owing to quarrels with the Queen and Prince Consort in 1851, he was Prime Minister almost continuously until his death in 1865. Intensely, John Bullishly, English, and therefore immensely popular, he undoubtedly preferred to remain aloof from European squabbles. But events constantly forced his hand. Not even in the time of Elizabeth I had England been able to tolerate a potentially hostile great power in possession of the Belgian coast, and a Belgian revolution in 1830 had produced a threat of European war or of a French annexation such as had forced England to war in 1793. By what his enemies called 'Bounce and Bluff', sending the fleet to Antwerp and threatening to fight the French, and by eight years of patient negotiation, Palmerston achieved a settlement by which Belgium became an independent nation whose neutrality was guaranteed by all the European powers.

Apart from this interest in Continental affairs, forced on England by the narrowness of the Channel even before the days of air-power, the problems of the Empire itself thrust her back into European politics. The vital maintenance of peace in and around the Indian Ocean could be guaranteed by the British Navy, only provided that no great military power seized the land bridge of Asia Minor, which would open ways into India and Africa uncontrollable by seapower. This was the threat which had sent Nelson chasing after Napoleon to the Nile in 1798. It had led Pitt to lay down the doctrine of British support for the decrepit Turkish Empire which, sprawling from the Danube to Egypt, alone kept the Russians back from Constantinople. It forced Palmerston in the 1830s to use the Mediterranean fleet and every weapon of bounce and bluff to stop both Russia and France from exploiting to their own profit a war between the Sultan and his own most powerful subject, the Pasha of Egypt. And it was the rather muddled pursuit of Pitt's principle of support for Turkey which involved the inept government of Lord Aberdeen, while Palmerston was out of office, in the Crimean War in 1854.

For different reasons Austria, France and England were all interested in preventing Russia from exploiting Slav nationalism in the Balkans to destroy the Turkish Empire and in maintaining Turkish control of the Straits of the Dardanelles so as to keep the Russian fleet penned in the Black Sea. By firm joint action and more skilful diplomacy they might have prevented a number of trivial disputes leading to a Russo-Turkish war. But in this they failed; and, though Austria held aloof, England and France felt bound to go to Turkey's help. Neither government had any clear idea of how or where to fight the Russians, or with what object, and in the end they found themselves committed to the capture and destruction of the great naval base at Sebastopol on the Crimean peninsula. It was a disastrous campaign in which the British troops fought and suffered with a courage never equalled before or since. They were landed, mostly straight from India, in tropical kit and without greatcoats or tents in a sultry heat which made the commanders forget the imminence of a Russian winter. Under the fumbling leadership of senior officers who had last seen service, if at all, at Waterloo, they cleared the way to Sebastopol by the victory of the Alma and fought off Russian attempts to interrupt their siege at Balaclava and Inkerman—'soldiers' battles' all three—in which both Heavy and Light Brigades of the Cavalry Division earned immortal fame and the 93rd Highlanders created the legend of the 'thin, red line'. But frostbite and cholera and sheer maladministration, lack of supplies and abominable conditions at the base hospitals, killed far more men than the Russians did, in spite of the heroic labours of Florence Nightingale and her band of devoted young women who laid the foundations of our modern nursing service. The fall of Sebastopol and the

Peace of Paris of 1856 in fact achieved the objects of the war: the Black Sea was neutralized and the Turkish power propped up for another twenty years. But the cost in unnecessary suffering and in casualties was appalling.

It was this mismanagement which brought Palmerston back to office for the last ten years of his life, nominally at the head of a Liberal government, but himself powerful enough to prevent any sweeping changes. It was only after his death that the two-party pattern of English politics, so long foreshadowed, became finally fixed in the familiar modern form, with Gladstone and Disraeli facing each other across the floor of the House as leaders of recognized and highly organized Liberal and Conservative parties. But, deeply though the political questions agitated the educated public opinion of the day, their policies were in fact almost of secondary importance in the scramble of industrial, commercial, and imperial development. When Gladstone at last got free from Palmerston's control and returned to power in 1868 with a mandate for reform, he did indeed carry an act to give free state primary education to all, and he overhauled the organization of the army. Disraeli in turn, between 1874 and 1880, finally legalized strikes, peaceful picketing, and all the manifold activities of trade unions, established the beginnings of a national health service, and made a start with slum clearance. But the great political battles of the day turned on issues which had little direct connection with England's progress: Disraeli's government fell because, chiefly, public opinion would not tolerate any longer support of a Turkey which massacred Bulgarian Christians; Gladstone was increasingly occupied with problems of Irish land and the Irish Church, and his third and fourth administrations fell because they could not carry Home Rule for Ireland.

In consequence politics took on a slightly amateurish, almost sporting quality, and men followed the battle of giants between Gladstone and Disraeli with the same enthusiasm that they devoted to the performances at Lord's of

8. Victorian prosperity. 'The Derby Day' by Frith
(By courtesy of the Trustees of the Tate Gallery)

W. G. Grace. Lord Rosebery achieved an altogether unique prestige by being Prime Minister and winning the Derby in the same year in 1895; and it was not until the outbreak of the Boer War in 1899 and the gradual realization at the turn of the century of growing dangers in Europe that Englishmen were forced to face the fact that industrial, commercial, and social progress could no longer be left to happen of themselves without close political control and guidance. Statistically it could be shown that the tide of English prosperity was still rising. By 1914 the population was 45 million and the Empire's trade was valued at the staggering annual total of about £1,100 millions. One-fifth of the world's surface and more than a fifth of the world's inhabitants—some 410 million people—came under the rule direct or indirect of the English Crown. But there were other statistics more alarming for the future, and the carefree days when England monopolized the world's markets more or less as she pleased were over.

The first industry to suffer disaster from foreign competition was agriculture. Quick, cheap transport and refrigeration enabled American and Canadian wheat and meat from Australia, New Zealand, and the Argentine to drive home-grown products almost from the market. After 1878 there was no recovery of arable farming. With the great turnover to grazing something like 150,000 agricultural labourers fell into unemployment and thronged the town with a fresh mass of unskilled labour, and the rapid depopulation of the more purely agrarian southern counties swelled the already alarming urban growth. Old England—the England of the Wessex novels of Thomas Hardy—vanished with terrifying speed. The skills and the crafts, the local industries and customs and idiosyncrasies, and in the end even many of the village schools, which had made up the life of the English rural community, disappeared, and the life went out of the English countryside. It has meant the loss of much that was valuable and irreplaceable and the complete subordination of the country to the overflowing needs of town housing and townsmen's recreation: a process which twentieth century governments have sometimes tried half-heartedly to resist, but which still continues, apparently irresistibly.

England was thus committed irrevocably to becoming an almost totally industrialized nation at a most dangerous moment, when the rising competition of German heavy industry and of the U.S.A. was already crowding her out of her traditional markets. The rest of the world began to exploit its coalfields at the moment when the most profitable seams of English coal were worked out and the English miner's annual output had begun, through no fault of his own, to fall. Nursed behind high tariff walls, European and American industry were undercutting English, and the fresh markets which the textile manufacturers, for example, sought among undeveloped peoples in Africa and Asia only gave a temporary respite until India and Japan in turn nursed their own cotton industries to a competitive level. England had thus thrown her agriculture overboard at the very moment when she was entering into an inevitable industrial decline. The high quality of many of her finished products was to slow up this decline and avert total disaster; and until 1914 the still rising profits of shipping, of foreign banking and foreign investment were to mask it altogether. But these were precarious sources of wealth, and dependence on them, coupled with agricultural ruin, was to leave the country terrifyingly vulnerable not only in war, but to the peace-time policies of economic nationalism increasingly practised by the twentieth century world.

From 1900 onwards, then, behind the façade of still rising wealth and the lavish comfort of upper and middle class life, real wages were beginning to fall again; there were new housing shortages and a failure to deal with many surviving slum areas; one in every three army recruits was being found medically unfit and social research revealed a dangerously large proportion of the population undernourished. The spreading practice of birth control was reducing numbers fast in the classes from which hitherto the nation's leaders had been largely drawn, and a rising flow of emigration was drawing off annually nearly a quarter of a million of the most enterprising and energetic of the artisan population. It is small wonder that to many thoughtful and serious people in the first decade of the twentieth century Edwardian society seemed to be dancing on the edge of catastrophe.

In contrast to these signals of decline at home imperial expansion had gone steadily forward. There had been a moment of appalling crisis immediately after the Crimean War, when the bulk of the Indian Army mutinied, massacring its officers and their families, and all but displacing British rule. The heroism of a few garrisons and of the handful of British and loyal Indian regiments saved the situation, and a wise policy of clemency afterwards, with a greater respect for native needs and prejudices, healed most of the wounds. The anomaly of a trading company ruling an empire was at last ended, the British government taking over direct and complete control; and in 1877 Disraeli persuaded Queen Victoria to assume the title of Empress of India, symbolizing the fact that, for a brief space at least, Mohammedans and Hindus, and all the diverse races and sects of the peninsula were united in comparative contentment under a single rule. Their freedom from foreign invasion had been further safeguarded by the acquisition by Britain of a majority interest in the French-built Suez Canal, which led in turn to a temporary protectorate over Egypt and the conquest of the Sudan. Meanwhile, amidst a hectic rush of international land-grabbing in South and Central Africa, thanks largely to the genius of Cecil Rhodes following up the labours of that greatest of all missionary explorers, Dr. Livingstone, Britain found herself ruling fresh tracts of undeveloped African territory, big with the menace of racial problems and already involving her in Kaffir and Zulu wars and in perpetual trouble with the Boers—descendants of the original Dutch settlers of Cape Colony.

The Boer War was the climax of a century of bickering.

The Dutch irreconcilables who had trekked north to the Orange Free State and the Transvaal rather than accept British rule were bent only on keeping the independence they had won and on sabotaging the British dream of a Union of South Africa in which they thought they would be in danger of being swamped by British immigrants. A mixture of motives drove the British forward—imperialist dreams, greed to exploit the newly discovered gold and diamonds of the Transvaal, resentment of the Boers' political intolerance and of their brutal approach to native problems—while the weakness of the government in London only encouraged President Kruger and his friends to extremist courses.

The best men on the spot thought war already inevitable in 1897; yet two years later it caught the British unprepared, with only 14,000 troops in South Africa to face 60,000 Boers. This initial weakness, out-of-date tactics which sent red-coated soldiers in close order against Boer farmers who were born marksmen and stalkers, and a fumbling high command, resulted in four major defeats—three of them in one 'Black' week—and in the prolonged sieges of Mafeking and Ladysmith. But once Lord Roberts got going as Commander-in-Chief with adequate reinforcements and equipment the result could not be in doubt, though it took two years to round up the Boer mobile columns and turn victory into conquest. In May 1902, a generous treaty offset the annexation of the Boer republics with the promise of early self-government and a gift of £3 millions for reconstruction. The final result seven years later, thanks largely to the wise administration of Lord Milner and the brilliant team of young men he collected round him, was the emergence of yet another self-governing Dominion—the Union of South Africa of which Rhodes had dreamed.

It was the Boer War which really woke England from her Victorian calm. The dogged effort which had been needed to win it had revealed a military weakness unsuspected since the Crimean War, and the unmistakably hostile reaction of foreign public opinion made many Englishmen aware for the first time of their country's dangerous isolation. Queen Victoria had died in 1901, ending the epoch to which she had given her name, in a very different world from that of her accession. The Franco-Prussian War of 1870 had created the new and overmighty power of Germany which not only, in permanent alliance with the old Austrian Empire, dominated Europe, but was a formidable industrial rival, clamoured for a larger share of colonies, and was building up a fleet to back the claim which could only be intended to threaten Britain's rule of the seas. With these two went the newly formed kingdom of Italy, to make up the Triple alliance. In a second armed camp was the Dual Alliance of France and Russia, drawn together in mutual protection from the mounting armaments and hysterical aggressiveness of the new Germany, but not for that reason less hostile to Britain. Russia, our enemy for a century in the Balkans, now seemed, after her startling expansion into Asia, to be threatening the northern passes into India, while the British position in Egypt and the Sudan, frustrating the ambitions of France in North Africa, had made a jealous enemy of that declining but still formidable power. Even the Americans, closely knit though they still were by blood and language to Great Britain, remained suspicious of a British imperialism which they had once had to fight for their own freedom.

In such a situation it was virtually impossible for the British Empire, scattered, vulnerable, and commercially involved in every corner of the world, to aim at political isolation and economic self-sufficiency. Some English statesmen already saw in Prussian militarism and in the ill-judged, excitable, sabre-rattling speeches of the German Emperor, William II, a threat of world dominion which would have to be resisted as Napoleon's had been a century before. Almost all agreed that we could no longer afford to remain friendless. So, after a tentative attempt to come to an understanding with Germany, frustrated by her refusal to abandon her naval challenge and by her continued clamour for 'a place in the sun', Britain drifted into a position of half-commitment to the other side—the Dual Alliance, extended gradually to a Triple Entente. Theoretically such arrangements left Parliament still free to choose peace or war in the event of a general conflagration. In practice, by 1914 Britain was morally committed to France in the event of German aggression by a whole series of naval and military arrangements, and an Expeditionary Force of six infantry and one cavalry divisions had been planned to co-operate with the French armies.

Against this international background the reign of Edward VII from 1901 to 1910 and the few years of his son, George V's, before the outbreak of war formed an interlude: a short, self-contained period of English history which can be seen socially and economically as a rich, mellow afterglow of the Victorian era, but which in politics both home and foreign was one of upheavals, foreshadowing the changes which the war was to precipitate. With the election of a Liberal government in 1906 the centre of vital interest shifted back again to Westminster, and there opened a period of unrest and political strife such as had not been seen since the 1830s. For, though the Liberal leaders, Campbell-Bannerman, and after his death Asquith, were sober Gladstonians, there was now a Labour group more than fifty strong, drawing support from the trade unions and socialist theories from the intellectuals of the Fabian Society, and determined on remedies which would mean the end of *laissez-faire*. Above all there was David Lloyd George, the fiery Welsh solicitor who became Chancellor of the Exchequer, and whose Liberalism was to be expressed in Old Age Pensions and in the Acts which gave the country a still rudimentary but more effective health service and a system of insurance against unemployment—ideas far removed from the world of either Lord Grey or Mr. Gladstone.

Meanwhile the rising clamour of the suffragette movement produced a militant wing which sought to force votes for women from a man-made Parliamentary system by every kind of outrage: the smashing of works of art, bombs in pillar-boxes, arson, and assault. Women had already made themselves prominent in every department of local administration and had broken into the universities; Australia and New Zealand had given them the vote and the reform in England was long overdue. But violence only antagonized Parliament and added one more element to the factious discord into which national politics suddenly degenerated. Under the stimulus of Liberal reforms the trade unions expanded more rapidly than their existing organization really allowed and their leaders temporarily lost full control. Industrial relations were embittered by lawless, unauthorized strikes, and there was a movement on foot to use something like a general strike as a weapon of political revolution.

Against this background of mounting disorder two great political battles—over reform of the House of Lords and Home Rule for Ireland—produced a crisis so grave that King George V, when he summoned the leaders of both parties to conference in July of 1914, wrote that 'civil war is on the lips of the most responsible and sober-minded of my subjects'. But for the irresponsibility and lack of judgment of the Conservative leaders, the House of Lords might well have continued to this day as a hereditary second chamber with an absolute veto on legislation; for, though clearly obsolete by modern social standards, it was venerable and it worked reasonably well. But from 1906 onwards the Conservatives openly boasted that they would use their majority in the upper House to keep control of the government of the country, even though they had been voted out of office. Thus the House of Lords had already exasperated public opinion by throwing out a whole string of Liberal measures when they took the dangerously unconstitutional step of rejecting Lloyd George's budget of 1909. It was a revolutionary budget, designed to finance both naval rearmament and the government's social schemes largely by an increased income tax and a new super tax on incomes over £5,000 a year. But it had been well-established usage for centuries that the Lords could not touch a money bill, and their action now forced the Liberals to bring in a Parliament Act which would restrict the Lords' veto so that it could only delay a measure for two years.

The battle over the Parliament Act forced two general elections in 1910 and brought into politics passionate hatreds which seemed at times to endanger the monarchy itself and the whole constitution. Once again, as in 1832, the King had to promise to create the number of peers needed to force the bill through the Lords, and once again the threat was enough; in August, 1911, the Lords passed it by seventeen votes. But the Conservatives were left in a state of embittered unreason, determined to be revenged at whatever cost to the constitution; and the Liberals were so weakened in numbers by the battle that they now depended for a majority on the Irish members, who made Home Rule for Ireland the price of their support. This was the issue which brought the country to the verge of civil war. For the Conservatives made common cause with the Protestant unionists of Northern Ireland, encouraging them to resist, if necessary by force, any attempt to incorporate Ulster in a self-governing Ireland. By 1914 the import of arms and the drilling of thousands of volunteers had provoked the Southern Irish nationalists to similar measures, while the refusal of a large number of English officers to serve against the Ulstermen made it unlikely that the government would be able to do much to prevent a civil war.

But, three weeks before the all-party conference met, an Austrian Archduke had been murdered by a Serb fanatic at Sarajevo. Unwisely, perhaps gambling on the reluctance of Great Britain to intervene in a quarrel so remote, the Germans had pledged unlimited support to the Austrian plan to seize the opportunity of eliminating Serbia as a dangerous neighbour. They certainly hoped that quick action by Austria might avoid a general war. In fact the Russians were bound to come in to help the Serbs or see their whole Balkan policy crash in ruins, and that meant that France would come in too. This brought Sir Edward Grey, the Foreign Secretary, face to face with the dilemma always concealed in the half-commitments to France. It is conceivable that, had the Germans clearly known that Great Britain would fight for France, they would have held the Austrians back. But Grey and Asquith could not even unite their own cabinet, let alone the whole country, in a decision to fight for what many thought an obscure, purely Balkan issue. Throughout the last week of July, therefore, while Austria sent Serbia an unacceptable ultimatum and one by one the great powers set in motion the uncontrollable machinery of mobilization, Grey could utter no specific threats and could only plead for a conference before it was too late. It was only on August 1st that Germany's refusal to guarantee that she would not invade Belgium convinced English Liberals that they would have, after all, to fight. For the guarantees of Belgian neutrality of 1839 had been renewed in 1870, and an absolute treaty obligation was added to all the other interests—anxiety for the Channel ports, and fears of Germany's later intentions—which would have made Grey himself, and all the Conservatives, intervene to save France in any case. On August 2nd a German ultimatum demanded the free passage of troops through Belgium, and on the 3rd Grey could at last speak for a united Britain in pledging support for the Belgians. Not only Conservatives, but even the Irish nationalists, were behind him. On August 4th the Germans entered Belgium, and by that night England was at war.

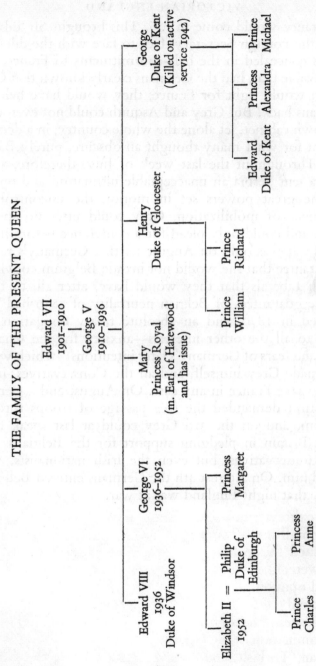

THE FAMILY OF THE PRESENT QUEEN

Edward VII
1901–1910

George V
1910–1936

Edward VIII
1936
Duke of Windsor

George VI
1936–1952

Mary
Princess Royal
(m. Earl of Harewood
and has issue)

Henry
Duke of Gloucester

George
Duke of Kent
(Killed on active
service 1942)

Elizabeth II = Philip
1952   Duke of
           Edinburgh

Princess
Margaret

Prince
William

Prince
Richard

Edward
Duke of Kent

Princess
Alexandra

Prince
Michael

Prince
Charles

Princess
Anne

Chapter Fourteen

THE WORLD WAR
AND ITS AFTERMATH

Readjustment in a changed World

★

Asound political instinct, both in 1914 and since, has
led Englishmen to set aside the difficult arguments of
diplomatic historians seeking to allocate a due share
of blame for the catastrophe to this or that Power's mistakes,
and to see the war as basically a simple and familiar issue.
Once again a force was loose which threatened the liberties
of Europe and the world, as Philip II and Louis XIV and
Napoleon had seemed to do; which unbalanced the equilibrium of Europe, glorified armed might, scorned the
triumphs of peace, and believed that power justified all
things. Nothing that can be said in criticism of Britain's
imperialism, or of British selfishness in exploiting the industrial and commercial advantages accident and history
had given her, invalidates that fundamental belief. In 1914,
and again in 1939, not England only, but the whole British
Empire threw into a struggle for its own and other peoples'
freedom all the accumulated wealth and power which had
so excited the jealousy of other nations. For Englishmen
these were, like Pitt's war a century before, struggles against
'armed opinion'.

Not only was the nature of the struggle the same; the
same strategic factors dominated the conduct of the war.
The domination of the German Staff over the policy of their
Austrian, Turkish, and Bulgarian allies made the Central

Powers a single unified enemy which, like Napoleon, could only be defeated by a coalition of allies and by blockade. Within days of the outbreak of war screens of British cruisers had closed every sea route into Germany and begun a slow strangulation which was in the end to be the most decisive single factor in winning the war. Unless Germany's High Seas Fleet could defeat the Grand Fleet concentrated in the Orkneys, she could not break that blockade. It was the maintenance of the Continental battle, of which the brunt must be borne by France and Russia, which presented the most serious problems. Britain's front-line strength on land was by European standards 'contemptible', and the European Alliance could not be allowed to go under. For it was unlikely that a German victory would leave any opportunity to manufacture fresh coalitions against her as Pitt had against Napoleon.

It has often been argued, and it is probably true, that the B.E.F. could have been used more decisively by a landing in Belgium or northern France in rear of the advancing Germans, as Sir John Moore had been landed in Napoleon's rear in Spain in 1808. But the necessity of preventing the quick defeat of France which the Germans planned as a prelude to the more leisurely conquest of Russia cannot be disputed; and it had in fact been long decided that the B.E.F. under Sir John French should work in close collaboration with the French armies. In this role it had its baptism of fire at Mons on August 22nd, and was engulfed in the great swinging retreat southwards before the right hook through Belgium which the Germans designed to fold the French back on their own fortified frontier line south of Verdun. German mismanagement and the genius of the French general Galliéni combined to frustrate this plan in the battle of the Marne; but the Allies in turn missed the chance of decisive victory and by October the Western Front had stabilized with both sides entrenched behind barbed wire in unbroken lines from the Vosges to Verdun and thence north-eastwards to the sea. Meanwhile in the east the vast, ill-equipped, ill-directed armies of Russia blundered to defeat through the sandy wastes of Poland and East Prussia, and on that side too, from the Carpathians to the Baltic, there was a single front, though less fortified and less continuously held than that in the west.

This substitution of siege warfare for mobility, the overwhelming defensive power of machine-gun fire, and the increasing difficulty of movement over shell-torn, waterlogged ground, set the generals on both sides a problem which none of them was able to solve. Frontal attacks, however, strongly supported by artillery, failed again and again to achieve the longed-for break through. Each side in turn produced a weapon which might have achieved a decision if properly appreciated and exploited—the Germans poison gas, which punched a four-mile gap in the allied line at Ypres in April 1915, and the English the tanks which could break clean through the German trench system—but neither general staff had the imagination to see the possibilities in time. So the costly assaults went on, gaining little except valueless tracts of ground at an appalling cost in human lives.

Into this war of attrition England flung armies on a scale never before contemplated; first the regular and then the territorial divisions; then, in 1915, the two millions of the volunteer armies raised by Lord Kitchener, the conqueror of the Sudan, who had become Minister of War; and finally, when the nation at last overcame its dislike of compulsory military service in 1916, further millions of conscripts; and to these the Dominions added hundreds of thousands more. Production of heavy guns, machine-guns, and shells did not really get going until Lloyd George took over a munitions ministry in 1915, and in consequence the flower of English young manhood was flung away in costly attacks which often even our generals knew to be valueless in themselves, but justified by the necessity of relieving our allies from a strain under which they were breaking. There were 300,000 British casualties on the Western Front in

1915, 60,000 of them in the unwanted battle of Loos alone. In the Battle of the Somme the following year there were 60,000 on the first day; 400,000 in all. Moreover, tactical clumsiness and inflexibility made British losses higher proportionately than French or German; worst of all for the future was the fact that for every two German officers killed, the British lost five. By the end of 1917 the Passchendaele offensives, though they had produced the first crack in the morale of the German high command, had brought England near the end of her man-power. Every fit man available up to the age of forty-one had been combed out of industry, so that the army with which Sir Douglas Haig, French's successor, was to win the war at last in the summer of 1918 was the last England could put in the field.

In face of this it was inevitable that British statesmen should look for some way to use sea power to turn the unbreakable German line in France. Lloyd George made himself a consistent advocate of an 'Eastern' strategy, in opposition to the allied generals; and Winston Churchill, who as First Lord of the Admiralty had already pleaded in vain for a more imaginative use of the army in 1914, hatched the most promising of these schemes in 1915: the attempt to seize the Gallipoli peninsula which commanded the Dardanelles, thereby freeing a vital supply line to Russia and going far to knock Turkey out of the war. Had enough troops been made available in time, had the operation been launched at the speed its originators demanded and a reasonable secrecy been observed, and even the minor administrative blunders been avoided such as those which entailed the reloading of all the transports at Alexandria before the assault, it must have been an almost bloodless victory which might have shortened the war by years. As it was, the joint military and naval attack failed by the narrowest of margins in April, and after eight months of costly fighting, in which the Australians and New Zealanders especially suffered and distinguished themselves, the whole force was evacuated in the most brilliantly successful operation of the campaign.

After that, attempts to find a key to Germany's back door, at Salonica on the Greek frontier, in Mesopotamia, and in Palestine, were too late to bring decisive results, though the most spectacular of them, Allenby's 1917-18 campaign, brilliantly assisted by Colonel Lawrence and his Arabs, re-covered Jerusalem for Christendom and largely helped to knock Turkey out at last.

Meanwhile, at sea, though the blockade slowly strangled German supplies of food and munitions, the great victory of which every British sailor dreamed always eluded them. In a pitched battle with Admiral Jellicoe's Grand Fleet the German High Seas Fleet, fast and hard-hitting though it was, must be annihilated; if Jellicoe pursued the enemy rashly into a minefield or submarine trap he could, in Churchill's vivid phrase, 'lose the war in an afternoon'. Therefore, the only battle fleet encounter, off Jutland in 1916, was almost inevitably indecisive: tactically a German victory in that they inflicted the heavier casualties, but broken off in the dusk at a moment when the British super-iority had just decisively asserted itself and, through a series of unhappy accidents, never renewed.

After that the Germans abandoned adventures in the North Sea, such as the bombardment of east coast towns which only stiffened English morale, and turned instead to the weapon which all but snatched them victory: the sub-marine. An effective blockade of Britain by U-boats could only be achieved by a policy of indiscriminate sinking of all merchant shipping at sight, without respect for the rules of warning and search or the rights of neutrals. Germany had tried this once in 1915, but had abandoned it when the out-cry at the sinking of the Cunard liner, *Lusitania*, at the cost of 1,200 civilian lives, made it clear that its pursuit would bring the United States into the war. Now, desperate at their failure to break the allied line in France while supplies steadily dwindled, the German leaders resumed unrestricted submarine warfare, bringing the expected American declara-tion of war, but hoping to knock England out before

American numbers and industrial wealth could be effectively mobilized. In this they all but succeeded. By the end of 1916 they were sinking 300,000 tons of merchant shipping a month; in April 1917, they sank 900,000 tons, and one in every four ships sailing from English ports was being sunk. England, in spite of stringent rationing and a drive on home agricultural production, was within six weeks of starvation before the tide was turned by counter-measures, the most effective of which was the system of protected convoys.

The bleakest year of the war for Britain was 1917. There was no outward sign that either the tremendous efforts made on the Western Front or the naval blockade were achieving anything. American help was still far off and Russia had collapsed in revolution, while the Italians, who had joined the allies in 1915, were all but destroyed by their defeat at Caporetto in October. But on what was beginning to be called the home front the nation was at last getting properly organized for a war which demanded a complete reversal of the ideas which had underlain Victorian society. Conscription and rationing had put an end to individual rights which had too often meant total sacrifices by the best while the worst skulked in safety or hoarded food. After many errors, press censorship was beginning to find the happy mean between disclosing secrets and telling so little that the worst was immediately feared. The Defence of the Realm Act over-rode Habeas Corpus; and in industry men had learnt to adjust their union rules on hours and standards, on dilution of skilled labour and the employment of women, and on the right to strike. All the sacrifices, the pigeon-holing of just rights and claims until better times, and the ungrudging voluntary co-operation demanded by total war, familiar enough to the Englishman of 1950, seemed to many in 1915, both inside Parliament and out of it, merely the negation of the very freedom for which the nation believed itself to be fighting. Inevitably the machinery worked badly at first and provoked some bitter grumbling. But on the whole the English people swallowed their traditional dislike of regimentation and responded with admirable self-discipline to the demands made on them.

One of the most necessary reorganizations had been at the centre, in the composition and practice of the Cabinet. Asquith, scholarly and urbane, every inch a man of peace, was quite incapable of providing the needed drive in the war effort, or of dealing with the seething intrigues, the rising influence of the press, and the conflicts of views which surrounded him. Even the Coalition government and the unwieldy cabinet of 1915-16 proved themselves clearly incapable, and it was Lloyd George who saved the situation at the end of 1916, forming a small cabinet within the government which he himself admirably directed to the sole purpose of winning the war. His dynamic energy and Welsh fervour and his intolerance of opposition, which often led him astray in peacetime politics, were wholly beneficial in 1917, and his was probably the greatest individual contribution to final victory.

Once the dogged struggle of 1917 had been survived in Flanders and at sea, that final victory was never really in doubt. But in March 1918, Ludendorff, the brain behind all the later German strategy, made a last gigantic effort to use the divisions set free by Russia's collapse to snatch victory in the West before the two million Americans who were beginning to pour into France put it out of reach for ever. Using new infiltration tactics which showed up the fallacies of all previous commanders on both sides, he struck at the junction of the British and French armies and all but succeeded in folding them back, the one on Paris, and the other on the Channel ports. The main blows fell on the British 5th and 4th Armies—120 divisions thrown against fifty-eight; and it was only by heroic efforts, at the cost of 400,000 casualties and 80,000 prisoners, that the line was patched and the key town of Amiens held. Haig, too inflexible in mind to make a great general, showed himself at this crisis one of the greatest of leaders. The British armies did as he asked them and fought it out with their 'backs to the wall'. Subsidiary blows against the French carried the enemy once again to the Marne, but no further. In July, over-riding the doubts and hesitations of his seniors, Haig flung Britain's last army back on to the attack on the Somme. The 300,000 Americans now landing each month made possible a converging Franco-American attack in the Argonne, and by August Ludendorff knew that he was beaten. Blockade and the war of attrition had broken German morale, civilian and military, and on November 11th the enemy surrendered unconditionally.

So once again, as in 1815, England faced the consequences of the total effort she had made. Foreigners, deprived of British goods for four fatal years, had developed industries of their own or sought supplies elsewhere. Trade with China and India had been disrupted and the cotton industry was never to get back again on to competitive terms with the Indians and Japanese. Similarly the competition which had threatened the coal and steel industries before the war had become ruinous by the 1920s. The whole world's system of credit, distribution, and exchange on which English commerce and finance had depended had all but broken down. Britain had lent her allies far more than she had borrowed from the United States and was to recover far less of her debt than she paid back. Direct taxation was seven times greater than in 1914; prices had more than doubled; the annual budget which had totalled about £200 millions when the war broke out was now to be over £700 millions. Behind high tariff walls the United States hoarded the bulk of the world's gold and developed incomparable natural resources to secure an unchallengeable position for their industries, while their bankers led the world's credit system along dangerously speculative courses. Everywhere the nations, new and old, were driving towards an economic self-sufficiency, making English recovery infinitely more difficult.

As in 1815, too, there was a mass of social and imperial problems, pigeon-holed in the stress of war, which now urgently demanded solution. The trade unions had claims left over from 1912, and were also clamouring for the return of rights and safeguards reluctantly given up in the crisis of the war. The vote could no longer be withheld from young men who had been called on to fight and die for the country, nor from women when more than a million of them had been replacing men in auxiliary services and in the munitions industry. The government had proclaimed that it fought to 'make the world safe for democracy', and was bound at least to make the claim good at home. It had promised its soldiers 'homes fit for heroes' and must try to redeem that promise out of the nation's shrunken resources or face the possibility of revolution on Russian lines. It had pledged itself to self-determination for the subject peoples of the Austrian and Turkish Empires, and must sooner or later honour the pledge in Ireland, Egypt and India.

When it is remembered that this gigantic problem in reconstruction had to be met by a generation which had lost a million of its best young men and been spiritually weakened by seeing the beliefs and securities of centuries destroyed or threatened and the accumulated capital of civilization thrown away, the recovery which England in fact made between the two wars, though partial only and very troublous, was remarkable. Lloyd George completed the democratic process begun in 1832 by giving all men over twenty-one and women over thirty the vote immediately after the Armistice and before seeking the re-election of his Coalition, and in 1928 women of twenty-one also got the vote. At the same time Fisher's education act raised the school-leaving age to fourteen, provided for part-time education to the age of eighteen, and finally abolished child labour. Moreover, within four years the Coalition had pledged itself to reward India for the 1½ million men she had sent to fight by the gradual extension of self-government, had ended the protectorate over Egypt, leaving only a garrison to guard the Suez Canal, and had patched up an Irish settlement. Disappointed of Home Rule by the outbreak of war, the Irish extremists had by the Easter Rebellion of 1916 started a chain of murder, arson and reprisal which pinned down more than 60,000 British troops, and it was not until 1921 that a treaty was signed giving Ireland two parliaments and making the south into a self-governing Dominion. But the Irish Free State was only established after a savage civil war among the Irish themselves, and was in due course to vote itself out of the Empire altogether as the Republic of Eire and to remain neutral in the second world war. Partition remains an issue to this day, and no final solution to the problem is yet in sight.

Against the hard facts of a falling balance of trade it was easier to achieve political justice than social. Nevertheless, by 1929 the value of real wages had risen again by 8 per cent and was second only to that of the United States, while the working day was shorter. There were more insured workers in employment than ever before. There had been further extensions of social services—pensions to widows and orphans and increase for the old—and housing acts to do something to lighten the burden of rent on working-class homes. But, partly perhaps through this fierce determination to maintain and even improve the general standard of living, and partly, too, because British industrial methods had become dangerously inflexible in the years before they had to meet the fierce blast of foreign competition, industry as a whole found it hard to meet the rising cost of social progress. Only the 'invisible' exports provided by banking, insurance, shipping, and foreign investments kept trade precariously in balance; and a dangerously deflationary policy, culminating in the return to the pre-war gold standard in 1925, coupled with interminable muddles over foreign debts and German reparations, made the balance even more precarious. Moreover, though England's exports of manufactured goods were still the highest in the world, the black depression which had settled on the textile industries, on coal mining, ship building, and engineering, offset and vitiated all the progress of recovery elsewhere.

These heavy industries were the ones which had been the most artificially inflated by the demands of the war, and it was on them that the main burden of the post-war slump fell. Not only was there a hard core of a million unemployed which seemed irreducible; it was concentrated in a few black areas, chiefly in Durham and South Wales. The miners, hardest hit of all, faced in 1925 a wage level lower than that of 1914, in a clumsily organized industry in which ill-feeling had long run high. It was this which brought all the unions out in a sympathetic general strike in 1926—a turning point in English industrial and political history. For the nation as a whole, if only partly consciously, rejected this use of an industrial weapon to force upon it the political views of a minority. An improvised volunteer organization kept the minimum essential services going. Instead of the mounting bitterness culminating in revolution which the world expected, good humour and tolerance prevailed, and within a week it was clear that the strike had failed; broken, not by the government or the army, but by the deep, instinctive Englishman's sense of fairness, which is his ultimate test of all political action. But that same test of fairness made the nation also uneasily aware that the conditions into which the workers of Tyneside and South Wales had been allowed to fall were indefensible. The meagre unemployment relief, supplemented by the offensively named 'dole', which could only be drawn for limited periods subject to hated tests of means and willingness to work, was no adequate method of dealing with this problem, moral as much as economic, of the semi-permanent degradation and despair of a million families. In 1929 it was this feeling which more than anything threw out of office Baldwin's Conservative government—successor to the Coalition—and returned Ramsay MacDonald and the Socialists to power.

This appearance of Labour as the largest party in the Commons completed the change which the war had brought into English politics. For Liberalism as an effective political force had perished; broken partly by intrigues and quarrels among its own leaders, partly because it clung still to the remnants of *laissez-faire* principles, which even Gladstone had found inapplicable in practice. Since 1918 there has been overwhelming agreement among Englishmen that only collective action can meet the massive social problems bequeathed by the Victorians, and the modern 'Welfare' state is not the creation of any one party. The cleavage in politics between Socialist and Conservative is one of method rather than principle: as to how close the control of the state should be over every department of national life so as to combine efficiency with social justice.

But the Socialists were given no real chance to carry out the schemes to nationalize all basic industries, in which their principles have become increasingly embodied, until after the Second World War. In 1929 they started handicapped by dependence on Liberal votes for an absolute majority; and before they got fairly going they were swept away in the disaster of the slump which dominated all the world's politics of the 1930s and intensified all the difficulties under which English recovery was labouring. The great crash of the Wall Street stock market in 1929 started a spreading financial collapse, reduced the world's growers of food and raw materials to ruin, and forced England again off the gold standard and into an industrial depression which raised the number of the unemployed to over 3 millions. In this crisis, as grave as any war, there emerged another coalition government, first under Ramsay MacDonald, and then Baldwin, under which the nation doggedly weathered the storm. High protective duties salvaged the most dangerously threatened industries, helped by a modest scheme of imperial preferences worked out by the representatives of all the Dominions at Ottawa in 1932. Sound and skilful finance restored British credit; something at last was done for agriculture by subsidies, quotas and tariffs; and there was a great extension of social services. By this curiously English method of Socialist policies carried though by a government and majority overwhelmingly Conservative in texture a partial recovery was made, and unemployment fell back to a million and a half. But it was made under the shadow of a new and growing threat of war, in which in 1939 all this achievement was to be engulfed.

The men of 1918 believed that they had fought 'a war to end war'; that once the military autocracies of Central Europe with their dangerously swollen armaments were destroyed, a democratic world would be able to settle down in amity. English disarmament, far beyond the point of safety and persisted in down to 1935, was a proof of the depth and sincerity of the nation's passionate desire to avoid another catastrophe. But the truth was that only adequate armaments and active support of a policy of collective security could maintain peace; and neither the British public nor the British leaders were prepared for the effort which this would require. The Treaty of Versailles and its subsidiary treaties which ended the war contained a number of basic mistakes: they imposed on Germany promises of reparations in kind for the damage she had done which, if she met them, must cripple her for a generation, while at the same time destroying the economics of those who received them; and they created a multiplicity of small nations out of the ruins of Austria and Turkey whose jealousies and economic insufficiency were to bedevil world politics for the next twenty years. But, under the inspiration of President Wilson of the United States, they created the machinery of the League of Nations which might have been used both for treaty revision and for collective security, had not all the great powers either misused it or refused to use it at all. The United States, on a wave of isolationist feeling, repudiated Wilson and would not join. Germany, treated as an outcast, was only admitted in 1926, and Russia did not join until 1934. France, meanwhile, terrified for her security, twice violated within fifty years, organized a bloc of small nations round Germany's frontiers and used the League rather to prevent treaty revision, as a machine designed solely to keep Germany permanently under. Finally, Great Britain, banking everything on the League, refused to face the fact that it could only be effective if supported in the last resort by force. Once the impression got abroad that Britain would make any concession rather than fight, her influence for peace lost all value, and neither the League nor her allies in Europe could defy with any confidence the new forces which the advent of Mussolini in Italy and Hitler in Germany let loose again in the world.

Thus England, too, contributed to the series of disasters which culminated in the Second World War. The inept politicians who conducted her foreign affairs dared not face a war-weary people with the possibility of further sacrifices. And the people, spiritually and materially exhausted not only by the war but by the struggle to restore their own standards of civilization, and unduly obsessed with a guilty sense that Germany had been treated too harshly at Versailles, were willing enough to shirk all the issues throughout the 1930s, when peace might have been saved at far less risk and sacrifice than was in the end demanded of them.

In this ignoble period of English history, amidst the unheeded warnings of a few far-sighted politicians, and most notably of Winston Churchill, Japan seized Manchuria from China, Hitler and a German army which had skilfully evaded the disarmament clauses of Versailles combined to destroy the German Republic, and the Italians conquered Abyssinia; Hitler reoccupied the Rhineland in 1935, seized Austria in 1937, and in 1938 by the threat of war forced Britain and France to abandon Czechoslovakia, and with it the last hope of combining an alliance which could stop Germany overrunning Europe. At each stage, mistrustful of their possible allies and conscious of the frightening weakness of army, navy and air force, British politicians gave way, without taking the only logical step of rearming to meet the next aggression. Anthony Eden, the only statesmanlike Foreign Secretary of the period, resigned when the government refused to risk war over Abyssinia; nobody else had the courage to risk unpopularity by facing the

British people with unpalatable truth. For this no party, and few individuals, can escape a share of blame. The hysterical crowds which greeted Neville Chamberlain when he returned from Munich in 1938, having sold the Czechs for a handful of worthless paper guarantees, represented a nation which was glad enough to be helped by its leaders not to face the facts.

Yet the revulsion of English feeling the following winter as it became clear that Hitler, secure in south and west, was now going to turn on Poland, should have warned the Dictators, if anything could warn them, that the 'degeneracy of Western Democracy' which they preached was a dangerous myth. Already rearmament was on the way and there was a hope that there would be enough fighter squadrons to save the country from the one form of attack which the Channel would not check. But what was decisive was the sudden, apparently unanimous resolution to make up by feverish, belated activity what was possible of the neglect of twenty years. England had no direct interest in Poland and had made no promises to her. But there was solid approval for the guarantee of her integrity jointly with France which did not waver even when the Russians signed a treaty of non-aggression with Hitler the following summer. It was clear that we could do little, in fact, to save Poland. But the feeling that a stand must be made for freedom and peace was at last overwhelming and there was hardly a doubting voice raised when the attack came and Britain and France honoured their pledges in September 1939.

Chapter Fifteen

ENGLAND'S FINEST HOUR

The Last and Greatest Crisis

★

I
t is easy and has been fashionable to criticize and belittle the leaders of the English nation between the wars;
and it is in fact difficult to tell anything of their story
without dwelling on the mistakes they made, for which the
present generation inevitably feels that it is paying. Every
theorist and reformer can point to some shortcomings: some
necessary reform which was postponed or shirked. Their
glaring errors in the field of foreign affairs have obscured
their positive achievement, just as the vices and weaknesses
of the nation as a whole, so obvious to the historian to-
day, have obscured the solid qualities—the patience and
good humour—which had gone to the transformation and
modernization of England. Yet, considered dispassionately,
the achievement of the years between the wars was in some
ways the most remarkable of all English history.

The changes since 1914 in the relationship between the
classes, in the attitude towards industrial disputes, poverty,
and unemployment, and in the duties of the state towards
its subjects, were in total revolutionary; and they had been
accomplished without revolution. The idle, pleasure-loving
rich of Edwardian days had willingly surrendered a great
part of their unfairly large share of the national wealth in
taxation and death duties to finance enlarged schemes of
education and social welfare. A Socialist party which had
grown out of a theory of class war had accepted the limita-

tions and responsibilities of the English system of government and had reached with the Conservatives that agreement on the fundamentals without which democratic
government by a party system is impossible. The venerable
institution of Parliament had adapted itself with truly amaz-
ing flexibility to the swelling demands of an ever more complicated, speeded-up civilization, delegating to local authori-
ties and government departments details of legislation, while
keeping general control of the whole. Above all the
Monarchy, the most venerable institution of all, had established itself in the new democratic age, in which theoretically
it should have been out of date and useless, as the greatest of
all stabilizing and unifying forces in the country. The simple,
homely, and essentially Christian virtues of George V and
his Queen had rooted the throne more firmly in the hearts
of the English people than any more spectacular sovereign
could have done, as the national rejoicing at their Jubilee of
1935 showed. This new prestige of monarchy survived even
the sad episode of King Edward VIII, when the man who,
as Prince of Wales, had enjoyed a personal popularity un-
equalled in English history was forced to abdicate in 1936 in
order to marry a woman whom the English people felt they
could not accept as Queen; and the unassuming devotion to
the public service of George VI, the brother who reluctantly
took the throne, still further strengthened that English institution which has most of all puzzled and excited the envy of
foreign peoples.

The fruit of all this was seen in the summer of 1940, when
Britain stood alone against a triumphant Germany, with no
support save that of a distant Empire; when Churchill was
to claim for her, in one of his greatest speeches, that, whatever the outcome, future generations would say: 'This was
their finest hour.' That the claim could be made—and made,
the historian can already say, with justice—was in itself a
tribute to a generation which had preserved English unity
and peaceful progress when elsewhere there was little
but demoralization, disintegration, and revolution. For

the England which had just recovered its army miraculously from Dunkirk and was feverishly preparing for what seemed the inevitable final assault, was united as never before in its history: more aware than ever before of the issues involved; more consciously and deliberately prepared for the sacrifices and sufferings and the unstinted effort which would alone save the nation from destruction. Moreover, the statesmen of that between-wars period had not only preserved a united nation to face the crisis, but, perhaps more remarkably still, a united empire. The great Dominions, which the Victorians had expected to cut themselves away from the mother country as soon as they had achieved maturity and self-government, and which had in fact by the Statute of Westminster of 1931 been given complete freedom of action, had used it to form with Britain an association more closely bound by ties of common sentiment and outlook than ever it had been by political controls or economic dependence. Though Britain for the moment bore the brunt, her loneliness was only the loneliness of an outpost behind which the industrial and military forces of Canada, Australia, New Zealand, and South Africa were mustering on an unprecedented scale; while the theoretically neutral United States of America furnished an industrial support which was already invaluable.

This time the European alliance against the aggressor, so narrowly preserved in the first war, had really collapsed. After the swift conquest of Poland and the long, cold winter of the 'phoney' war, when France strove behind her Maginot line to heal her spiritual and political ills, and a British army, inadequate still in numbers, training, and equipment, waited on the familiar ground of northern France, the blow had fallen swiftly and disastrously in the spring of 1940. Norway, Denmark, Holland and Belgium, and finally France, had been overrun, and Hitler was triumphantly proclaiming the new order which was to last in Europe for 1,000 years. That England survived this—the third and greatest of the crises of her modern history—was due to the indomitable leadership of Churchill and the courage and skill of a handful of fighter pilots who, by Christmas, had fought off Germany's air attack and so made invasion by her, for the moment, invincible army impossible.

This latest of England's wars against a Continental aggressor reproduced to a remarkable degree all the factors and situations of previous struggles. The Armada this time was airborne, but the Spitfires and Hurricanes 'plucked its feathers' as surely and successfully as Drake had plucked those of the Spaniards. There was the same tightening blockade of the Continent as in the last war against Germany and the same dour struggle to defeat the submarine threat to British shipping, more dangerous this time, because assisted by aircraft and based on a coastline uninterruptedly in enemy control from the Baltic to the Pyrenees. Baffled, as Napoleon had been, by the inaccessibility of an island power, Hitler, too, had to turn to the east and seek to open a land route to India. With laughably inadequate forces General Wavell fought off the first German-Italian assault on Egypt, and at Alamein in October, 1942, Montgomery won one of the world's decisive battles and began the clearance of North Africa which was to pave the way for the invasion of Sicily and Italy: that attack on what Churchill called 'the soft under-belly of the Axis' which was to play against Hitler the same role as the Peninsular campaigns had against Napoleon. Finally, all this had brought Hitler, as it had brought Napoleon, to see the only solution of his problems in an invasion of Russia which came nearer to success than Napoleon's but was to end in 1944 with a retreat as disastrous as that of 1812.

But at the same time there had entered in wholly new factors, and the theatre of the war had been extended from the historic and traditional battlefields to the remotest corners of Asia and the Pacific. Japan's simultaneous attack on the British and Dutch possessions in the East Indies and on the American fleet at Pearl Harbour in December 1941, had a twofold effect. It brought to the aid of the hard-pressed British the massive support of the United States without which the liberation of western Europe would scarcely have been possible. But it also produced an attack on the rear of the British position in the area of the Indian Ocean for which no adequate preparation had been made, so that Malaya and Burma were overrun, the great base at Singapore surrendered, the Dutch islands occupied, and India and Australia faced with the possibility of direct invasion. Not even the most tentative assessment can yet be made of the effects of this sudden and disastrous interruption of the Pax Britannica which had kept major war from southern Asia for two centuries. Forces of nationalism and Communism were released which still endanger all peaceful, rational development. The aftermath of the war still drags on in Malaya, Indo-China, and Korea. A Communist China and two independent great powers in India and Pakistan have added new elements to an incalculable situation, and what began as a defensive war against Japanese imperialism has turned into a dogged struggle against a different enemy of which the outcome is still uncertain.

The challenge to the United States, ultimately fatal to Japan, also sealed the doom of Germany in Europe. American manpower and industrial strength made possible the liberation of North Africa and of the Mediterranean. Its reinforcement transformed the already formidable British air assault on Germany into a crippling pressure which slowly paralysed the German armies both in east and west; and it made possible the triumphant invasion of Normandy in 1944. The American break through at Avranches and Montgomery's destruction of the German armies at Falaise freed France and Belgium and much of Holland; and the final push across the Rhine in the spring of 1945 combined with the Russian advance in the east to force a German surrender before Hitler's new secret weapons could snatch for him victory from defeat. Victory in Europe was won on 8th May 1945. Three months later two atomic bombs broke the Japanese will to resist; and so the allies from the east and west were left face to face with their own ideological differences which the necessities of a joint campaign had so far made it possible to gloss over.

A final assessment of the results is no more possible in the west than in the east, and it will be many years before historians can see with any clarity the war's effects, social, political, and economic, in England. War, as the Prussian militarists have constantly proclaimed, can regenerate and revitalize a nation grown too soft and comfortable. It can also, as the history of Europe between 1918 and 1939 showed, sap all vitality and sense of responsibility, even when it has ended in victory. In the years which followed the apparently barren triumphs of V.E. and V.J. days there were many who saw evidence everywhere in England of moral collapse; of a people exhausted by the tremendous effort of the past six years and daunted by the still greater efforts ahead if peace was to be more than a breathing space, intent only on snatching what personal comfort there was at the maximum wage for the minimum effort. But there are plenty of signs which point the other way.

In general England's situation at the end of the war showed most of the processes noticeable at the start of the century almost complete. The incomparable sacrifices she had made to mobilize all her resources, industrial and military, to defeat Germany had, in spite of the generous help of the Dominions and of the United States, left her on the verge of bankruptcy. The last of her accumulated wealth had gone; every foreign investment had been sold; essential modernization and capital replacement had everywhere been postponed in the urgency of war and there was no surplus immediately available out of which these arrears could be made good and war damage repaired. Her slender reserves of gold began quickly to run out and the abrupt cessation of the lease-lend arrangements by which the United States had supported her in war time left her debilitated industry to adapt its antiquated and inadequate plant as best it could, while at the same time providing the visible exports to pay for the food from abroad without which she must starve. An immense American loan, granted on terms which seemed to many at the time unduly harsh, tided over the immediate crisis. But the struggle was long and difficult and, though it has seemed easier lately, is not over yet. It has had to be carried on, moreover, under the unexpected burden of rearmament. The hopes of world peace fostered by the great inter-allied conferences of the war and by the preliminary arrangements for a United Nations' Organization which would remedy the defects of the old League, were frustrated by the hostility and suspicion of Russia and the forcible communization of eastern Europe, which has left the western World holding the frontier of the Iron Curtain in a cold war which might at any moment degenerate into open hostilities. In consequence a vastly disproportionate part of the world's effort has had to be devoted to military needs, and the peace for which men fought and died has not yet been won.

On the other hand, when all the difficulties are borne in mind, what has been achieved is remarkable. The passionate determination of ordinary men that there should be some reward in terms of social welfare for the efforts and sacrifices which had won the war gave Mr. Attlee and the Socialists a clear-cut victory in the General Election of 1945. But the scheme for universal social security on a predominantly contributory basis, by which every man and woman in England has been insured against the worst consequences of unemployment, sickness, and old age; the provision of a free health service as part of this; and the final opening of the opportunity for free secondary and university education for all who can show the necessary ability to profit from it: these were not exclusively Socialist measures, though socialist in conception and execution. They had been planned in war time by the National government, and represent the basic agreement of all shades of political opinion. It was, indeed, a Liberal, Sir William Beveridge, who formulated and gave his name to this first general system of social security. This was the final victory over the last lingering remnants of *laissez-faire* thought: a triumphant return both to the mediaeval sense of responsibility towards the needy and the infirm and to the Tudor method of using government action to meet it. Mr. Churchill and the Conservatives who replaced Attlee again in 1951 have thrown a greater value on free enterprise and individual initiative in industry and commerce, but always within a framework mainly socialist. Utilitarian individualism is dead.

The field of political controversy has in fact narrowed to the degree of state control desirable in industry and the methods of its application. The nationalization by the Socialist government of the industries where industrial discontent most prevailed between the wars—coal mining and railways—has launched a gigantic experiment in state enterprise whose results have yet to work themselves out; and the Conservative victory of 1951 was in time to halt and reverse for the time being the project to carry the same experiment into the steel and transport industries. In such vital matters as the rehousing of a great part of the nation the two parties are rivals only; on the necessity of checking the inflationary rise of prices and wages and profits so as to preserve some of the value of the pensions and benefits of social security, and the principle of close co-operation with the leaders of the trade unions to ensure that a sense of injustice does not interfere with maximum output, both parties are substantially agreed. Of the results of all this activity this much, perhaps, may be said: that, provided no world disaster again shatters all peaceful development, England's gains of the past century and a half in living standards, welfare, and security can yet be held by the economic policies of postwar governments. All still depends on the quality of the effort which the nation is prepared to make to secure them.

The extinction of Britain as a great power has often before seemed imminent to outside watchers. As early as 1776 an American champion of Independence wrote a prayer that 'when the change comes, and come it must, that America must become the seat of Empire, may Britain gently verge down the decline of life, and sink away in the arms of American sons'. If Britain in fact maintains her place in the world it will be greatly due to the generous help of American and other sons. But it is permissible to hope that she is not yet verging down the decline of life and that the moral and spiritual impetus of her great stand for freedom in 1940 may carry her forward in spite of her present material handicaps to a new greatness in a new Elizabethan age. To see only an overcrowded population unable to grow its own food, too exhausted for the effort of reconstruction, industrially paralysed by obsolete equipment and conservative habits of mind of both management and labour, and only anxious to finance social welfare with American charity, is to miss the invisible assets: the immense patience and good humour which survived unimpaired the nightly bombing, the queues and the rationing; the political maturity and sense of responsibility inherited from ten centuries of uninterrupted experiment in the exercise of freedom; above all, the tremendous sense of unity, strengthened by war, and much more easily perpetuated in the more equal, unprivileged society which emerged from it.

There is of course in this Britain much that has gone and is going irretrievably wrong. The ruin of the countryside, begun in the agricultural depression of the 1880s, is being rapidly completed by the motor car. Ribbon development has produced a straggling, unsightly suburbia whose inhabitants lose all the intangible advantages of living in a community. Each year fresh acreages of good farming land disappear beneath new towns and estates of new houses, neat, trim, and sanitary, but mass-produced and architecturally uninspired, while more are engulfed in the airfields whose lengthening runways must accommodate not only the transcontinental airliners, but the many-engined bombers which garrison the frontier of western civilization. The disappearance of slums is offset by the gradual ruin of so many of the country houses which are woven into the nation's history and are a large part of its finest architectural inheritance. Though sport flourishes, far too many watch and too few play, and the amusements of the people are more and more those which demand the least effort of the imagination: the cinema, the wireless, and, potentially the most powerful and dangerous of them all, television. There would seem, moreover, to be a danger that universal education is being achieved at the expense of some loss of standards and it could be argued that in an age when most people enjoy more leisure than ever before there is less ability than ever to employ leisure profitably. There are no signs as yet of a new Elizabethan age bringing forth any but a cheap, mass-produced culture.

Yet, however conscious Englishmen may be of a continuing wastage of the nation's inheritance, the grounds for satisfaction with what has been achieved in the teeth of a series of world disasters are very solid. By adapting her ancient institutions to modern purposes England has preserved her mediaeval liberties from both the extremes of current thought and has achieved a social and political stability unique in the modern world. 'England', Pitt said in his last speech, 'has saved herself by her exertions, and will, as I trust, save Europe by her example.' The claim might be made to-day not to Europe only, but to the whole free world. The most characteristic of all English transformations, by which the monarchy defeated by Parliament in the seventeenth century has become the greatest of all democratic institutions in the twentieth century holds the Commonwealth together in a solidarity which makes nonsense of the expectation of England's collapse as a world power. For England's power, once expressed in terms of a pulverizing industrial and commercial supremacy, is none the less real now that it is changed into a leadership of a free association of peoples whose general will to peace and co-operation transcends all temporary and local differences. The adherence of India to this association, even if on terms which seem to the legalist and the logician fantastic, gives good grounds to hope that Afrikander nationalism and the impatient aspiration of coloured folk all over Africa may yet be prevented from plunging that continent into violence and disorder, and that the peaceful evolution of backward races throughout the Empire may be possible under British leadership in spite of the visible and immense difficulties. That is the conclusion which may be drawn from a Coronation which stirred the loyalties of the peoples of the Commonwealth as never before, and roused, even outside the Commonwealth as well as within it, emotions which many thought long dead. These are the terms in which the task of the new Elizabethan age has been set. What is perhaps most significant in England's story is that the objects are still such as Alfred would have understood and approved and that the effort we are called upon to make is still the same effort to which he gave the initial impulse when he marched out of Athelney in 878: 'virtuously and fittingly' to administer an inheritance of great responsibility.

SOME SUGGESTIONS
FOR FURTHER READING

★

GENERAL. This list is not comprehensive or systematic, but rather a series of personal recommendations of some of the more readable history books. There is an excellent comprehensive list for more detailed reading at the end of Keith Feiling's *History of England*, a work on which I have drawn enormously in the writing of this book, and which is strongly recommended to anyone who wants the whole of English history in one volume in much greater detail than it is to be found here. Bryant's 3-volume *Story of England* promises to be admirable; and those who want an authoritative survey in even greater detail should go to the fourteen volumes of the *Oxford History of England*, almost all of which are now published. Trevelyan's *English Social History* is a wholly fascinating survey, and the most readable of the many economic histories is probably Lipson's *Economic History of England*.

SAXON ENGLAND. Most of the available books are too specialized for the general reader. Oman, *England before the Norman Conquest*, covers the whole period more shortly than the Oxford History. *The Anglo-Saxon Chronicle* itself is the best reading of all and Asser's *Life of Alfred* is amusing and vivid, though inaccurate.

MEDIAEVAL ENGLAND. Once again most of the studies are too detailed for the general reader. But Oman's *Art of War in the Middle Ages* is interesting. There are plenty of good surveys of mediaeval church architecture, but Mrs. Esdaile's recent *English Church Monuments* deserves special mention. K. B. McFarlane's *John Wycliffe and the Lollards* and E. F. Jacob's *Henry V and the Invasion of France*, both in the 'Teach Yourself History' series, though specialized, are short and very readable. Kingsford's *Prejudice and Promise in Fifteenth Century England* gives an excellent series of pictures of the background of the Wars of the Roses.

TUDORS AND STUARTS. It is difficult to choose from the multitude of books, especially biographies, available for these periods. Pollard's *Henry VIII* and Neale's *Queen Elizabeth* are both excellent surveys which between them cover most of the sixteenth century. Strachey, *Elizabeth and Essex* deserves mention on literary grounds alone; and Baskerville, *The English Monasteries* fills in some of the background of the Reformation. There are also Rowse's *Queen Elizabeth and her Age* and *Elizabethan England*. There are learned but readable commentaries on the early Stuarts by David Mathew, *The Jacobean Age* and *The Age of Charles I*. Trevelyan's *England under the Stuarts* and Miss C. V. Wedgewood's biographies of *Strafford* and *Montrose* are all easy to read. Bryant's *Charles II* and his 3-volume *Samuel Pepys* are both admirable for the general reader; and for those who like their history romanticized the novels of Margaret Irwin, *Royal Flush*, *The Proud Servant*, and *The Stranger Prince*, are also admirable.

EIGHTEENTH AND NINETEENTH CENTURIES. Most of the eighteenth century can be covered in three biographies: Oliver, *The Endless Adventure*, three delightful and discursive volumes mainly about Walpole; Basil Williams, *Chatham*; and Holland Rose, *Life of William Pitt*. Namier's *England in the Age of the American Revolution* is essential for the understanding of eighteenth century politics. Bryant's three volumes on the Napoleonic era, *The Years of Endurance*, *The*

Years of Victory, and *The Age of Elegance*, are excellent reading, as is G. M. Young's *Portrait of an Age* for the following period. Disraeli's two novels, *Sybil* and *Coningsby*, give as much insight into the England of the Reform Bill as anything which has been written since. Mantoux, *The Industrial Revolution*, gives a more solid survey of a different aspect of the same period. The *Letters of Queen Victoria* make an excellent running commentary on the events of her reign. Sidney and Beatrice Webb, *The History of Trade Unionism*, is irreplaceable as a survey of industrial relations in the nineteenth century, and Dangerfield's *The Strange Death of Liberal England* is an amusing and vivid account of the politics of the period just before the First World War.

RECENT TIMES. As we approach our own day the list of books available for further study becomes quite unmanageable. Churchill's four volumes, *The World Crisis* is the best, though not always the most accurate, account of the First World War, and Cruttwell and Liddell Hart have each written a *History of the Great War* in a single volume. Among the many biographies of soldiers and statesmen Wavell's *Allenby* is outstanding, while T. E. Lawrence's own account of the Arab revolt and the Turkish campaign in *The Seven Pillars of Wisdom* is immortal. For the period between the wars there is little that is authoritative or outstanding, and for the last war Churchill's *The Second World War* is likely to be without a rival for some years to come.

INDEX

★

Aberdeen, George Hamilton Gordon, 4th Earl of, 223
Abingdon, 41
Act of Settlement (1701), 171
Act of Union (1707), 172
Adam Smith, 186, 201
Addison, Joseph, 170, 201
Adela, wife of King Stephen, 71
Aelfhere, Ealdorman of Mercia, 45
Aelfric, Ealdorman, 45, 47
African Company, 170
Agincourt, Battle of, 103–4, 120
Alamein, Battle of, 253
Alexander I of Scotland, 43
Alexandria, 238
Albert of Saxe-Coburg-Gotha, Prince Consort, 211–12, 222
Alfred, King of Wessex (871–99), 13–22, 24, 26–8, 30–1, 33, 35–6, 39–41, 43, 46, 51, 53, 56, 58, 77, 119, 260
Alfred, brother to Edward the Confessor, 43, 49, 51
Allenby, Edmund, Field Marshal Lord, 239
Alma, Battle of the, 223
Amalgamated Engineering Union, 217–18
Amiens, 241
Amiens, Peace of (1802), 191
Anglo-Saxon Chronicle, 14, 15, 38, 46
Anlaf of Dublin, 39
Anne, Queen of England (1702–14), 162–3, 165, 170–3
Anne of Bohemia, Queen of Richard II, 101

Anne Boleyn, Queen of Henry VIII, 121, 123, 127
Anne, Princess, daughter of Queen Elizabeth II, 234
Anne, Duchess of Savoy, 163
Anselm, St., Archbishop of Canterbury, 80–1
Anti-Corn Law League, 213–14
Antwerp, 193, 196, 222
Appellant, Lords, 101–2
Appledore, 16
Arkwright, Sir Richard, 182
Arlette, mother of William I, 60
Armada, Spanish, 137–8, 145, 160, 253
Armed Neutrality, The, 191–2
Arnold, Dr. Thomas, 221
Arnulf, The Emperor, 32
Arthur, King of Britain, 20
Arthur of Brittany, 71, 83
Arthur, Prince of Wales, son of Henry VIII, 129
Ashdown, Battle of, 14
Ashington, Battle of, 48
Aske, Robert, 127
Asquith, Herbert, later Earl of Oxford and Asquith, 230, 233, 241
Asser, Bishop of Sherborne, 29
Athelney, 13, 15–17, 26, 29, 39, 260
Athelstan, King of England (924–40), 27, 33, 35, 37–9, 52, 56, 58
Attlee, Clement, 256–7
Augustine, St., 16, 30
Authorised Version of the Bible, 143
Avignon, 95, 98
Avranches, 254

Babington Conspiracy, 138
Bacon, Francis, Viscount St. Albans, 144, 149
Balaclava, Battle of, 223
Baldwin, Stanley, 1st Earl, 245–6
Ball, John, 99–100, 123
Bamborough, 37
Bank of England, 167
Bannockburn, Battle of, 87–8
Barbados, 170
Barebones Parliament, 155
Barham, Admiral Sir Charles Middleton, 1st Lord, 194
Barlings Abbey, 126
Barnet, Battle of, 109
Bastille, Paris, 188
Bastwick, John, 149–50
Bate's Case, 143
Bath, 41
Battle Abbey, 61
Beaconsfield; see Disraeli
Beaufort, Edmund, 2nd Duke of, 90, 107, 112
Beaufort, Henry, Cardinal, 90, 107
Beaufort, John, 1st Duke of, 90, 106, 107, 112
Beaufort, Margaret, Countess of Richmond, 90, 110
Becket, Thomas, Archbishop of Canterbury, 80–1, 123
Bede, The Venerable, 22, 30
Bedford, 35, 37
Bedford, John, Duke of, son of Henry IV, 106–7
Benfleet, 33
Bentham, Jeremy, 218
Berkhamstead, 63
Beveridge, Sir William, 256
Bill of Rights (1689), 164–5
Birmingham, 199
Bishops' War, 148
Black Death, 92, 94–5, 101, 115
Black Hole of Calcutta, 177
Black Prince, Edward the, son of Edward III, 71, 90, 93–4
Blake, Admiral Robert, 155
Blanche of Lancaster, 71, 90
Blenheim, Battle of, 167

Blücher, Marshal Gebhard von, 197
Board of Trade, 186
Bodleian Library, 106
Boer War, 225, 227–8
Boethius, 30
Boleyn, family, 113; see also Anne
Bolingbroke, Henry St. John, Viscount, 171
Bonaparte; see Napoleon
Bosworth, Battle of, 110–11
Boulogne, 193
Bow Street Runners, 198
Boyne, Battle of the, 166
Brentford, Battle of, 48
Brest, 194
Brétigny, Treaty of, 94
Brian Boru, King of Ireland, 45
Bridgnorth, 37
Bright, John, 214
Brindley, James, 183
Bristol, 41, 151, 209
Bromesberrow, 37
Browning, Robert, 219
Bruce, Robert, King of Scotland, 87–8
Brunanburh, Battle of, 38–9
Brunswick, Augusta, Duchess of, 185
Brussels, 197
Buckingham, George Villiers, 1st Duke of, 144–7
Burghley, William Cecil, 1st Lord, 135–6
Burgoyne, General John, 181
Burke, Edmund, 188–9
Busaco, Battle of, 196
Byng, Admiral George, Viscount Torrington, 173
Byng, Admiral John, 177
Byrhtnoth, Ealdorman of Essex, 46
Byron, George Gordon, 6th Lord, 202
Byzantium, 60

Cabot brothers, 117
Cade, Jack, 107
Cadiz, 138, 145–6, 194
Caister Castle, 105
Calais, 93–4, 107, 115, 133, 139

Cambridge, 35, 37, 100, 114
Cambridge, Richard, Duke of, 90, 104
Campbell-Bannerman, Sir Henry, 230
Camperdown, Battle of, 192
Canning, George, 197, 205, 207, 221
Canterbury, 20, 26, 28–9, 69, 95, 97, 125
Canterbury Tales, 97–8
Canute, King of England (1016–35), 43, 48–50, 52–3, 56, 73
Cape Colony, 196, 227
Cape Passaro, Battle of, 173
Cape St. Vincent, Battle of, 192
Capet, Hugh, Count of Paris, 39
Caporetto, Battle of, 240
Carlisle, 127, 154
Caroline of Anspach, Queen of George II, 175
Caroline of Brunswick, Queen of George IV, 185
Castlereagh, Robert Stewart, 2nd Viscount, 196–7, 202–5, 221
Câteau Cambrésis, Treaty of, 137
Catherine of Aragon, Queen of Henry VIII, 121, 132
Catholic Emancipation, 193, 207
Cato Street Conspiracy, 204
Cavalier Parliament, 156–7
Caxton, William, 114
Cecil, family, 113; see also Burghley and Salisbury
Chamberlain, Neville, 249
Charlemagne, The Emperor, 26
Charles I of England (1625–49), 145–52, 154–6, 163
Charles II of England (1660–85), 155–61, 163, 167, 172, 178
Charles, Prince, Duke of Cornwall, 234
Charles V, The Emperor, 121
Charles Edward, the Young Pretender, 163, 176–7
Charlotte, Princess, daughter of George IV, 185, 198
Chartism, 212–13, 215
Chatham, 158
Chatham, William Pitt, 1st Earl of, 177, 179, 184, 190

Chaucer, Geoffrey, 97–8, 118, 122
Chester, 33, 36, 41, 53
Chichester, 33
Chippenham, 13–14, 16, 26
Christ Church, Oxford, 120, 162
Churchill, John; see Marlborough
Churchill, Sir Winston, 238–9, 248, 251, 253, 257
Cirencester, 20
Clarence, Lionel, Duke of, 90
Clarence, George, Duke of, 91, 109, 112, 116, 127
Clarendon, Edward Hyde, 1st Earl of, 149, 156–7, 159
Clarendon Code, 157
Clement VII, Pope, 121
Clifford, family, 112
Clive, Robert, Lord, 177
Cluny, Abbey of, 41
Cobbett, William, 207
Cobden, Richard, 214
Colchester, 37
Coleridge, Samuel Taylor, 202
Colet, John, 119, 122
Combination Laws, 205–6
Common Pleas, Court of, 77
Concert of Europe, 197
Consolations of Philosophy (Boethius), 30
Constantine III, King of Scots, 37–8
Constantinople, 222
Continental system, 195
Corfe Castle, 44
Corn Laws, 203, 212–13
Corpus Christi College, Cambridge, 100
Corunna, Battle of, 196
Council of the North, 117, 126, 150
Council of Wales, 117, 150
Cranmer, Thomas, Archbishop of Canterbury, 123, 127, 130, 133
Crécy, Battle of, 93
Crimean War, 223–4
Cripplegate, 104
Cromwell, Oliver, Protector, 152, 154–6, 158
Cromwell, Thomas, Earl of Essex, 124, 126–7

Culloden, Battle of, 177
Cumberland, William, Duke of, 177, 185
Cumberland, Ernest, Duke of, 185, 208, 212

Dacre, family, 112
Danegeld, 46-7, 50, 54
Dardanelles, The, 223, 238
Darwin, Charles, 218
David I of Scotland, 43
Declaration of Indulgence (1672), 160; (1688), 162
Defoe, Daniel, 170
Dent, 126
Derby, 37, 177
Despenser, family, 88
Dettingen, Battle of, 176
Dickens, Charles, 219
Disraeli, Benjamin, later Earl of Beaconsfield, 217, 224, 227
Dives, River, 59
Domesday, Survey, 65, 70, 79
Dover, Secret Treaties of, 159-61
Drake, Sir Francis, 135, 138, 253
Droitwich, 53
Dublin, 13, 37-8, 45, 52
Dudley, Edmund, 119
Dudley, John; see Northumberland
Dunbar, Battle of, 155
Duncan, Admiral Adam, 1st Viscount 192
Dundee, John Graham of Claverhouse, 1st Viscount, 166
Dunkirk, 155, 159, 252
Dunstan, St., Archbishop of Canterbury, 40-1, 44-5, 69
Durham, 17, 69, 124, 245
Durham, John Lambton, 1st Earl of, 220

Eadred, King of England (946-55), 27, 39
East India Company, 139, 170, 187-8, 210, 220, 227
Easterlings, 113
Eastern Association, 152
Ecclesiastical Commission, 210

Ecclesiastical History (Bede), 30
Eden, Anthony, 248
Edgar, King of England (957-75), 27, 40-1, 43-4
Edgar Atheling, 43, 56-7, 63, 69, 74
Edgehill, Battle of, 151
Edinburgh, 177
Edinburgh, Philip, Duke of, 234
Edington, Battle of, 26
Edith of Scotland, Queen of Henry I, 43, 71, 74
Edmund, King of England (940-46), 27, 39
Edmund Crouchback, Earl of Lancaster, 71
Edmund, Earl of Kent, 71
Edmund Ironside, King of England (1016), 43, 48-9, 50-1, 56
Education Act (1876), 224; (1918), 243
Edward I of England (1272-1307), 71, 83, 85-7, 89, 95, 98, 103
Edward II of England (1307-27), 71, 87-9, 101
Edward III of England (1327-77), 71-2, 89, 90, 92-5, 98, 103, 107
Edward IV of England (1461-83), 91, 108-110
Edward V of England (1483), 91, 109
Edward VI of England (1547-53), 129-30, 132, 134
Edward VII of England (1901-10), 185, 230, 234
Edward VIII of England (1936), 234, 251
Edward the Confessor, King of England (1042-66), 43, 49, 51-2, 55-6
Edward the Elder, King of Wessex (899-924), 27, 31, 33, 35-7, 54
Edward the Exile, son of Edmund Ironside, 43, 49
Edward the Martyr, King of England, (975-8), 43-4
Edward of Lancaster, Prince of Wales, 91, 108-9
Edwin, Earl of Mercia, 56, 58, 60-1, 63, 69

Edwy, King of England (955–9), 27, 39, 40
Egbert, King of Wessex (802–39), 27
Eleanor of Aquitaine, Queen of Henry II, 80
Eleanor de Montfort, 71
Elfthryth, Queen to Edgar, 43
Eliot, Sir John, 146
Elizabeth I of England (1558–1603), 129, 133–43, 222
Elizabeth II of England (1952–), 222
Elizabeth, Princess, Electress Palatine, 144, 163, 171
Elizabeth Woodville, Queen of Edward IV, 108
Elizabeth of York, Queen to Henry VII, 91, 110, 111
Emma of Normandy, Queen of Ethelred the Unready and Canute, 43, 49, 51
Empson, Sir Richard, 119
Engels, Friedrich, 215
Enniskillen, 166
Erasmus of Rotterdam, 119
Eric, Earl of Northumbria, 50
Eric Bloodaxe, 399
Essex, Robert Devereux, 2nd Earl of, 139
Ethelbald, King of Wessex (858–60), 27
Ethelbert, King of Wessex (860–6), 27
Ethelflaed, Lady of the Mercians, 27, 35–7
Ethelflaed, Queen of Edgar, 43
Ethelgifu, 40
Ethelnoth, Ealdorman of Somerset, 15, 33
Ethelred, King of Wessex (866–71), 14, 24, 27
Ethelred, the Unready, King of England (978–1016), 43–50, 54, 73
Ethelred, Ealdorman of Mercia, 35–6
Ethelwine, Ealdorman of East Anglia, 45
Ethelwold, Bishop of Winchester, 41
Ethelwulf, King of Wessex (839–58), 27
Eton College, 114

Evesham, Battle of, 85
Excise Scheme, 175, 186
Exclusion Bills, 161, 171
Exeter, 17, 33
Eynsham, 118

Factory Act (1833), 209
Fairfax, Thomas, 3rd Lord, 152
Falaise, 254
Fire of London (1666), 158
Fisher, Cardinal, Bishop of Rochester, 125
Fisher, H. A. L., 243
FitzUrse, Reginald, 81
Flodden, Battle of, 120
Fotheringay Castle, 138
Fox, Charles James, 189–90, 195, 207
Fox, Richard, Bishop of Winchester, 124
Frederick, Prince of Wales, son of George II, 185
Frederick, Elector Palatine, 144, 163
French, Sir John, later 1st Earl of Ypres, 236, 238
Frobisher, Sir Martin, 135

Gag Acts, 189, 204
Gaveston, Piers, 88
Galliéni, General, 236
Gaunt, John of, Duke of Lancaster, 90, 102, 106
Genoa, 95
Geoffrey of Anjou, 43, 71
Geoffrey of Brittany, 71
Geoffrey de Mandeville, 73
George I of England (1714–27), 163, 171–3, 185
George II of England (1727–60), 175–6, 185
George III of England (1760–1820), 177–8, 185–6, 192–3, 198, 211
George IV of England (1820–30), 185, 198, 208
George V of England (1910–36), 230–2, 234, 251
George VI of England (1936–52), 234, 251
Gibraltar, 167, 193

Gilbert, Sir Humphrey, 135
Gladstone, William Ewart, 218, 224, 230, 246
Glastonbury, 13, 41
Glorious 1st of June, Battle of, 191
Gloucester, 13
Gloucester, Humphrey, Duke of, 106–7, 118
Gloucester, Henry, Duke of, 234
Gloucester, Richard, Duke of; see Richard III
Gloucester, Thomas of Woodstock, Duke of, 102
Goderich, Frederick Robinson, Viscount, 205
Godstow Nunnery, 124
Godwin, Earl of Wessex, 51–2, 55, 73
Golden Hind (ship), 138
Grace, W. G., 225
Grand Remonstrance, 151
Green Ribbon Club, 160
Gregory the Great, Pope, 30
Grenville, Sir Richard, 135, 138
Gresham Manor, 105
Grey, Charles, 2nd Earl of, 207–9, 230
Grey, Henry; see Suffolk
Grey, Lady Catherine, 129
Grey, Lady Jane, 129, 132
Grey, Sir Edward, later Viscount Grey of Falloden, 233
Grimbald, Abbot of Winchester, 29
Grindal, Edmund, Archbishop of Canterbury, 140
Grocyn, William, 119
Guildford, 51
Guthrum the Dane, 13, 16, 26, 28, 35
Guy Fawkes, 143, 160
Gyrth, brother of Harold, 62

Habeas Corpus Act, 189, 203, 240
Haig, Sir Douglas, 1st Earl, 238, 241–2
Hakewill, William, 141
Hamburg, 193
Hampden, John, 148–9
Hampton Court, 120
Hampton Court Conference, 143
Hanseatic League, 113
Harcourt, Sir Robert, 118

Hardy Thomas (fl. 1800), 190
Hardy, Thomas, the writer, 225
Harold, King of England (1066), 55–63
Harold Hardrada, King of Norway, 56–7, 59–63
Harold Harefoot, King of England (1036–40), 51–2
Harthacanute, King of England (1040 2), 43, 51–2, 56
Hastings, Battle of, 61–3
Hatfield, 133
Hawkins, Sir John, 135, 138
Henrietta Maria, Queen of Charles I, 145, 147
Henrietta, Duchess of Orleans, 159, 163
Henry I of England (1100–35), 43, 71, 74–5, 77–8, 81
Henry II of England (1154–89), 43, 71, 75, 77–86, 94, 103, 111, 118, 123
Henry III of England (1216–72), 71, 82, 84–5, 101
Henry IV of England (1399–1413), 90, 102–4, 107–8
Henry V of England (1413–22), 90, 102–4, 107
Henry VI of England (1422–61), 91, 102, 104, 106–9
Henry VII of England (1485–1509), 110–11, 113–14, 116–20, 127, 129
Henry VIII of England (1509–47), 113, 117–21, 123–30, 132–3, 137, 167
Henry Stuart, Prince of Wales, son of James I, 163
Hepburn, Miners' Leader, 206
High Commission, Court of, 135–6, 149–50
History of the World (Orosius), 30
Hitler, Adolf, 248–9, 252–4
Hogarth, William, 183
Hogg, Stephen, 157
Hooper, John, Bishop, 130, 133
Horne Tooke, Parson, 190
Hounslow Heath, 162
Howard of Effingham; see Nottingham

Howe, Admiral Richard, 1st Earl, 191
Hubba, Danish king, 13, 15–16
Hudson Bay Company, 170
Hull, 151
Huntingdon, 17, 35, 37
Huskisson, William, 205
Hyde, Edward; see Clarendon

Impositions, 150
Indemnity and Oblivion, Act of (1661), 156
India Act (1784), 187–8
Indian Mutiny, 227
Inkerman, Battle of, 223
Inquest of Sheriffs (1170), 79
Instrument of Government, The, 155
Ipswich Grammar School, 120
Ironsides, 152

Jamaica, 155
James VI of Scotland and I of England (1603–25), 43, 129, 140, 142–5, 163, 171
James II of England (1685–88), 159–66, 176
James, The Old Pretender, 162–3, 165–6, 171–2
James IV of Scotland, 118, 120, 129
James V of Scotland, 129
Jellicoe, Admiral Sir John, 1st Earl, 239
Jerusalem, 239
Joan of Arc, St., 104
Joan of Kent, 71
John, King of England (1199–1216), 71, 82–4
John, King of France, 93
John VII, Pope, 31
John Ball, 99–100, 123
John, the Old Saxon, Abbot of Athelney, 29
John of Salisbury, 118
Joyce, Cornet George, 154
Joyce, William, of Bristol, 105–6
Jumièges; see Robert of
Jutland, Battle of, 239

Kateryn of Bayonne (ship), 105

Katherine of France, Queen of Henry V, 90
Kay's Fly Shuttle, 182
Kent, Edmund, Earl of, 71
Kent, Edward, Duke of (d. 1820), 185
Kent, Edward, Duke of, 234
Kent, George, Duke of (d. 1942), 234
Kent, Princess Alexandra and Prince Michael of, 234
Kett, Robert, 132
Kildare, Gerald FitzGerald, 9th Earl of, 116
Killiekrankie, Battle of, 166
King's Bench, Court of, 77
King's College, Cambridge, 119
King's Friends, 178, 181, 193
Kitchener, Horatio, 1st Earl, 237
Knollys, family, 113
Kruger, President Paul, 228

Labourers, Statutes of (1351), 96; (1563), 136
Ladysmith, Siege of, 228
La Hogue, Battle of, 166
Lambert Simnel, 116
Lancaster; see Edmund Crouchback and Gaunt
Lancaster, Thomas, Earl of, 88
Lanfranc, Archbishop of Canterbury, 69, 73
Langland, William, 98, 122
Latimer, Hugh, Bishop of Worcester, 123, 130, 133
La Rochelle, 145
Laud, William, Archbishop of Canterbury, 147–50, 219
Lawrence, Col. T. E., 239
League of Nations, 247–8, 256
Leeds, 182, 199
Leicester, 35, 37
Le Mans, 80
Leofric, Earl of Mercia, 56
Levellers, 154–5
Lewes, Battle of, 85
Limoges, 93
Linacre, Thomas, 119
Lincoln, 35, 37, 127
Lincoln's Inn, 114, 141

Lisbon, 196
Lizard, The, 139
Lloyd George, David, 1st Earl, 230–1, 237–8, 241, 243
Lollards, 98
London, 18–19, 46–7, 50, 53, 55, 59, 61, 63, 75, 99–102, 105, 107–8, 112–13, 127, 131, 133, 136, 151, 156, 178–9, 183–4, 199, 209, 214
Londonderry, 166
Long Parliament, 148–9, 152–5
Loos, Battle of, 238
Lords Appellant, 101–2
Lords Ordainers, 88, 101
Louis XIV of France, 159, 170, 191, 235
Louis XVIII of France, 196
Ludendorff, Erich, 241–2
Ludlow, 117
Lusitania (ship), 239
Luther, Martin, 121

Macadam, John, 183
Macaulay, Thomas, 1st Lord, 219
MacDonald, J. Ramsay, 245–6
Madrid, 145
Mafeking, Siege of, 228
Maginot Line, 252
Magna Carta, 84–5
Malcolm III, King of Scots, 43
Maldon, 37; Battle of, 46
Malplaquet, Battle of, 167
Malta, 196
Malthus, Thomas, 201
Manchester, 35, 182, 199–200, 203–4, 214
Mandeville; see Geoffrey
Map, Walter, 118
Mar, John Erskine, 11th Earl of, 172
March; see Mortimer
Marchall, William, 115
Marden, Battle of, 14
Margaret, St., Queen of Scotland, 43
Margaret of Anjou, Queen of Henry VI, 107–110
Margaret Tudor, Queen of Scotland, 118, 129
Margaret, Princess, 234

Marlborough, John Churchill, 1st Duke of, 166–7, 171
Marlowe, Christopher, 135
Marne, River, 242
Marston Moor, Battle of, 151–2
Martinique, 191
Marx, Karl, 215
Mary I of England (1553–8), 121, 129, 132–4
Mary II of England (1688–94), 162–5
Mary, Princess of Orange, 163
Mary, Princess Royal, Countess of Harewood, 234
Mary Stuart, Queen of Scots, 129
Mary Tudor, Duchess of Suffolk, 129
Matilda, The Empress, 43, 71, 75
Medina, Sidonia, Duke of, 139
Melbourne, William Lamb, 2nd Viscount, 208–9, 211
Merchant Adventurers, 113
Metropolitan Police, 205
Middlesex Election, 179
Milner, Alfred, Lord, 228
Milton, John, 150
Minorca, 167, 177
Mississippi River, 176
Molasses Act (1733), 175
Moleyns, Bishop Adam de, 107
Moleyns, Robert, Lord, 105
Monck, General George, later Duke of Albemarle, 156
Monmouth, James Scott, 1st Duke of, 160–1
Monopolies, 141–2, 147, 150
Mons, Battle of, 236
Montfort, Simon de, 85–6
Montgomery, Field Marshal Lord, of Alamein, 253–4
Montrose, James Graham, 1st Marquis of, 152
Moore, Francis, 142
Moore, Sir John, 196, 236
Morcar, Earl of Northumbria, 56, 58, 60, 61, 63, 69
More, Sir Thomas, 119, 122, 125
Mortimer, Anne, Duchess of Cambridge, 90, 104, 106

Mortimer, Edmund, 5th Earl of March, 90
Mortimer, Philippa, Countess of March, 90
Mortimer, Roger, 1st Earl of March, 89
Mortimer, Roger, 4th Earl of March, 90, 104
Morton, Cardinal, 119, 124
Munich, Treaty of, 248-9
Mussolini, Benito, 248

Napoleon Bonaparte, 191-7, 229, 235-6, 253
Naseby, Battle of, 151-2
Navigation Laws, 117
Nelson, Admiral Horatio, 1st Viscount, 192, 194-5, 222
Neville, family, 112; see also Salisbury and Warwick
New Amsterdam, 159
New England, 148
New Model Army, 152, 155-7
New York, 159
Newcastle, Thomas Pelham, 1st Duke of, 176
Newfoundland, 167, 170
Nightingale, Florence, 223
Nile, Battle of the, 192, 222
Non-jurors, 171
Norfolk, John Howard, 1st Duke of, 105
Norfolk, Thomas Howard, 3rd Duke of, 126
Northampton, 35, 37
Northumberland, Henry Percy, 4th Earl of, 116, 118
Northumberland, Henry Percy, 6th Earl of, 126
Northumberland, John Dudley, 1st Duke of, 130-2
Nottingham, 35, 37, 151
Nottingham, Charles Howard, Lord Howard of Effingham, 1st Earl of, 139, 144
Norwich, 76, 100, 132
Nova Scotia, 167
Novgorod, 60

Oates, Titus, 160
O'Connor, Feargus, 213
Odda, Ealdorman of Devon, 15-16
Odo of Bayeux, 74
Ohio, River, 176-7
Olaf of Sweden, 49, 51
Olaf Tryggveson, 46
Orosius, 30
Oswald, St., Archbishop of York, 40-1, 44, 69
Otford, Battle of, 48
Ottawa Agreements, 246
Oudenarde, Battle of, 167
Overbury, Sir Thomas, 144
Oxford, 114, 119, 124, 152, 162
Oxford Movement, 219
Oxford, Robert de Vere, 9th Earl of, 101-2
Oxford, John de Vere, 13th Earl of, 116

Paine, Thomas, 188
Palatinate, 144-5
Palmerston, Henry Temple, 3rd Viscount, 222-4
Paris, 188-9, 202, 241
Paris, Peace of, 224
Parliament Act (1910), 232
Parma, Alexander Farnese, Duke of, 139
Passchendele, Battle of, 238
Paston, family, 105
Pastoral Care (Gregory the Great), 30
Pearl Harbour, Battle of, 253
Peasants' Revolt, 97, 99-100
Peel, Sir Robert, 205, 210-11, 214, 222
Pembroke, Aymer de Valence, Earl of, 88
Penpons, Richard, 105
Penselwood, 48
Percy, family, 112; see also Northumberland
Percy, Sir Thomas, 126
Perkin Warbeck, 116
Peterborough, 73, 76
Petition of Right, 146
Peterloo Massacre, 203-4

Pevensey, 61
Philip II of Spain, 133, 137-9, 235
Philip, Duke of Orleans, 159, 163
Philippa of Clarence; *see* Mortimer
Pilgrimage of Grace, 126-7
Pitt, William, the Elder; *see* Chatham
Pitt, William, the Younger, 184, 186–195, 205, 211, 222-3, 235-6
Place, Francis, 205
Plague, The Great (1665), 158
Plegmund, Archbishop of Canterbury, 29
Plymouth, 105, 138, 151
Poitiers, Battle of, 93
Political Register (newspaper), 207
Pole, Cardinal Reginald, 133
Pole, de la; *see* Suffolk
Pontefract, 88, 102
Poor Law (1563), 136; (1834), 210
Popish Plot, 160
Portsmouth, 107, 145
Praemunire, Statute of (1353), 94
Preston, Battles of (1648), 154; (1715) 172
Prestonpans, Battle of, 177
Pride's Purge, 154
Provisors, Statute of (1351), 94
Pym, John, 149

Radcot Bridge, Battle of, 102
Raleigh, Sir Walter, 135, 138-9
Ramillies, Battle of, 167
Redruth, 106
Reform Bill (1832), 208-9, 212
Rhodes, Cecil, 227-8
Richard I of England (1189-99), 71, 80, 82-3
Richard II of England (1377-99), 90, 98, 100-2, 106
Richard III of England (1483-5), 91, 109-12
Richard; *see also* Cambridge and York
Richelieu, Cardinal, 145
Ridley, Nicholas, Bishop, 130-1, 133
Ridolfi Conspiracy, 138
Robert I of Scotland; *see* Bruce

Robert, Duke of Normandy (d. 1134), 71, 74
Robert of Bellême, 73
Robert of Jumièges, Archbishop of Canterbury, 55
Roberts, Field Marshal Lord, 228
Robinson; *see* Goderich
Rochefort, 194
Rochester, 32
Rodney, George, Admiral Lord, 181
Rosebery, Archibald Primrose, 5th Earl of, 225
Rowland Hill, 210
Royal Charles (ship), 158
Rugby School, 221
Runnymede, 84
Rupert, Prince, of the Rhine, 151-2
Russell, family, 113
Russell, Lord John, 208
Rye House Plot, 161
Ryswick, Peace of (1697), 166

St. Albans, Battles of, 95, 108, 124
St. Helena, 197
St. Ives, 106
St. John; *see* Bolingbroke
St. Valéry-en-Caux, 59-60
St. Vincent, John Jervis, 1st Earl of, 192
Sta Lucia, 191
Saints, Battle of the, 181
Salamanca, Battle of, 196
Salic Law, 212
Salisbury, Richard Neville, Earl of, 108
Salisbury, Sir Robert Cecil, Earl of, 139, 142, 144
Salisbury, Margaret, Countess of, 127
Salisbury, John of, 108
Salonica, 239
Sarajevo, 181
Saratoga, 232
Savile, Sir John, 150
Saye and Sele, James, Lord, 107
Scone, Stone of, 87
Sebastopol, Siege of, 223
Sedgemoor, Battle of, 161
Septennial Act (1715), 173

Seymour, Edward; *see* Somerset
Seymour, Jane, Queen of Henry VIII, 127, 130
Shaftesbury, 29
Shaftesbury, Anthony Ashley Cooper 1st Earl of, 160–1
Shaftesbury, Anthony Ashley Cooper 7th Earl of, 209
Shakespeare, William, 135
Sheerness, 158
Shelley, Percy Bysshe, 202
Sherborne, 29
Sheriffmuir, Battle of, 172
Ship Money, 140, 150–1, 155
Shrewsbury, 37, 104
Sidney, Sir Philip, 135
Silchester, 20
Singapore, 254
Six Acts (1819), 204
Six Articles (1540), 130
Slavery and Slave Trade, 187, 195, 197, 210
Smithfield, 100–1
Society for Promoting Christian Knowledge, 184
Somerset, Edward Seymour, 1st Duke of, 130, 132
Somerset, Robert Carr, Earl of, 144
Somerset; *see also* Beaufort
Somme, Battle of the, 238
Sophia, Electress of Hanover, 163, 171
South Sea Company, 173–4
Southampton, 46
Speenhamland Decision, 201
Spinning Jenny, 182
Spitalfields, 183
Spurs, Battle of the, 120
Stamford, 17, 35, 37
Stamford Bridge, Battle of, 60–1
Stanley, Lord, 116
Star Chamber, Court of, 117–18, 150
Steele, Sir Richard, 170
Steelyard, 113
Stephen, King of England (1135–54), 71, 75–6, 103
Stigand, Archbishop of Canterbury, 55, 59, 63, 69
Stirling, 87

Strafford, Thomas Wentworth, 1st Earl of, 147, 149–50
Streona, Eadric, Ealdorman, 43, 45, 47–8, 50
Strickland, Mr., 140
Sudan, 227, 229, 237
Suez Canal, 227, 243
Suffolk, Charles Brandon, Duke of, 129
Suffolk, William de la Pole, 1st Duke of, 107
Suffolk, Henry Grey, Duke of, 129
Suffolk, Frances, Duchess of, 129
Suffolk, Mary Tudor, Duchess of, 129
Supremacy, Act of (1534), 125
Surrey, Thomas Howard, Earl of, 2nd Duke of Norfolk, 120
Sweyn Forkbeard, King of Denmark, 47–8
Sweyn Estrithson, King of Denmark, 51, 56
Sweyn, brother of Harold, 55
Swift, Jonathan, 170
Swynford, Catherine, 90, 106
Sybil (novel), 217

Talavera, Battle of, 196
Temple, The, 114
Tenchebrai, Battle of, 74
Tennyson, Alfred, Lord, 219
Test Act, 160, 175
Tewkesbury, Battle of, 109
Thackeray, William Makepeace, 219
Thirty-Nine Articles, 135
Thirty Years' War, 144
Thorney Island, 33
Throckmorton Conspiracy, 138
Tilbury, 139
Tiptoft, John, Earl of Worcester, 110, 118
Torbay, 164
Torres Vedras, Lines of, 196
Tostig, Earl of Northumbria, 57–61
Toulon, 194
Toulouse, 196
Towcester, 37
Towton, Battle of, 108
Trades Union Congress, 218

Trafalgar, Battle of, 195
Treasons' Act (1352), 94
Tudor, Owen and Edmund, 90
Tunnage and Poundage, 141, 146, 150
Tyburn, 89

United Irishmen, 192
United Nations' Organization, 256
Utopia (book), 122
Utrecht, Treaties of, 167, 171, 173

Verdun, 236
Vere; see Oxford, Earl of
Versailles Treaty, 247–8
Victoria, Queen of England (1837–1901), 185, 211–12, 222, 227, 229
Victory (ship), 195
Vienna Congress, 196–7
Villeneuve, Admiral Pierre de, 194
Villiers; see Buckingham
Virginia, 139
Vision of Piers Plowman (book), 98
Vittoria, Battle of, 196

Wakefield, Battle of, 108
Walcheren, Isle of, 196
Wallace, Sir William, 87
Wallingford, 63
Walpole, Sir Robert, later Earl of Orford, 174–5, 186
Walsingham, Sir Francis, 135
Walter, Hubert, Archbishop of Canterbury, 83
Walworth, Sir William, Lord Mayor, 100
Warminster, 16
Warwick, 37
Warwick, Richard Neville, Earl of, 108–9, 112, 115
Warwick, Guy de Beauchamp, Earl of, 88
Warwick, John Dudley, Earl of; see Northumberland
Warwick, Edward Plantagenet, Earl of, 91, 116
Washington, George, 177, 181
Wat Tyler, 99–100
Waterloo, Battle of, 197, 223

Watling Street, 39
Watt's steam engine, 182
Wavell, Field Marshal Lord, 253
Wedmore Treaty, 26, 28
Wellington, Arthur Wellesley, 1st Duke of, 196 7, 204, 207, 209, 214
Wentworth, Peter, 141–2
Wentworth, Thomas; see Strafford
Werferth, Bishop of Worcester, 15, 29
Wesley brothers, 184
Westminster, 63, 78, 84, 95, 114–15, 117–18, 204–5, 230
Westminster, Statute of (1931), 252
Wexford, 13, 45
Weymouth, 95
White Ship, 74
Whitehall, 120, 150, 154
Whittington, Richard, 113
Wilberforce, William, 187
Wilkes, John, 178–9
William I of England (1066–87), 56–7, 59–63, 67, 69, 71, 73–4
William II of England (1087–1100), 71, 74, 80
William III of England (1688–1702), 162–6, 167, 170, 173
William IV of England (1830–7), 185, 208–9
William Atheling, son of Henry I, 71, 74
William Clito, 71
William of Wykeham, 114
William II, German Emperor, 229
Wilson, President Woodrow, 247
Winchester, 41, 52, 55, 65, 70, 114
Witan, The, 24, 31, 39, 44, 49, 51–2, 56, 63
Witham, 37
Wolsey, Cardinal, 119–21
Woodville, Elizabeth, Queen of Edward IV, 108–9
Worcester, 15, 155
Wordsworth, William, 202
Wotton, family, 113
Wren, Sir Christopher, 158, 165
Wyatt, Sir Thomas, 133
Wycliffe, John, 98, 118, 122

York, 37–8, 52, 60–1, 69, 76, 108, 117, 126–7

York, Edmund Langley, Duke of, 90

York, Richard Plantagenet, 3rd Duke of, 90, 106–8

York, Richard, Duke of, son of Edward IV, 91, 109, 114

York, Elizabeth of, Queen of Henry VII, 91, 110–11

Ypres, 237

Ypres, Earl of; see French